STUDIES IN CHRISTIAN HISTORY AND THOUGHT

Protestant Nonconformity and Christian Missions

STUDIES IN CHRISTIAN HISTORY AND THOUGHT

Protestant Nonconformity and Christian Missions

Edited by Martin Wellings

WIPF & STOCK · Eugene, Oregon

Wipf and Stock Publishers
199 W 8th Ave, Suite 3
Eugene, OR 97401

Protestant Nonconformity and Christian Missions
By Wellings, Martin

ISBN 13: 978-1-62654-773-3
Publication date 3/1/2014
Previously published by Paternoster, 2014

To Alan Sell, whose vision gave birth to ADHSCL

STUDIES IN CHRISTIAN HISTORY AND THOUGHT

Series Preface

This series complements the specialist series of Studies in Evangelical History and Thought and Studies in Baptist History and Thought for which Paternoster is becoming increasingly well known by offering works that cover the wider field of Christian history and thought. It encompasses accounts of Christian witness at various periods, studies of individual Christians and movements, and works which concern the relations of church and society through history, and the history of Christian thought.

The series includes monographs, revised dissertations and theses, and collections of papers by individuals and groups. As well as 'free standing' volumes, works on particular running themes are being commissioned; authors will be engaged for these from around the world and from a variety of Christian traditions.

A high academic standard combined with lively writing will commend the volumes in this series both to scholars and to a wider readership

Contents

Notes on Contributors

Clyde Binfield is Emeritus Professor in History at the University of Sheffield. He is a Past President of the Ecclesiastical History Society, the United Reformed Church History Society, and the Chapels Society. He is President of the Friends of Dr Williams's Library and is a Trustee of that Library, the Historic Chapels Trust, and the Yorkshire Historic Churches Trust. He has written widely on English Dissenting History, especially of the nineteenth and twentieth centuries.

John H. Darch is the author of a number of publications about Victorian missions. He has worked in Church of England parish ministry and in education (in both secondary and HE sectors). He is currently Director of Ordinands and Curate Training for the Diocese of Blackburn.

Tim Grass is an associate tutor at Spurgeon's College, London, and assistant editor for the Ecclesiastical History Society. Among his other works are *Gathering to His Name: The Story of Open Brethren in Britain and Ireland* (2006), *Generations: British Brethren Mission to Spain, 1834-1990* (2011), and *F.F. Bruce: A Life* (2011).

J. Gwynfor Jones, formerly Professor of Welsh History, School of History, Archaeology and Religious Studies, Cardiff University, has published extensively on early modern Welsh religious, social and cultural history and nineteenth-century Welsh nonconformity.

Margaret Jones is a Methodist minister living in Salisbury. Before retirement she served in circuit appointments, in theological education and in the Methodist Church's Connexional Team. Her main research interest is the history of women in eighteenth and nineteenth-century British Methodism.

John Pritchard is a Methodist minister, former General Secretary of the Methodist Missionary Society and author of a two-volume history, *Methodists and their Missionary Societies, 1760-1900* and *1900-1996.*

Geoffrey Roper has worked with Council for World Mission over nine years, after retiring from Churches Together in England where he served as secretary of the Free Churches Group for nonconformist denominations in both England and Wales.

John Handby Thompson is a retired Civil Servant, sometime President of the Chapels Society and Chairman of the Friends of the Congregational Library. His publications include *A History of the Coward Trust* (1998), *Highgate Dissenters* (2001)and *The Free Church Army Chaplain, 1830-1930* (2012), based on his doctoral thesis.

Derek Tidball, a Baptist minister and former Principal of London School of Theology, is currently Visiting Scholar at Spurgeon's College. His PhD (Keele University) was entitled 'Nonconformist Home Missions 1796-1901'. Although publishing occasionally in the area of history, his chief writing interests have been in pastoral and biblical theology.

Martin Wellings is Superintendent Minister of the Oxford Methodist Circuit and Past President of the World Methodist Historical Society. He has written widely on Methodist and evangelical history, co-editing *The Ashgate Research Companion to World Methodism* (2013).

INTRODUCTION

Martin Wellings

In his definitive account of the Edinburgh World Missionary Conference Brian Stanley observes that '[m]uch of the literature designed for students and general readers reinforces the debatable assumption that the ecumenical movement actually began at Edinburgh in 1910'.[1] One tag-line used for the 2010 commemoration of the Edinburgh Conference was 'a centenary celebration of ecumenism'.[2] In reality, Edinburgh 1910 was the latest in a series of interdenominational and international missionary conferences, with immediate predecessors in London in 1888 and New York in 1900, and with roots in pan-evangelical aspirations and gatherings reaching back into the mid-nineteenth century.[3] Edinburgh 1910 was neither comprehensively ecumenical in its scope nor authoritatively ecclesiastical in its representation: the delegates were nominated by missionary societies, not churches, and there was neither Roman Catholic nor Orthodox presence at the conference. That said, the meeting at Edinburgh offered a snapshot of largely Anglo-American Protestant missions in the heyday of the Protestant missionary movement, and through its Continuation Committee it proved seminal for the development of missionary thinking and ecumenical trajectories in the twentieth century. As such, the 2010 commemoration and reappraisal were well merited.

The Edinburgh centenary suggested a theme for the 2010 conference of the Association of Denominational Historical Societies and Cognate Libraries, an association bringing together Baptists and Congregationalists, Methodists and Unitarians, the Society of Friends and the 'New Church', the United Reformed Church and the Huguenots, the Welsh Presbyterians and the Chapels Society, with libraries in London, Oxford, Cambridge and Manchester. The ADHSCL conference addressed the topic of 'Protestant Nonconformity and Christian Missions', deliberately reaching beyond the 'foreign missions' agenda of Edin-

---

1 Brian Stanley, *The World Missionary Conference, Edinburgh 1910* (Cambridge: Eerdmans, 2009), p. 7.

2 See <http://connection.ebscohost.com/c/proceedings/51271264/edinburgh-1910-centenary-celebration-ecumenism>, accessed 25 June 2013.

3 Stanley, *World Missionary Conference*, pp. 18-19.

burgh 1910 to include missions at home. A selection of the conference papers, with several additional essays, is offered in the present volume. This collection does not claim to be a comprehensive history of Nonconformist missions, but it does give suggestive angles of approach to a vast subject.

Reflecting on the motivation for missions in his Fernley Lecture of 1913, *Religions and Religion*, the Wesleyan Methodist James Hope Moulton acknowledged that a transformation had occurred in Christian attitudes to people of other faiths. It was no longer the case that Christians supported overseas missions because they were convinced that those who had failed to make an explicit commitment to Christ were destined for hell. Moulton welcomed this development, insisting that the Christian obligation was to share with all people the empowering love and grace of God, which alone enabled human beings to live in accordance with God's will: Christians are 'bound by the very fundamental law of our religion to pass it on to every man who does not yet possess it, *because* it is incomparably the mightiest power in enabling weak humanity to achieve the life that God demands'.[4] Moulton was equally clear that the missionary commission of the Church, enshrined in the New Testament, owed its origin to the teaching of Jesus, and he rebutted the suggestion of Adolf von Harnack that it represented a later development of the gospel tradition.[5]

Missionary motivation is woven through the essays in the present volume. The theological imperative is discussed by J. Gwynfor Jones, who sets Welsh Nonconformist missions in the widest sweep of Christian history. Attitudes to other faiths are discussed by John Pritchard, in relation to India, and by Clyde Binfield, who shows that mid-nineteenth century Congregationalists were as alert to the presence of God in 'heathen' lands as were Edwardian Wesleyans like Moulton. Tim Grass brings out the priority of evangelism in the Brethren mission in Spain, and the active propagation of the gospel is the underlying assumption of the Baptist Home Missions described by Derek Tidball.

One of the vexed issues preoccupying the organisers of Edinburgh 1910 was the definition of the 'mission field'. Anglo-American evangelicalism had a long history of missionary activity in Latin America, southern Europe and the Middle East: lands which were officially Roman Catholic or Orthodox. In order to secure the participation of the Society for the Propagation of the Gospel, to retain the support of Bishop Charles Gore and other High Church leaders, and to achieve the endorsement of Archbishop Randall Davidson, the Edinburgh organisers excluded 'Christendom' from the scope of the conference. Edinburgh officially represented the mission of 'Christendom' to the non-Christian world.[6]

4 James Hope Moulton, *Religions and Religion* (London: Charles H. Kelly, 1913), p. 132.

5 Moulton, *Religions and Religion*, pp. 137-46.

6 Stanley, *World Missionary Conference*, pp. 49-72.

Such territorial considerations did not hamper Nonconformist missions. Mention is made here by John Handby Thompson of the Wesleyan William Harris Rule's ventures into Spain, and Brethren outreach in that country is discussed by Tim Grass. Evangelical Nonconformity was not inhibited by ecclesiastical boundaries; indeed, the emphasis on a personal response to the gospel made such distinctions meaningless. The unconverted, whether at home or overseas, and whether nominally Protestant or Roman Catholic, Christian, Muslim or Hindu, needed to appropriate new life in Christ. The scope of mission therefore was worldwide, reaching out to the 'home heathen' as well as to 'regions beyond'. This understanding was reflected not only in the evangelical imperative but also in the approach of specialised agencies, like the Wesleyan Mission to Soldiers whose origins are narrated here.

If the mission field was broad and the agencies diverse, so were the methods and strategies deployed by Protestant Nonconformists in spreading the gospel. Derek Tidball's essay on Baptist Home Missions surveys itinerant preaching, the employment of village missionaries, the use of tracts, and the adoption and then repudiation of American revivalist techniques by British Baptists, setting these strategies alongside a theological evolution from hyper-Calvinism to the missionary advocacy of Andrew Fuller and J. Howard Hinton. The reminder that organised itinerancy was not the sole preserve of Methodists in the tradition of the Wesleys, but was adopted by evangelicals in older Dissenting groups, is very timely.[7] In his account of Brethren missions in Spain Tim Grass looks at evangelism, colportage, educational work and medical missions: all familiar missionary methods. Less familiar, and much more provocative, is John Darch's exploration of the use of violence by Victorian missionaries in the Tropics. Although thankfully infrequent, always controversial, and generating indignant comment among contemporaries, both critics and supporters of missions, there seems to be evidence that some missionaries were prepared to invoke the civil power, or even to deploy force themselves, in pursuit of their ends.

Linked to this latter point is the relationship of missions and missionaries to a range of other agencies, institutions and individuals. The key relationship for these voluntary bodies, dependent as they were on donations, was with their network of supporters: consumers of anniversary sermons and lantern lectures, readers of 'missionary notices' in the denominational magazines, purchasers of edifying literature, patrons of bazaars, regular subscribers, collectors, and missionary box-holders. These individuals, gathered into local fund-raising auxiliaries and sometimes serving on national committees, supplied the money and the personnel for the missionary societies.[8] Clyde Binfield provides 'a Congrega-

---

7 Compare Deryck Lovegrove, *Established Church, Sectarian People. Itinerancy and the Transformation of English Dissent, 1780-1830* (Cambridge: CUP, 1988).

8 See, for example, Brian Stanley, *The History of the Baptist Missionary Society, 1792-1992* (Edinburgh: T & T Clark, 1992), chap. 7; for evocations of Victorian Noncon-

tional dimension', looking at the involvement of Thomas Thompson and Jemima Luke, particularly with the London Missionary Society. This study of engagement by the Congregational elite is complemented by Margaret Jones' exploration of women and missions in Wesleyan Methodism, through the 'Ladies' Committee for the Amelioration of the Condition of Women in Heathen Countries, and for Education etc.' and its successor-bodies. These essays examine how supporters engaged with missions, what they offered, and what they received, and how involvement with overseas missions expressed Christian discipleship.

The relationship of the societies to the civil power is addressed directly by John Darch, by John Pritchard in discussing the 1857 Indian Rebellion, and by Tim Grass in his portrayal of the Brethren mission in the often unwelcoming environment of Spain. John Handby Thompson's essay on Wesleyan chaplaincy in the British Army details the stages through which the Wesleyan mission to soldiers came to be recognised by the Horse Guards, paving the way for a broader Nonconformist chaplaincy to the Forces from the First World War onwards.

Finally, the relationship between missionary societies and churches, and between 'sending' and 'receiving' lands is picked up by Geoffrey Roper in his account of the evolution of four British-based mission bodies into Council for World Mission in the latter half of the twentieth century. Here, as elsewhere, changing structures reflected adaptation to context and new theological and missiological priorities.

Missionaries, and supporters of missions, have been regular targets for criticism, and this has overlapped with popular and literary attacks on Nonconformity and evangelicalism in general.[9] From the ludicrous Mrs Jellyby in Dickens' *Bleak House* (1852-53) to the sanctimonious hypocrite Godfrey Ablewhite in Wilkie Collins' *The Moonstone* (1868) to the portrayal of the Wesleyan revival and its counterpoint, the bazaar, in Arnold Bennett's *Anna of the Five Towns* (1902), and beyond, missions have been held up to ridicule. Besides the mockery of Victorian and Edwardian chapel culture, more serious questions have been asked about missions and imperialism, and about the imposition of beliefs and values by Western Christians on people in other parts of the world and by the affluent on the poor.[10] Some of these issues are addressed in these essays,

---

formity, including the paraphernalia of activities and fund-raising, see Charles D. Cashdollar, *A Spiritual Home. Life in British and American Reformed Congregations, 1830-1915* (University Park, PA: Penn State UP, 2000) and W. Haslam Mills, *Grey Pastures* (London: Chapels Society, 2003).

9 Valentine Cunningham, *Everywhere Spoken Against: Dissent in the Victorian Novel* (Oxford: OUP, 1975).

10 See, for example, Andrew Porter, *Religion versus Empire? British Protestant Missionaries and Overseas Expansion, 1700-1914* (Manchester: Manchester UP, 2004), and Brian Stanley, *The Bible and the Flag. Protestant Missions and British Imperialism in the Nineteenth and Twentieth Centuries* (Leicester: Apollos, 1990).

both in the exploration of changing attitudes towards other faiths and cultures, and in the recognition that the missionary enterprise was not an exclusively male, middle-class operation. Margaret Jones' essay, in particular, shows some of the opportunities offered to women by involvement in the missionary movement, and gives examples of the empowerment of the 'ladies in the gallery'. The Brethren missionaries traced by Tim Grass and Derek Tidball's Baptist itinerants were not members of the elite, but skilled manual workers seeking to share their faith.

The rhetoric of Edinburgh 1910 looked forward to the triumph of Christendom in the immediate future. Scientific advances, technological improvements, progress in education and political reform all seemed conducive to 'the evangelisation of the world in this generation.'[11] Those who were anxious about the state of the Western churches asserted that a commitment to foreign missions would stimulate spiritual renewal at home as well.[12] A century later, secularization preoccupies the Western churches, particularly in Britain, while the predictions of 1910, in terms of the acknowledgment of Christianity as the 'crown' of the 'advanced' religions of the East have not been realised.[13] Instead, the real growth in global Christianity in the twentieth century took place in Africa, among peoples largely ignored at Edinburgh, and through the instrumentality of independent and Pentecostal denominations not represented at the conference. Large and flourishing congregations in contemporary Britain reflect the new Nonconformity of a global Christian diaspora bringing Nigerian, Ghanaian, Zimbabwean and Korean missionaries to this country, and promising a very different retrospective on Protestant Nonconformity and Christian Missions in a century's time.

---

11 Stanley, *World Missionary Conference*, pp. 1-3, 8. The quotation formed the 'watchword' of the Student Volunteer Missionary Union, adopted in 1896: Tissington Tatlow, *The Story of the Student Christian Movement* (London: SCM Press, 1933), p. 75.

12 For instance, Moulton, *Religions and Religion*, pp. 187-98.

13 The description of Christianity as the 'crown' of Hinduism was associated particularly with J.N. Farquhar, for whom see Eric J. Sharpe, *Comparative Religion: A History* (London: Duckworth, 1986 [2nd ed.]), pp. 151-54.

CHAPTER 1

'Spiritual Adventure': Some Aspects of Welsh Nonconformist Missionary Activity in Foreign Lands

John Gwynfor Jones

This theme is vast, even in relation to Welsh missionary activity. It deserves a substantial volume to examine it in any depth mainly because its author would have at his or her command an immensely rich source of socio-religious material which would unravel the complexities involved in the organization of Christian mission, particularly among the Welsh Nonconformists, broadly from the latter half of the eighteenth century onwards. That is why the title has been deliberately limited to include a few aspects of the subject, thus allowing the opportunity to select what are considered to be some of the main features of missionary work—regarded, with some necessary qualification, as the 'modern nursery of heroes'—conducted beyond British shores. That does not imply that the home mission has, in the past, been neglected. It also has its own story to tell, but not fully researched maybe, most of it housed in archival material embedded mainly in repositories and denominational journals.[1]

The Welsh Nonconformist tradition can boast a very strong and enduring missionary history extending back to the seventeenth century. The Puritan background associated with the early dissenting groups which emerged during the course of the seventeenth century laid a foundation upon which subsequent nonconformist bodies built a remarkable missionary enterprise which had al-

---

1 For general studies on missionary activity including Wales see Carlos F. Cardoza-Orlando: *Mission: An Essential Guide* (Nashville, TN: Abingdon, 2002); J. Andrew Kirk, *What is Mission?: Theological Explorations* (London: Fortress, 1999); idem, *Mission under Scrutiny: Confronting Contemporary Challenges* (London: DLT, 2006); D. Ben Rees (ed.), *Vehicles of Grace and Hope: Welsh Missionaries in India 1870–1970* (Pasadena, CA: William Carey Library, 2002). For the Welsh context see J. Meirion Lloyd (ed.), *Nine Missionary Pioneers: The Story of Nine Pioneering Missionaries in North-East India* (Caernarfon: Mission Board, 1989); idem, *History of the Church in Mizoram: Harvest in the Hills* (Aisawl: Synod Publication Board, 1991); Nigel Jenkins, *Gwalia in Khasia* (Llandysul: Alun Books, 1995); J. Hughes Morris, *The History of the Calvinistic Methodists' Foreign Mission to the end of the year 1904* (Liverpool: Calvinistic Methodist Book Room, 1910): D. Andrew Jones, 'From Darkness to Light: The Home and Foreign Missions' in J. Gwynfor Jones and M. Beech Hughes (eds.), *The History of Welsh Calvinistic Methodism*, 3 *Growth and Consolidation (c. 1814–1914)* (Presbyterian Church of Wales) [forthcoming].

most world-wide repercussions by the mid-nineteenth century. Indeed, the concept of missionary activity has a history extending back to the origins of the Christian faith. Missiology basically means the action taken by Christian bodies to send men and women forth with spiritual authority to preach the Christian faith and administer the sacraments at home or in foreign lands, an authority given by God to the Church to preach and convert 'the heathen'.[2] It can also mean extensive evangelization and the offer of spiritual instruction to improve the moral quality of people's lives. Doubtless one of the most famous and indeed notorious organizations during the Reformation was that associated with the Jesuit Society founded by Ignatius Loyola. Its campaigns were aimed at destroying Protestant heresies in the sixteenth century. It was in September 1540 that the Bull *Regimini militantis ecclesiae* established the Society of Jesus to teach Christianity to children and the uneducated and to serve as soldiers in the vanguard of the Catholic Reformation inspired by the Papacy.[3]

In a wider context, missionary activity, less stringent than that of the Jesuits, embraced a much broader spectrum of religious personalities within the Christian Church. That Church had a sense of mission since its inception in the first century AD. Mission, in fact, supplied the Church with its lifeblood from its inception. Jesus's commission to his disciples is central to the mission, as the Gospel according to St Mark records (16:15-16): 'Go forth to every part of the world and proclaim the good news to the whole creation.' He also instructed them in Acts (1:8): 'But you will receive power when the Holy Spirit comes upon you, and you will bear witness for me in Jerusalem, and all over Judea and Samaria, and away to the ends of the earth.' The aim, as revealed in the Book of Acts and the activities of St Paul and other missionaries, was to save souls.

'Mission' is a short word which has an extraordinarily complex meaning. It lies essentially at the very roots of Christian life. The call to serve God is to inaugurate a mission, a statement which requires further elucidation. The word, in itself, has immense implications and can be interpreted in various ways. In this post-modernist (or post-Christian) age, a fundamental question is posed: how do we go about interpreting our duty as Christians in the process of spreading the gospel? Occasionally we see and hear street-preachers with their placards these days in the main thoroughfares of our towns and cities, and another question then arises: do we seriously consider them to be missionaries for the Christian faith with their fundamentalist slogans or merely regard them as an annoyance to busy shoppers and commuters attending to their own business?

---

2 G. Hartwell Jones, *Celtic Britain and the Pilgrim Movement* (London: Hon. Society of Cymmrodorion, 1912); J.E. Lloyd, *A History of Wales* (London and Carmarthen: Longmans, Green and Co., 1989 ed.), 1, chap. 5, pp. 124–61; C. Thomas, *Christianity in Roman Britain to AD 500* (London: Batsford, 1993).

3 G.R. Elton, *Reformation Europe 1517–1559* (London: Collins, 1964), pp. 200–201. For a full study of the Society see William V. Bangert, *A History of the Society of Jesus* (St Louis, MO; Institute of Jesuit Souces, 2nd ed. 1986).

Despite their unpopularity in some quarters they do proclaim a moral and often concisely worded message. Moreover, does mission entail being engaged in a much broader act of extending the message of the Christian Church, whether it be in a pulpit or in a community, among people with whom we are acquainted or those who lie outside our sphere of activity? God is central in all Christian mission: '. . . God initiates all missionary activity,' it has been stated, 'and that God, as a missionary God, participates with those whom God sends . . . the mission of God is the mission of the church, and those who are sent on such a mission are in close relationship with both God and the world.'[4]

A large number of books and pamphlets have been published over the years on the vast subject of Christian mission, offering a multitude of interpretations, most of them based on biblical teaching. When examining the early faith in Britain, for example, attention needs to be given to the early Celtic traditions associated with the saints, notably St David, St Teilo, St Illtud and, in a broader context, St Patrick, St Columba and St Aidan, together with the preaching friars and the extended role of the medieval Church in Christendom.[5] In its heyday the Roman Catholic faith had its mission plan worked out among secular priests and monastic orders well before the Reformation, thus representing the ecclesiastical arm of secular power in Western Europe.

It is now fully accepted that mission is no longer regarded merely as a Christian activity overseas in a foreign cultural environment. The mission frontier is not primarily a geographical one, but rather one of belief, conviction and commitment. Christ's last commission, noted above, involved the use of men (and later women) in the task of extending the central message of the gospel. This commitment entailed assuming a continuing role in the life and survival of the Church, a factor which, despite its many challenges, has served to maintain the faith to this day.

The Christian missionary activity in Wales deserves consideration because, although geographically small, it did contribute immensely to the mission work from the Protestant Reformation onwards. Mention needs to be made of the Catholic missionaries of the latter sixteenth century onwards, and the zeal of individuals like Father John Roberts, the anniversary of whose death was celebrated in 2010,[6] and seminary priests Philip Evans and John Lloyd, executed in Cardiff in 1679.[7] In the Protestant fold John Penry, the fiery Brecknockshire

---

4 Cardoza-Orlando, *Mission*, p. 14.

5 For background, see G.H. Doble, *Lives of the Welsh Saints*, ed. D. Simon Evans (Cardiff: University of Wales Press, 1971); E.G. Bowen, *Saints, Seaways and Settlements in the Celtic Lands* (Cardiff: University of Wales Press, 1969); N.K. Chadwick, *The Age of the Saints in the Early Celtic Church* (London: OUP, 1961).

6 T.P. Ellis, *Welsh Benedictines of the Terror* (Newtown: Welsh Outlook Press, 1936), pp. 43–54; idem, *The Catholic Martyrs of Wales* (London: Burnes, Oates and Washborne, 1933), pp. 79–91.

7 Madge O'Keefe, *Four Martyrs of South Wales and the Marches* (Cardiff, 1970).

Puritan of late Elizabethan days,[8] and the dissenting fathers of the seventeenth century, notably William Wroth, Walter Cradock and Vavasor Powell, pursued their own Puritan mission in days of strong Anglican opposition.[9] Among others of this dissenting tradition they served to lay the foundation of Protestant sectaries, and later Nonconformist denominations in Wales of the nineteenth century. In his own inimitable way Rhys Prichard, the Puritan vicar of Llandovery, Carmarthenshire, in the mid-seventeenth century used his own method of propagating the gospel by composing a large corpus of religious carols in Welsh to serve the needs of his simple parishioners.[10] When the portable edition of the Welsh Bible appeared in 1630, known as 'Y Beibl Bach' (The Small Bible), financed by Thomas Middleton and Rowland Heylin, two prosperous London-Welsh merchants, he urged his fellow-countrymen to purchase copies (at five shillings a copy) to improve their moral standards. Two carols (in translation) will reveal his missionary appeal to his readers:

> The Word's a candle, to give light,
> The Word will shew thee where to tread,
> The Word will guide thy airy flight,
> The Word to heaven will thee lead.
>
> The Bible, in thy native tongue,
> May e'en for a crown be got,
> Sell then all, and be not long,
> E'er thou the precious book hast bought.[11]

Despite his puritanical tendencies Prichard faced no opposition and enjoyed a reputable career in the church. Days of persecution, however, had, decades earlier, sent 'the Pilgrim fathers' to the New World in 1620, followed by Quakers and other dissidents in subsequent generations after the restrictions imposed on Protestant Dissenters after the Restoration of monarchy in 1660–62.[12]

In the late seventeenth and early eighteenth centuries educational and philanthropic societies, such as the Welsh Trust (1674–81), established by Thomas Gouge of London and Stephen Hughes of Meidrim, Carmarthenshire, and the SPCK (1699) spread the Christian Word through their educational establishments and devotional publications, many of them through the medium of the

---

8 William Pierce, *John Penry: His Life, Times and Writings* (London: Hodder and Stoughton, 1923).

9 Geraint H. Jenkins, *Protestant Dissenters in Wales, 1639–89* (Cardiff: University of Wales Press, 1992).

10 R. Jones, *'A Lanterne to their feete': Remembering Rhys Prichard 1579–1644, Vicar of Llandovery* (Llanwrda: Drovers Press, 1994).

11 Jones, *'A Lanterne to their feete'*, p. 60.

12 Jenkins, *Protestant Dissenters*, pp. 39–71.

native Welsh language.[13] By then the emphasis on piety and philanthropy had become a major theme in the Anglican Church and in Dissenting circles. Griffith Jones of Llanddowror, Carmarthenshire, an Anglican priest, set up his circulating schools in Wales from the 1730s onwards at a time when the powerful Methodist revival increasingly left its deep impact on the nation in a period when the Anglican Church had lost much of its momentum but still commanded the loyalty of the majority of Welsh people.[14] Jones's aim was to improve literacy among the Welsh people in north and south Wales by instructing children and adults to read the Bible and the catechism through the medium of their native language. It can be said that his whole life, like that of other missionaries dedicated to advancing education, was a mission. In March 1738, in one of his letters, Jones stated:

> Tis humbly conceived there cannot be higher acts of charity, nor alms so much to the glory of God, the good of others, and the joy of the giver, in any other way than in contributing to help immortal society to a blessed welfare in the eternal state. . . . As the gospel . . . was first preached to the poor, and from them went forth and spread over all the earth, what if the Lord will think fit again to restore the gospel as its primitive force and lustre by the same method? . . . If it should be but to prepare and preserve a seed or remnant to transmit the gospel light to a succeeding generation, it deserves to be esteemed a work worthy of the greatest zeal and expense to promote it in every place where God in his providence opens a way for it.[15]

This statement was essentially the very foundation of his ministry and mission, and he did not detract from it throughout his life.

Griffith Jones lived in an age when emphasis was placed on 'promoting Christian knowledge' and before his time, in 1691, a Society for the Refor-

---

13 E.D. Evans, *A History of Wales, 1660–1815* (Cardiff: University of Wales Press, 1976), pp. 43–56; M.G. Jones, *The Charity School Movement: a Study of Eighteenth-Century Puritanism in Action* (London: Cass, 1964[2nd ed.]); Mary Clement, *The SPCK and Wales, 1699–1740: a History of the SPCK in Wales from its Foundation to the early years of the Welsh Methodist Movement* (London: SPCK, 1954).

14 F.A. Cavenagh, *The Life and Work of Griffith Jones of Llanddowror* (Cardiff: University of Wales Press, 1930); T. Kelly, *Griffith Jones, Llanddowror: Pioneer in Adult Education* (Cardiff: University of Wales Press, 1950); Geraint H. Jenkins, '"An old and honoured soldier": Griffith Jones, Llanddowror', *Welsh History Review*, 11 (1983), 449–68; Glanmor Williams, 'Griffith Jones, Llanddowror (1683–1761)', in C.E. Gittins (ed.), *Pioneers of Welsh Education* (Swansea: Faculty of Education, 1960), pp. 11–30. For loyalties to the Anglican Church see Eryn M. White, 'A "poor benighted church"?: church and society in mid-eighteenth-century Wales', in R.R. Davies and Geraint H. Jenkins (eds), *From Medieval to Modern Wales: Historical Essays in Honour of Kenneth O. Morgan and Ralph A. Griffiths* (Cardiff: University of Wales Press, 2004), pp. 123–41.

15 W. Moses Williams (ed.), *Selections from the Welch Piety* (Cardiff: Gwasg Prifysgol Cymru, 1938), pp. 22–23.

mation of Manners was established to promote a healthy concern for the cause of religion in the world. In the field of education Gouge and Hughes, both evicted clergy who became Dissenters, pursued their mission through the auspices of the Welsh Trust, particularly through the publication of religious and devotional literature and by providing education for children with emphasis on Christian charity. Thus was established among Dissenters the 'parent body' of the charity movement in eighteenth-century Wales. The sense of mission was unmistakable. It was a powerful force and an example for forward-looking pioneers in the extension of the faith into foreign parts.

The outbreak of the evangelical revival in the 1730s following the conversion of Howell Harris of Trefeca witnessed yet another, more dynamic thrust forward in missionary activity. Harris was an enigmatic and forceful religious leader.[16] His relations with his fellow Methodist leaders, namely Daniel Rowland, William Williams, Pantycelyn, the famous Welsh hymn writer, and others became increasingly antagonistic, especially after 1750 when the Methodist movement was split between Harris's supporters and those of Rowland. However, Harris is still universally regarded as the pioneering leader of Methodism in Wales, who, despite his theological disagreements with others, was persistently determined to fulfil his mission. In his own account of his life he stated as follows when referring to his failure to obtain holy orders:

> After my dismission, I was more established in my own soul that my mission was from God. . . . I felt no scruple ever since, but have been more and more established and confirmed . . . feeling the love of Christ in my heart, I saw an absolute necessity of going about to propagate the gospel of my dear Master and Redeemer.[17]

Such a declaration followed an equally powerful private testimony by him at Llangasty parish church, Brecknockshire, in May 1735, when his conversion was finally consummated: 'My soul being filled and satiated, crying 'Tis enough, I am satisfied. Give me strength and I will follow thee through fire and water.'[18] This was the ultimate declaration of total submission to Christ, not dissimilar to John Wesley's words on his conversion three years later, on 24 May 1738, at Aldersgate:

---

16 Geraint Tudur, *Howell Harris: From Conversion to Separation 1735–1750* (Cardiff: University of Wales Press, 2000), pp. 15–16.

17 Howell Harris, *Brief Account of the Life of Howell Harris, Esq*. (Trevecka, 1791), pp. 41–42.

18 Harris, *Brief Account*, p. 18.

> I felt my heart strangely warmed. I felt that I did trust in Christ, Christ alone, for salvation: and an assurance was given me, that He had taken away *my* sins, even *mine*, and saved me from the law of sin and death.[19]

The home mission conducted by the Welsh and English Methodists was a phenomenon which was to have significant repercussions on social and moral issues in future generations. Moreover, missionary movements abroad led the way to the establishment of mission work among Dissenters of varying theological persuasions, again driven by conscience. Griffith Jones, mentioned above, who, in 1713 was a local correspondent of the SPCK in west Wales, considered becoming a missionary with the Danish mission at Tranquebar in India. The SPCK was interested in developing that mission but Jones, for health and other reasons, changed his mind, and refused the opportunity to pursue 'an outlet for his evangelical zeal'.[20] The Methodist fathers, with whom Jones was in close contact (although he disagreed with their evangelical fervour), made a tremendous impact on the growth of mission among their successors in what became, in 1811, the Calvinistic Methodist (later Presbyterian) Church of Wales, a body which was to extend the foreign missionary ventures of future generations.

Of the second generation of Calvinistic Methodists in Wales doubtless Thomas Charles stands out as the most significant leader.[21] He was an ordained Anglican priest who became a Methodist and who promoted the Sunday School movement in Wales from about 1789 onwards. He was a noteworthy theologian, a *litterateur*, biblical lexicographer and reluctant leader of his followers in forming an independent Connexion, the two-hundredth anniversary of which was commemorated in 2011. Charles was not the founder of the Sunday Schools, and praise must be accorded to others like Robert Raikes of Gloucester and Edward Williams of Wrexham for initiating them.[22] Nevertheless, Charles established the system on a missionary basis in Wales. He was truly the architect of the new denomination and his mission was firmly based on the need to secure the salvation of souls through the medium of Welsh, an aim which he promoted throughout his life. With regard to his charity schools Charles again emphasized his main ambition

---

19 *John Wesley's Journal, abridged by N. Curnock* (London: Epworth Press, 1958), p. 51, quoted in J.H. Plumb, *England in the Eighteenth Century (1714–1815)* (Harmondsworth: Penguin, 1961), p. 92.

20 H.C.G. Matthews and B.H. Harrison (eds), *Oxford Dictionary of National Biography from the Earliest Times to the Year 2000* (Oxford, 2004) [hereafter *ODNB*], 30, pp. 501-02; E.D. Evans, *History of Wales*, pp. 98–99.

21 D.E. Jenkins, *The Life of the Rev. Thomas Charles of Bala* (Denbigh: Llewelyn Jenkins, 1908), 2, chap. 32, pp. 185–90; I.G. Jones, 'Thomas Charles of Bala', in *Pioneers of Welsh Education*, pp. 31–56.

22 For Edward Williams see J.E. Lloyd and R.T. Jenkins (eds), *Dictionary of Welsh Biography down to 1940* (London: Hon. Society of Cymmrodorion, 1959) [hereafter *DWB*], pp. 1034–35.

> . . . to teach the children to read their native language correctly, and to instruct them in the principles of Christianity, and nothing more, as the salvation of their souls is the only point we have in view we excluded everything from our little seminaries that has no direct tendency to promote that most important end.[23]

The mission was clear and it is hardly surprising, given Charles's enterprising spirit, that he expanded his interest enthusiastically into the field of foreign mission.

It was in September 1795 that the Mission Society was formed in London, later to be named the London Missionary Society (the forerunner of the Council for World Mission (CWM)).[24] The nature of the period in which evangelical and educational activities thrived gave tremendous impetus to such a society to stimulate foreign and home missions. Anglicans and Dissenters became involved in promoting the faith, principally through evangelical channels. The spiritual condition of non-Christian countries of the world drew the attention of religious leaders in their hymns, sermons and prayers. William Williams of Pantycelyn's English hymn, later translated into Welsh, made a poignant reference to this:

> Let the Indian, let the Negro
> Let the rude barbarian see
> That divine and glorious conquest
> Once obtained on Calvary.
> Let the gospel
> Loud resound from pole to pole.
>
> Kingdoms wide that sit in darkness,
> Let them have the glorious light,
> And from Eastern coast to Western
> May the morning chase the night,
> And redemption,
> Freely purchased, win the day. [25]

Such a subversive racialist attitude in verse would not now be considered appropriate for inclusion in a Christian hymnbook, but in Pantycelyn's day it was considered vital to view Christian mission at home and abroad as a matter of urgency. In his view, by now discounted, the mission needed to extend its mes-

---

23 D.E. Jenkins, *Thomas Charles*, 1, p. 566.

24 C. Silvester Horne, *A Popular History of the Free Churches* (London: James Clarke, 1903), pp. 273, 334, 336, 337.

25 R. Brinley Jones, *Songs of Praises: English Hymns and Elegies of William Williams, Pantycelyn* (Llanerch: Felinfach, 1991). For extensive studies of Williams see Eifion Evans, *Bread of Heaven: The Life and Work of William Williams, Pantycelyn* (Bridgend: Bryntirion Press, 2010); Glyn Tegai Hughes, *Williams Pantycelyn* (Cardiff: University of Wales Press, 1983).

sage 'o'er the gloomy hills of darkness'.[26] William Williams was foremost in the propagation of the Christian mission in the late eighteenth century and followed the Puritan tradition of the previous century which believed in the end of the world and the second coming of Christ. The millenarians believed that Christ would return to eradicate sin and to reign on earth for an extended period before the end of the world, and they prophesied that the thousand years was nigh. It was a version of that belief that evangelicals held, including Williams of Pantycelyn and Griffith Jones, Llanddowror. This meant that Christ's appearance on earth would be prefaced by a long period of success for the Christian mission, a thousand years when Christ would reign in spirit. This was regarded as the 'Puritan hope', and it appeared in Williams's prose as well as his poetry, especially from the mid-1760s onwards. In 1762 this belief was spurred on by the powerful revival at Llangeitho, symbolising the move forward to promote the world-wide mission and ultimate success of the Christian Church.[27] Students from the Countess Huntingdon's college at Trefeca had, between 1769 and 1772, gone abroad to North America to conduct their mission, though not an entirely successful one.[28] William Williams believed that, despite days when the world-wide mission temporarily lost its impetus, the desired end would, in due course, be achieved. This confidence was increasingly expressed when it was reassured that the 'Gentiles', having cast off their 'drowsiness, decay and backsliding', would be converted, aroused and caught up in a frenzy of religious fervor. That would bestir missionaries to greater activity and strengthen their conviction that they had a message of Christian love and charity to impart. Charles, like Williams, believed in the 'Puritan hope' and, as shown above, set about the task to hasten its coming. Williams made his message clear in a letter to Thomas Charles of Bala on 14 July 1787:

> . . . for the fullness of gentiles shall come in viz. the gentiles . . . shall hear of a Crucified Saviour; & shall believe in him . . . thus all the gentile world shall receive ye Gospel & believe; then drowsiness shall fall on 'em in the time of their drowsiness, decay & backsliding . . . & [th]yn the sleeping Gentile Church shall be roused up by ye zeal Love & faith and catch ye fire so ye whole world will be on blaze.[29]

---

[26] Jones, *Songs of Praises*, p. 90.

[27] Eifion Evans, *Daniel Rowland and the Great Evangelical Awakening in Wales* (Edinburgh: Banner of Truth, 1985), pp. 309–21.

[28] Edwin Welch, *Spiritual Pilgrim: A Reassessment of the Life of the Countess of Huntingdon* (Cardiff: University of Wales Press,1995), chap. 8, pp. 131–47.

[29] Edward Morgan, *Ministerial Record; or Brief Account of the Great Progress of Religion under the Ministry of W. Williams, of Pantycelyn* (Llandovery: William Rees, 1847), pp. 55–58; G.M. Roberts, *Y Pêr Ganiedydd (Pantycelyn)* (Aberystwyth: Gwasg Aberystwyth, 1949), 1, p. 162.

It was the Baptist William Carey who, in his book *An Enquiry into the Obligations of Christians* (1792), sought to propagate the Christian mission abroad.[30] He was regarded as the 'Father of modern missions', a man of conviction and a strong leader. In the same year he preached his famous sermon at Nottingham which led to founding the Baptist Missionary Society. At almost the same time the Missionary Society of London appointed a Board of Directors, its chief aim being to select a mission field, appoint potential missionaries and hire a ship to transport them to the South-Sea islands. It was on 27 May 1800 that John Davies, a weaver's son from Llanfihangel-yng-Ngwynfa, Montgomeryshire, who was influenced by Thomas Charles, a Director of the Mission Society, set sail with his wife for Tahiti.[31] Davies was a teacher in one of Charles's schools at Llanwyddelan, and that eventually led to his decision to board the *Royal Admiral* for the long arduous journey to that far-off island which took fourteen months to complete. On that journey he and his fellow missionaries were required to minister to 300 prisoners—a captive audience indeed—bound for Botany Bay. After landing in Tahiti Davies soon learnt the local language and produced a Tahitian grammar and dictionary as well as translating into that language Bunyan's *Pilgrim's Progress* and sections of the New Testament, the Psalms and the Westminster Catechism. His very long period of service there, however, was not easy owing to the various difficulties he encountered, such as conflicts between native tribes, his own domestic problems as well as personal rivalries, continued persecution and the opposition of Roman Catholic missionaries. Nevertheless, he remained on the island for fifty four years, and during that long period did not once visit his mother country. Judging by his own testimony he did not regret his decision to go to Tahiti, and he continued to correspond with his friends in Wales, even during his last years when he was totally blind. At that time his commitment still remained as strong as ever, and that became evident in his last letter to a friend:

> It is certainly with us a trying and discouraging time; it is a winnowing time . . ., the wind has blown away most of the Teachers and the churches under their care have been broken up, and the people scattered: but our consolation is that the farm is in His hand who is owner of the wheat. . . . I wish my friends not to be concerned about me as an individual. I am in the Lord's hands.[32]

---

30 *ODNB*, 10, pp. 90–1; B. Stanley, *The History of the Baptist Missionary Society, 1791–1992* (Edinburgh: T and T Clark, 1992).

31 *DWB*, p. 134. For background see C.W. Newbury, *The History of the Tahitian Mission, 1779–1830* (Cambridge: CUP, for the Hakluyt Soc.,1961); R. Watcyn James, 'John Davies, Tahiti: the Trade of the Missionary Awareness of the Early Welsh Calvinistic Methodists' (Ph.D. thesis, University of Wales, 1986).

32 CMA (Calvinistic Methodist Archive, National Library of Wales), 16237 (15 July 1845).

A remarkable pioneer indeed, fully committed to his labours despite his disability right to the end. He was a person of sterling qualities which he had inherited in his youth in his native Wales.

No detailed account can be given in this short study of all the Nonconformist missionaries from Wales who became involved in spreading the gospel in foreign lands. Much of their contribution has already been recorded elsewhere in individual studies recounting denominational activities. One of note was David Jones from Penrhiw, near Neuadd-lwyd, Cardiganshire, an Independent who became associated with the Madagascar mission supported by the London Missionary Society.[33] He arrived in that island in 1818 with Thomas Bevan, a co-student of his, whose life was cut short owing to his early death soon after his arrival. Jones himself endured personal tragedy, having buried his wife who caught a fever soon after her arrival. With the assistance of David Griffiths, another missionary, he published a Malagasy grammar, hymnbook and the Bible.[34] At Antananarvio, the capital city, he opened the first of a number of his schools in Madagascar, another of his pioneering ventures.

Thomas Morgan Thomas, another Independent from the Vale of Glamorgan, set sail for Matabele Land in 1858. He returned home in 1861 but collected sufficient funds to go back to continue his mission, this time independent of the London Missionary Society. On his second visit he published some elementary books including hymns in the local language.[35]

In 1840 the Welsh Calvinistic Methodists established their Foreign Missionary Society independent of the London Missionary Society to which Thomas Charles had been so closely attached.[36] There was a growing feeling that there was need for a Missionary Society in the Connexion. Several disagreements had occurred between the Methodists and the Independents, particularly in relation to the very nature of church mission and the Independent and Presbyterian systems. The London Missionary Society's organisation was run almost entirely by Independents who increased their control over its affairs. Some Methodist candidates were rejected, and it was generally felt that forming a new Calvinistic Methodist Society would enable the Connexion to contribute more forcefully and effectively to foreign missions. The Methodist mission extended principally into the Khasi Hills and Jaintia of India in 1841, followed by Serampore, the Lushai Hills (Mizoram) and Brittany.[37] It was in 1821 that the first attempt was made by the denomination to work in India, the inhabitants of the Khasi Hills being considered as 'having been covered in black darkness'. Thomas Jones was the first Calvinistic Methodist missionary in that region. He was a

---

33 *DWB*, p. 453.

34 *DWB*, p. 303.

35 *DWB*, p. 967.

36 Morris, *History of the Calvinistic Methodists' Foreign Mission*, pp. 160–61.

37 Morris, *History of the Calvinistic Methodists' Foreign Mission*, pp. 160-61; J. Meirion Lloyd, *History of the Church in Mizoram* (Aizwal: Synod Publications Board, 1991).

native of Llangynyw, Montgomeryshire and was one of Dr Lewis Edwards's first students at Bala Theological College in Merioneth.[38] He reached India in April 1841 and settled at Cherrapunji. Apart from his missionary duties be translated St Matthew's gospel into the native language, but his mission was dogged by controversy.[39] William Lewis, and his wife Mary, were two remarkable missionaries who laboured in the mission field of Cherrapunji. They set sail on the *Malabar* on 16 July 1842, and after a long tedious journey reached their destination on 21 January the following year. Despite their frustrating experiences during their period of almost twenty years in India they performed their duties valiantly and to a great degree successfully before returning home in May 1861, bringing with them a convert, U Larsing, to Wrexham where they settled.[40]

John Thomas of Meidrim, Dyfed, went to Tinneveli, near Madras, and by using the native language he prepared local leaders to establish and maintain churches. Daniel Jones, a native of Llanrhaeadr, Denbighshire, promoted his mission in the Khasi Hills but died a year after his arrival there.[41] D.E. Jones, who hailed from Llandderfel, Merioneth, went to Lushai, reaching Aisawl in August 1897, and the Mizo people heartily welcomed him.[42] In 1906 a revival occurred there which enabled his mission to see off its enemies and competitors. With financial support he established a publishing house in 1913 in the city, which led to an increase in schools and book publications. Jones translated parts of the New Testament into the native language and composed several hymns. He also strengthened the church's structure by insisting on maintaining and increasing church membership.

The Wesleyan Methodist, Hugh Penri Davies, became a successful missionary in India and Nigeria. A native of Dinas Mawddwy, Merioneth, he went to the Hyderabad region in 1914 and became headmaster of the high school at Secunderabad.[43] In 1918 he devoted his time entirely to missionary work, and eventually moved to Nigeria where he became an English and Religious Studies teacher in east Nicosia. Doubtless his mission was successful and he devoted most of his time to education.

---

38 *DWB*, p. 518; Rees, *Vehicles of Grace and Hope*, pp. 100–103; Jenkins, *Gwalia in Khasia*, pp. 49–53.

39 For a detailed investigation of broader aspects of Thomas Jones's mission and its impact on Christian expansion on an imperial frontier see Andrew J. May, *Welsh Missionaries and British Imperialism: The Empire of Clouds in North-East India* (Manchester: Manchester University Press, 2012).

40 Rees, *Vessels of Grace and Hope*, pp. 127–28; 'Mrs Mary Lewis', *Y Cenhadwr* [The Missionary), *The Missionary Journal of the [Welsh] Calvinistic Methodists*, 28 (n.7), July 1949, pp. 97–98; Elfed ap Nefydd Roberts, 'William a Mary Lewis Cherrapunji a Wrecsam', *Historical Society of the Presbyterian Church of Wales*, 36 (2012), pp. 78–92.

41 Rees, *Vessels of Grace and Hope*, p. 80.

42 Rees, *Vessels of Grace and Hope*, pp. 82–83.

43 Rees, *Vessels of Grace and Hope*, p. 22.

Turning now to the Far East, the Christian mission there also became a notable feature of life in parts of China. There was no admittance to missionaries in China but they worked on the perimeter at Malacca and Panang on the western coasts of Malaysia. The Methodist Josiah Hughes of Liverpool worked there between 1830 and 1840, and during his time there he began to translate *Yr Hyfforddwr* (*The Instructor*) into Portuguese.[44] More renowned for his missionary exploits was Griffith John from Swansea.[45] He departed for Shanghai in 1855, and five years later he travelled 250 miles up the Yangtze-Kiang river to Nanking and obtained permission for Christians to work in the city and the outlying areas. In 1863 he settled at Hankow to the west and was known to be a remarkable long-distance traveller in many parts of China. His movements did not end there for in 1885 he published a version of the New Testament in the Wen-li dialect. Of his many achievements it has been said that Dr Griffith John succeeded in harvesting much of the fruit of the seed he himself had helped to sow. He showed political interest in China and sympathized with the revolutionary Taiping Rising (1850–64) in south China against the Manchu–led Qing dynasty. His linguistic skills enabled him to criticize Chinese leadership and support peasant communities against its oppression. He was a man of strong words, often intensely outspoken in public affairs and 'highly influential within the larger missionary community'.[46] Equally renowned was John's near contemporary, Timothy Richard, a native of Carmarthenshire, regarded as 'one of the greatest missionaries whom any branch of the Church has ever sent to China'.[47] A Baptist by religious persuasion, he was educated at Haverfordwest Baptist College, and in 1869 the Baptist Missionary Society sent him to China. He settled in different places, such as Chefoo, Shantung, Shansi and Shanghai, and in 1891 he was appointed Secretary of the Christian Literature Society of China. He was highly acclaimed for his work in China, being honoured as a mandarin of the highest order and elevated to become a member of the Order of the Double Dragon. The University of Wales also acknowledged his vast contribution to missionary activity in China, honouring him with the degree of Doctor of Laws in 1916.

Many other missionaries could be mentioned in this study, all of whom were involved in missionary work, not only in north-east India but also in other places such as the South-Sea Islands, Malacca, China, St Petersburg, Siberia, South Africa, Madagascar, Brittany and southern Rhodesia. Times, however, were eventually to introduce new attitudes, and at the Missionary and Evangelical Council of the World Conference at Bangkok in 1973 a change of emphasis

---

44 Rees, *Vessels of Grace and Hope*, pp. 65–66.

45 *DWB*, pp. 440–41; N. Gibbard, *Griffith John: Apostle to Central China* (Bridgend: Gwasg Bryntirion, 1998); N. Bitton, *The Story of Griffith John the Apostle of Central China* (London: Sunday School Union, c.1915); W. Robson, *Griffith John, Founder of the Hankow Mission Central China* (London: F.H. Revell, 1888).

46 *ODNB*, 30, pp. 213–14;

47 *DWB*, pp. 849–50.

occurred. More concentration was placed in Mizoram in north-east India, for example, on the Calvinistic mission. There was also a growing feeling that the churches should maintain themselves. An opinion was emerging that the 'scaffolding' should be removed, thus enabling the Church to develop further, unobstructed by external factors and to initiate its own Christian strategy and organisation. A maturity had taken place in Indian society and many new developments were in the process of taking place in the modern age, particularly in science and technology. The years following Indian independence in 1947 prompted a new dynamic in the history of Christian missions and theology, and the growth of Indian nationalism threatened the confidence of many religious groups. New local leaders emerged leading to less demand for the importation of missionaries from Britain. The London Missionary Society realised that sending missionaries was no longer the absolute necessity but rather fostering co-operation with other missionary societies and local churches in the mission fields. The International Mission Council joined with the World Council of Churches meeting at New Delhi in 1961 and became the mission and evangelising branch of the Council. That, in part, led to the opportunity for the London Missionary Society to form the Congregational Council for World Mission in 1966. In 1977 that council was incorporated under the new name Council for World Mission (CWM).[48]

In view of the thriving mission work conducted in various parts of India and the Far East, it remains to assess briefly what specific contribution Welsh missionaries made to the propagation of the Christian faith in foreign fields. It is interesting to note that the majority came from the rural parts of the country, particularly the west and the north. They were mentored and recommended for the work by denominational societies, and down to the present a number of actively engaged men and women missionaries had firm roots in Wales. A number of volumes, mostly in Welsh, have been published on the missionary service, notably J. Hughes Morris's detailed study of the Welsh Calvinistic Methodist foreign missionary activity in 1907 and the three volumes published by the Presbyterian Church of Wales, namely on Khasia (Ednyfed Thomas, 1988), Mizoram (J. Meirion Lloyd, 1989 and Gwen Rees Roberts) and Sylhet-Cachar (D. G. Merfyn Jones, 1990).[49] Also, a very large and varied corpus of archival material survives, carefully catalogued in the National Library of Wales at Aberystwyth and elsewhere. The careers in the mission field of individuals such as Rev. T.B. Phillips, Dr and Mrs R. Arthur Hughes, Rev. and Mrs Lewis Men-

[48] See chapter 9 below.

[49] For J. Hughes Morris see Rees, *Vehicles of Grace and Hope*, pp. 151–52 and for Gwen Rees Roberts, Rees, *Vehicles of Grace and Hope*, pp. 151–52 and her interesting autobiography, *Memories of Mizoram: Recollections and Reflections* (Cardiff: Presbyterian Church of Wales Mission Board, 2001).

dus,[50] and many others, men and women, far too numerous to mention, amply testified in denominational missionary journals, to their faith and dedication to the cause of God in foreign parts. Their positive contributions extended into the fields of communal rehabilitation, theology, medicine and education, and despite increasing political, cultural, personal and nationalistic pressures, their expertise was offered in all these spheres of activity, all of which lie outside the scope of this study. The principal function of the Christian mission, however, wherever it was and is conducted, serves to advance God's Kingdom and acts as a powerful force to this day enabling churches, at home and abroad, to assist religious communities to find their role. Long may it continue to promote his Church on earth.

---

[50] Rees, *Vehicles of Grace and Hope*, pp. 151–52, 61–62, 66–69,137–38, 167–68. For R. Arthur Hughes see also D. Ben Rees, 'Robert Arthur Hughes', in *75 Anniversary, 1922–1997: Their Vision, Our Legacy. KJP Synod Hospital, Shillong* (Shillong, 1997), pp. 51–55; idem, (ed.), *The Call and Contribution of Dr Robert Arthur Hughes (1910–1996) and some of his Predecessors in North-East India* (Liverpool: Modern Welsh Publications, 2004).

CHAPTER 2

English Baptists and Home Missions, 1797-1865[1]

Derek J. Tidball

After his conversion, Joseph Donisthorpe, a blacksmith and clockmaker in Leicestershire, gathered his neighbours together in his kitchen to answer their questions about his recent conversion, but soon found himself preaching to them about their lost condition and need of salvation. Before long, Donisthorpe travelled the villages nearby as an evangelist, supporting himself through his trades as a blacksmith and clockmaker, before becoming, at his own expense, a more settled pastor.[2] Donisthorpe's local Baptist Church at Barton-in-the-Beans, Leicester, which had been founded itself only in 1745,[3] became the centre of a vigorous itinerant group which led to the planting of twenty other churches before 1815.[4] While perhaps unusually effective, the work of the Midland Group was typical of the commitment found among Baptists in the late eighteenth and early nineteenth centuries.

Deryck Lovegrove has rightly judged that a crucial factor in the transformation of Protestant Dissent 'from contemptible insignificance to the full flower of Victorian Nonconformity' was the utilization of itinerant evangelism.[5] The Baptist churches' use of itinerancy, however, characteristically reflected their divergent roots and congregational independency and so often lacked any strategic grasp of the task of evangelising England and, with a relatively weak

---

1 This chapter is based on Derek J. Tidball, 'English Nonconformist Home Missions 1796-1901' (Ph.D. thesis, Keele University, 1981), esp. pp. 20-36 and 119-148.

2 J.R. Godfrey, *Historic Memorials of Barton and Melbourne General Baptist Churches* (London and Leicester: Buck Winks, 1891), pp. 102, 105, cited by Frank W. Rinaldi, *The Tribe of Dan: The New Connexion of General Baptists 1770-1891* (Studies in Baptist History and Thought) (Milton Keynes: Paternoster, 2008), p. 101.

3 Barton-in-the-Beans Church probably had Moravian origins. See Fred M.W. Harrison, *It All Began Here: The Story of the East Midland Baptist Association* (London: East Midland Baptist Association, 1986), pp. 36-38.

4 Rinaldi, *Tribe of Dan*, pp. 101-102.

5 Deryck W. Lovegrove, *Established Church, Sectarian People: Itinerancy and the Transformation of English Dissent, 1780-1830* (Cambridge: Cambridge University Press, 1988), p. 14. The Moravian roots of the church may explain, in part, its missionary zeal.

central Home Mission body, responded to rather than shaped the wider currents around them.

The birth of Baptist Home Missions

In 1797, seven Particular Baptist London ministers together with a subscriber from each of their churches formed the first committee of The Baptist Society in London for the Encouragement and Support of Itinerant Preaching with the object of sending out suitably qualified Calvinistic ministers as itinerant preachers and of supporting settled ministers in village preaching.[6] The formation of such a society would have been difficult to envisage a generation or so earlier but was then part of a much wider movement resulting from several developments in the history of nonconformity, as well as the political ferment of the age.

Antecedents

The tradition of itinerant preaching stretched back to the seventeenth century and survived a little even during the period of eighteenth century decline.[7] So the development of home missionary or itinerant societies was not entirely novel but it took place on an unprecedented scale in the last decade of the eighteenth century. The *Societas Evangelica*, in which several of George Whitefield's preachers were influential, was formed among the Independents in 1776, although it did not really come to life until 1796.[8] The Evangelical Association for the Propagation of the Gospel, later generally known as the Village Itinerant Society, was also founded in 1796. The following year the Congregational Society for the Spread of the Gospel in England and the London Itinerant Society were formed.

A second contributory factor was the Methodist Revival which provided other denominational streams with the stimulus they needed to adopt a more aggressive style in presenting the gospel to those outside the church rather than being confined to providing pastoral support to those within. Edward Williams of Rotherham typified the change. Converted through the preaching of a Methodist lay preacher, he combined 'the best elements of' Old Dissent, with its emphasis on reason and education, with those of New Dissent, with its 'urge to save souls'.[9] Institutionally, it led to the formation of the (Arminian) New Connexion of General Baptist (of which Donisthorpe and Barton-in-the-Beans were

6 J. Rippon, *The Baptist Annual Register* [hereafter *BAR*], ii (1794-1797), p. 468.

7 Lovegrove, *Established Church*, pp. 22-23.

8 J. Wilson, *Memoir of the Life and Character of Thomas Wilson* (London: John Snow, 1849), p. 40.

9 W.T. Owen, *Edward Williams DD, 1750-1813. His Life, Thought and Influence* (Cardiff: University of Wales, 1963), p. 3.

a part) under Dan Taylor, who had been converted to Christ through Methodism,[10] and to a reconceptualising of the ministry as more than pastoral.[11]

The rise of the overseas missionary movement provided a provocative stimulus for home missions, particularly among Baptists. John Rippon, advocated the cause of overseas mission in his *Baptist Annual Register* but equally pleaded that his readers should not neglect the 'myriads' at home who were 'profoundly ignorant [of Christianity], if not notoriously profligate and profane'.[12] H.F. Burder, the Congregationalist, insisted, 'We must not postpone our obligation to one of these until our obligation to the other is discharged' but rather by giving attention to one 'we are at the same time promot[ing] the interests of the other...'[13] Some were stung into practical action by the rise of overseas missions and began to engage in village preaching at home. The *Societas Evangelica* and several other itinerant societies presented themselves as paralleling the work of overseas missions in their work at home. Overseas mission proved a particular catalyst to home missions among the Baptists as set out below. Yet others were less persuaded of the cause of overseas missions, with one correspondent objecting to the Methodist Thomas Coke's *Address* on overseas mission by reminding him that 'Charity begins at Home'.[14] Notwithstanding the objections, the rise of overseas mission overwhelmingly had a catalytic effect on the cause of home missions.

A further factor was the loosening of the old bonds of the dependency system, the redrawing of social class boundaries and the fledgling and often-fragile context of greater political freedom.[15] The itinerancy practised among revived Dissenters was considered by many in the Established Church to be politically motivated. John Newton believed all Dissenters were republicans and enemies of the government and claimed David Bogue, a leading Congregationalist from Portsmouth, to be 'as bitter against Government as any Frenchman or republican in the world!' He and others were unconvinced by the protestations of John Rippon who urged itinerants,

> In these labours, let them keep the great object constantly in view; which is, not merely to propagate a set of theological sentiments though ever so true; much less to disseminate political opinions, or to canvass the affairs of state; but in fear of

---

10 Rinaldi, *The Tribe of Dan*, pp. 3, 8-9.

11 J.H.Y. Briggs, *The English Baptists of the Nineteenth Century* (A History of the English Baptists, vol. 3) (Didcot: Baptist Historical Society, 1994), pp. 13-15, Lovegrove, *Established Church*, p. 27 and W.R. Ward, 'The Baptists and the Transformation of the Church, 1780-1830', *Baptist Quarterly* 25 (1973), pp.173-74.

12 *Evangelical Magazine*, ii (1794-97), p. 457.

13 H.F. Burder, *The United Claims of Home and Foreign Missions* (London: R. Baynes, 1824), pp. 13-14.

14 John Vickers, *Thomas Coke, Apostle of Methodism* (London: Epworth Press, 1969), p. 138.

15 A.D. Gilbert, *Religion and Society in Industrial England: Church, Chapel and Social Change 1749-1914* (London and New York: Longman, 1980).

> God, which much prayer, circumspection and self-denial to warn sinners of the wrath to come.[16]

However, the growth of new initiatives in home mission would never have taken place but for the reformulation of the Calvinism which was pervasive among Old Dissent. Given its commitment to the doctrines of election and of man's total depravity, it was not only unnecessary but considered an error to invite people to respond to the gospel. It was, in Joseph Ivimey's words a 'non-invitation, non-application system' of theology.[17] Andrew Fuller's judgment was harsher: it was 'a threatening and forbidding system of theology which seemed as a two-edged sword to protect the cross of Christ from intrusion of unbidden pilgrims' and make the gospel 'a poor shrivelled thing'.[18]

The pastor and theologian attributed with breaking the stranglehold of hyper-Calvinism among Baptists was Andrew Fuller.[19] Influenced by his own experience, by the biographies of people such as David Brainerd, and the writings of Jonathan Edwards, and above all by his own reading of the scriptures, he published his version of moderate Calvinism in *The Gospel Worthy of All Acceptation* in 1781. Without disputing the doctrine of election, he argued that it was the solemn duty of all who heard the gospel to believe it and set out his belief that the preaching of the gospel was to be the supreme end of the work of the ministry. 'Christ and his apostle,' he argued, 'without any hesitation, called on sinners to "repent and believe the gospel", but we considering them as poor, impotent and depraved creatures, have disposed to drop this part of the Christian ministry.'[20] The logic seemed incontrovertible since the *Evangelical Magazine* stated in his obituary, 'to talk of converting sinners by preaching only to saints is an absurdity as great as well can be conceived of'.[21]

Formation

The confluence of these influences made the time ripe for the formation of the Baptist Home Missionary Society, among Particular Baptists, in 1797. In July and August that year, the Revs John Saffery and William Steadman undertook an eight-week preaching tour of Cornwall at the request of the Baptist Missionary Society.[22] Starting at Landrake they visited each town on the south coast

---

[16] Rippon, *BAR* ii, (1794-7), p. 466.

[17] Cited by E.F. Clipsham, 'Andrew Fuller and Fullerism', *BQ* 20 (1963), p. 101.

[18] A.G. Fuller, *Andrew Fuller* (London: Hodder and Stoughton, 1882), p. 30.

[19] On Fuller, see Peter J. Morden, *Offering Christ to the World: Andrew Fuller (1754–1815) and the Revival of Eighteenth Century Particular Baptist Life* (Studies in Baptist History and Thought), (Carlisle: Paternoster Press, 2003). Among Independents it was Edward Williams who was the significant reviser of the theological system.

[20] Andrew Fuller (ed.), *The Complete Works of Andrew Fuller*, (London: William Ball, 1837), ii, p. 84.

[21] *Evangelical Magazine,* xxvi (1818), pp. 3-4.

[22] Rippon, *BAM,* ii (1794-7), p. 459.

before turning north at Land's End and doing the same on the north coast. They preached three times each Sunday and seven or eight times each week, sometimes using Methodist churches but, where these were not available, preaching in private houses or in the open air. On occasions they preached to crowds of over five hundred people. They encountered little opposition, finding the inhabitants 'civil, friendly, intelligent and inclined to hear the word'.[23] Saffrey and Steadman attributed their reception to the relative independence of the Cornish who, unlike those engaged in agriculture, were not integrated into the traditional dependency system. They also acknowledged the success of the Methodists in bringing the population 'into the habits of hearing the word'.[24] For all this, only three or four were converted.[25] Yet this tour inspired the formation of 'The Baptist Society in London for the Encouragement and Support of Itinerant Preaching' later that year.

Rev. Abraham Booth,[26] formerly a General Baptist, but now one who was to play a leading role in this essentially, if not exclusively, Calvinistic Baptist work, set out the justification for the Society. Booth argued that although there was always an obligation to support ministers in their preaching of the gospel there were times that 'more loudly called for exertions of this kind', of which the present time was one due to disturbance on the international scene and the spread of infidelity.

Membership of the society was open to all who subscribed one guinea per annum. A committee of seven was formed with the purpose of sending out, after proper examination, as many Calvinistic Baptist ministers for the work of itinerancy as possible. They could also support the work of settled village ministers if deemed appropriate.[27] In line with the pan-evangelical spirit of the time, their itinerants were permitted to work with paedobaptist ministers providing they shared the same general purpose of preaching the gospel.[28]

Development

Little is known of the society's activities until 1813 but it is likely to have spent the initial years supporting the work of ministers like Joseph Lee Sprague who had been ordained to be minister of Bovey Tracey Baptist Church, Devon, in 1796 and usually preached six times a week in the surrounding villages, and devoted four weeks every summer to itinerating in north Devon and Somerset.[29]

---

23 Rippon, *BAM*, ii (1794-7), p. 459.

24 Rippon, *BAM*, ii (1794-7), pp. 460-61.

25 Rippon, *BAM*, ii (1794-7), p. 460.

26 E.A. Payne, 'Abraham Booth 1734-1806)', *BQ* 26 (1975), pp. 28-42.

27 Rippon, *BAM*, ii (1794-7), p. 470, Rule XI.

28 R.H. Martin, 'The Pan-Evangelical Impulse in Britain 1795-1830, with special reference to four London societies' (D.Phil. thesis, Oxford University, 1974) and *Evangelicals United: Ecumenical Stirrings in Pre-Victorian Britain, 1795-1830* (Lanham, MD: Scarecrow Press, 1983).

29 Rippon, *BAM*, iii (1798-1802), p. 8.

Rippon's claim that the itinerants 'scarcely met any opposition' and the country was 'open for village preaching' was overly optimistic.[30] In Suffolk, Charles Farmery was fined £20 for preaching in a house at Wetheringsett that was not registered under the Toleration Act in 1800 and when Daniel Wilson preached at Orford in 1812 he recalls he collected nothing but missiles and abuse.[31]

An article in the *Baptist Magazine* of 1813 broke the silence about the Society's work and spoke of the way in which it had functioned 'for many years . . . doing good in a very silent and unostentatious manner'.[32] A year later the same publication claimed the Society was 'too little known' and gave details of its work in North Devon.[33] 1814 also saw its first public meeting which reported that thirty ministers had been granted occasional aid.[34] In East Kent, the missionary who was employed 'preached weekly in five villages, ran a Sunday School for fifty children and conducted two prayer meetings', conducted open airs and in addition fortnightly exchanged tracts and sold Bibles.[35] The West Country seems to have been a particular focus of the society's concern. Mr J. Jeffrey established a work on the Scilly Isles in 1816 where he was instrumental in a number of conversions including that of one couple who 'for many years were proverbial for iniquity'.[36] The work there soon became separately funded and the Society's focus shifted to the Channel Islands.

The Society's rather long name was changed in 1817 to 'The Baptist Itinerant and Home Missionary Society' but its aims remained the same and with a newly-formed sub-committee charged with forming auxiliaries to aid its work,[37] such as the one formed in Kent and Sussex,[38] the work expanded from then until the mid-1830s. The expansion enabled the appointment of full-time agents from 1820 onwards. The initial four appointments had risen to forty by 1831 and, according to Roger Hayden, this figure had grown to 100 by 1835.[39] This meant increased administrative burdens and the Rev. John Edwards, who had succeeded the original secretary, Mr W. Gale, in 1815, was joined in 1824 by the Rev. F.A Cox. Cox (1783-1853) was a talented and energetic man with

---

30 Rippon, *BAM*, iii (1798-1802), p. 40.

31 A.J. Klaiber, *The Story of the Suffolk Baptists* (London: Kingsgate Press, 1931), pp. 63 and 69.

32 *Baptist Magazine*, v (1813), p. 279.

33 *BM*, vi (1814), p. 251.

34 C. Brown, *The Story of Baptist Home Missions* (London: Veale, Chifferiel and Co., 1897), p. 29.

35 Roger Hayden, *English Baptist History and Heritage* (Didcot: Baptist Union of Great Britain, 2005^2), p.132.

36 *BM*, ix (1817), p. 474.

37 *BM*, ix (1817), pp. 397-98.

38 F. Bufford, *Kent and Sussex Baptist Associations* (Faversham: E. Vinson, 1963), p. 75.

39 Hayden, *English Baptist History*, p.132.

fingers in many pies[40] but during his joint-secretaryship of the Society he encouraged a policy of supporting missionaries who would give their full time to breaking up new ground and nursing infant causes, rather than supporting existing ministers on occasional journeys.

Throughout the period of its expansion, the society advertised its success. It estimated twenty churches had been formed through its activity between 1820 and 1827.[41] Five years later it spoke of 200 persons being added to the churches it served[42] and in 1835 it reported 300 additions.[43]

For all its successes, however, the Society was not without its problems, of which the shortage of money was chief. In 1826 the annual meeting met under circumstances of 'great discouragement' since for the previous six months agents had only been paid by the Society borrowing money, and it looked as if their operations were going to have to be cut back. The blame was laid at the door of a national economic depression. On this occasion five generous donors who met the debt rescued the Society.[44] But, national economic circumstances apart, the Society never found it easy to raise the money they thought 'commensurate with the claims of' the requests made to them.[45] *The Baptist Magazine*[46] of 1822 put its finances in perspective when it published the revenues received by several leading societies the previous year:

The British and Foreign Bible Society	£103,802. 17.11
The London Missionary Society	£29,437.00.00
The Baptist Missionary Society	£11,600.00.00
The Baptist Home Missionary Society	£930. 00.00

In truth, BHMS was the poor relation among larger missionary Societies. But the work of the Society was only one contribution among many Baptists were making at a more regional and local level. The idea of any national Union still lay a little in the future and much work was undertaken on the basis of individual initiative through Baptists operating a religious free economy. So the cumulative picture of Baptist home missionary enterprise would have been much larger.

A second problem BHMS encountered during this early stage concerned the calibre of its agents. Some agents had been criticized as having 'slender abili-

40 J.H.Y. Briggs, 'Cox, Francis Augustus', in D. M. Lewis (ed.), *The Blackwell Dictionary of Evangelical Biography 1730-1860*, vol. 1, (Oxford: Blackwell, 1995), records him as *inter alia* helping to launch the *Baptist Magazine,* Baptist Irish Society and London University, serving as Secretary to the General Body of Protestant Dissenting Ministers and active in the Anti-State Church Association.

41 *BM*, xix (1827), p. 282.

42 *BM*, xxv (1833), p. 328.

43 *BM*, xxvii (1835), p. 284.

44 *BM*, xviii (1826), pp. 286, 383 and 576.

45 *BM*, xvi (1824), pp. 362, xx (1828) p. 278 and xxiii (1831), p. 292.

46 *BM*, xiv (1822), p. 468.

ties' and the committee as a whole were criticized for being concerned about multiplying the number of agents rather than having men of the right qualities to employ. 'If the messengers who are sent to preach the gospel . . . be not possessed of prudence and talent above mediocrity,' the *Baptist Magazine* asserted, 'they will only injure the cause they were employed to promote.'[47] No consideration seems to have been given to any distinct training being offered to the agents. However, William Steadman who had become Principal of the Northern Academy in 1805, was a driving force in the Society and had as the goal of his training, 'Evangelism steadied by education'.[48] Other academies adopted the need to train ministers evangelistically (see below), although none seem to have taken on the training of itinerants as a separate exercise. So perhaps a separate initiative was considered unnecessary.

The Revivalist Phase

In spite of the challenges, the leaders of the BHMS evinced growing optimism about its work, fuelled by reports of revivals reaching it from the United States. While some, such as James Edmeston who warned that the long-term effects of revival were poor and that steady work in the churches was more fruitful,[49] the Society's leaders responded enthusiastically. They sided with H.F. Burder who argued that apathy was worse than fanaticism and that, 'The time may possibly come when we need refrigeration by some cooling process; but at present we need warmth.' He defended revival converts who might well, he admitted, lack the refinement seen in other converts but were often marked by 'a peculiarly elevated character of spirituality'.[50]

In 1835, Baptist ministers Francis Cox and James Hoby were sent to the United States to observe the revivals firsthand. On their return they jointly wrote of their experiences, and later Dr. Cox published *Suggestions Designed to Promote the Revival and Extension of Religion.*[51] His writing was to shape the policy of BHMS for the next decade.

Cox pointed to nine features of American religion which were worth imitation: (1) individual Christians accepted full responsibility for aiming at the conversion, not just moral reformation, of others; (2) there were many private associations for prayer; (3) enquiry meetings were found useful; (4) they expected the conversion of their youth since 'those who professed the earliest persevered the longest'; (5) maternal associations had been commenced by Mrs Payson in

[47] *BM*, xix (1827), p. 322.

[48] A.C. Underwood, *A History of English Baptists* (London: Kingsgate Press, 1947), pp. 175-76 and D.W. Lovegrove, 'Particular Baptist Itinerant Preachers during the late Eighteenth and early Nineteenth centuries,' *BQ* 28 (1979), pp. 130-32.

[49] *Evangelical Magazine*, NS, vii (1829), p. 190.

[50] *EM*, NS, vii (1829), pp. 246-48.

[51] The full title was *Suggestions Designed to Promote the Revival and Extension of Religion founded on Observations made during a journey in the U.S.A. in the Spring and Summer of 1835* (London: T. Ward, 1836).

1820 where mothers met to pray for and entreat their children to be converted; (6) new churches were planted in needy areas; (7) churches divided when they reached a certain size into two congregations; (8) ministers itinerated for the sole purpose of evangelizing; and (9) the use of protracted meetings, conducted judiciously, to provide a 'quickening zeal'.[52] This last point was to prove the most significant for the future of BHMS.

The new emphasis on revivalism coincided with the appointment of Rev. Charles Hill Roe of Middleton Tindale as travelling secretary of the Society. Roe was the son of an Irish clergyman who had been converted through a Baptist missionary and trained under William Steadman, whose son-in-law he became. Richard Carwardine calls him a 'wild Irishman' who personified the revivalist wing of the Baptist churches.[53] But Roe cannot have been without administrative abilities since he increased the annual income of the Society from £2000 to £5000 during his time as secretary and also increased the support base of the Society by augmenting the number of auxiliaries devoted to its cause, such as that established in Worcester in 1836 and Lancashire in 1841.[54] While much of the Society's work continued as before, he withdrew support from places where there was little success over a prolonged period.[55] Roe's real aim was to inject revivalist life into BHMS.

Shortly after his appointment, Roe undertook a tour of the United Kingdom and concluded that England was a century behind Wales in relation to evangelism. In Wales he met a more popular mode of preaching which was more suited to the capacity of the hearers. He also commended the Welsh 'evangelist system' where ministers frequently visited other churches and made their visits 'directly and ostensibly revival occasions'.[56] The new auxiliaries became channels of his revivalist emphasis.

During this optimistic phase Thomas Pulsford was widely employed by BHMS to promote revival. Pulsford had long been in touch with the Society, having started work as an evangelist in North Devon in 1818.[57] He had no difficulty in attracting an admiring crowd, especially among working class men, agricultural labourers and factory operatives,[58] and is described by Carwardine as the James Caughey of the Baptist churches.[59] Pulsford's novel approach involved preparing for a campaign along the lines advocated by Charles Finney

52 Cox, *Suggestions Designed*, pp. 5-21.

53 R. Carwardine, 'The Evangelist System: Charles Roe, Thomas Pulsford and the Baptist Home Missionary Society,' *BQ* 28 (1980), p. 212.

54 Brown, *Story of BHMS*, pp. 32 and 69; Carwardine, 'The Evangelist System' p. 212.

55 Minutes of the Baptist Home Missionary Society 1832-42 (Angus Library, Oxford), 8 Oct 1839 and 22 Sept 1841.

56 *BM*, xxix (1837), pp. 365-66.

57 D. Thompson, *A Book of Remembrance* (London: Alexander and Shepheard, 1885), pp. 78, 87 and 103-104.

58 Carwardine, 'The Evangelist System', p. 219.

59 Carwardine, 'The Evangelist System', p. 214.

in his *Lectures on Revival*. He shared much in common theologically as well as pragmatically with Finney, but without adopting some of Finney's extremes in either area.[60] He would rise at 4 a.m., hold protracted meetings twice daily and three times on a Sunday, climaxing in the evening sermon as the main reaping time.[61]

Pulsford's work was marked by success. In 1839 he was sent to Carlisle to work with the newly formed Northern Auxiliary of BHMS. During his two months in the city he baptized twelve and left a church of twenty-three members. Douglas, the historian of the northern churches, commented that, 'his labours were indefatigable; and his success, in exciting attention and in arousing careless sinners and the torpid among professors was remarkable'.[62] After Carlisle he turned south and produced results wherever he went. In Newark in 1841 his preaching resulted in 200 enquirers and ninety-eight new members a month after his departure. His most successful year was 1842-43 when his meetings resulted in some 500 conversions.[63]

Before long, the revivalist policy of Roe and Pulsford was called into question. Unsuitable candidates were still asking for support.[64] Roe resigned as Secretary in 1841 and took up a pastorate in Birmingham, despite the pleas of the committee and the temptation of a generous increase in salary. They believed God had blessed his work but that he had possibly overstretched himself. They feared his departure would discourage many who had come into the work under his leadership.[65] After Roe departed, they appointed the Rev. Stephen Davis as his successor. Severe financial strains in 1842 showed that the Society's income had not kept pace with its needs[66] and a number of older auxiliaries, including Cornwall, Devon, Kent, Buckinghamshire and Hertfordshire had become alienated by the Society's new policy and needed winning back 'by kindness and wisdom'.[67]

Increasing doubts about the policy of revivalism emerged, especially concerning its long-term results.[68] The Carlisle church remained open only for a few years[69] and Pulsford's work was subject to criticism.[70] In the late 1830s the

---

60 Carwardine, 'The Evangelist System', p. 217.

61 Carwardine, 'The Evangelist System', p. 216.

62 D. Douglas, *History of Baptist Churches in the North of England* (London: Houlston and Stoneman, 1846) p. 241.

63 The statistics here come from Carwardine, 'The Evangelist System', p. 218.

64 BHMS Minutes, 19 Jan 1841.

65 BHMS Minutes, 7 Jun 1841.

66 BHMS Minutes, 18 Jan 1842

67 BHMS Minutes, 18 Jan 1842.

68 E.g., J.H. Hinton, *Individual Effort and the Active Christian* (London: W. Ball, Arnold and Co., 1859), pp. xii-xxi.

69 W.T. Whitley, *Baptists of North West England* (London: Kingsgate Press, 1913), p. 119.

70 'Quarterly Register of the Baptist Home Missionary Society', *The Baptist Record* (1846), pp. 72-73 and 286-87.

fledgling Baptist Union applauded revivals such as those in Yorkshire,[71] Cradley Heath and Cardigan, and advocated their methods.[72] But from 1841 onwards it became increasing cautious and by 1844 was examining the statistics with greater realism. That year it reported 'with regret the fact now elicited, that the average increase of the year has been somewhat less than six members for each church, being the smallest increase since 1838'.[73] By 1846 it was four new members per church with a third of churches estimated to be stationary or in a retrograde state.[74] The following year, the fiftieth anniversary of BHMS, the problem was even more evident and new measures were called for to arrest decline.[75]

The situation compelled BHMS to reassess its strategy. *The Baptist Record*, while expressing some understanding for the decisions taken, accused BHMS of losing its direction.[76] It had never been the purpose of the Society, the *Record* asserted, to promote revivals in stagnant churches and the original policy of church extension, especially in the villages, should be rediscovered. Doing so had brought a measure of disorder and excitement to the church but had resulted in settled pastors being compared poorly to the more dynamic visiting preachers. Too much pressure had been put on securing results and not enough on the adequate preparation of people for baptism and church membership. The office of 'revivalist' and 'evangelist' should not be confused, and for every one revivalist the Society should appoint three evangelists. The revivalist policy, though wisely conducted and avoiding the excesses of revivals in the USA, had in the end, it claimed, been counter-productive.

The committee of BHMS accepted the criticisms and admitted that they had undervalued the more ordinary means of conversion and that their agents had been less and less cultivating virgin soil for the gospel. In 1846, therefore, they introduced a new constitution firmly stating that their aim was the growth and formation of churches.[77] Other changes involved the extension of the franchise of the society and greater autonomy for more local associations. At the Annual Meeting the following year it was said that providence had brought the revivalist system to a close and a new phase of Baptist evangelism had begun.[78]

Following the re-engineering of BHMS, its work limped along as it continually struggled financially. While it carried on receiving some support, many other home mission initiatives developed which bypassed its work while the Society itself failed to adapt to the claims of the new towns which had risen up the national mission agenda. In 1865 it combined with the Baptist Irish Society

[71] *Baptist Union Handbook* (1838), p. 27.
[72] *BUH* (1839), p. 30.
[73] *BUH* (1844), p. 6.
[74] *BUH* (1846), p. 73.
[75] *BUH* (1848), p. 46
[76] *BR* (1845), pp. 77-80 and Carwardine, 'The Evangelist System', pp. 220-21.
[77] *BR* (1846), p. 285.
[78] Carwardine, 'The Evangelist System', p. 221.

to form the British and Irish Baptist Home Mission but this did nothing really to revive its fortunes. Its real work was over and it became a trickling stream in a swelling ocean of other Baptist initiatives in evangelism until eventually swallowed up by the Baptist Union in 1882.[79]

Other dimensions of Baptist home missionary activity

The contribution of associations

Particular Baptists had been used to cooperating together since their earliest days but this cooperation was essentially expressed through regional Associations. The formation of the 'General Meeting of the Particular (or Calvinistic) Baptist Denomination' – the embryonic Baptist Union – took place in 1813 partly as a response to the need to support the work of the Baptist Missionary Society which was founded in 1797 and partly as a response to the growing denominational consciousness that was characteristic of the time. So while a national home mission body might have been relatively weak, much evangelistic work was undertaken through regional associations. Many historical associations were fairly moribund until the missionary vision renewed them and new associations were founded for the purpose of supporting itinerancy in the late eighteenth or early nineteenth centuries.[80] When the missionary impulse took hold it appeared, in W.R. Ward's words, as if 'the Kingdom of God seemed delivered over to the association principle'.[81]

Some associations were specifically founded for the purpose of supporting itinerancy, such as the Northern Evangelical Society, a joint Baptist-Independent initiative, which explicitly attributed its formation in 1798 to the formation of the BMS.[82] Among the existing Particular Baptist Associations, The Western Association wrote to its churches in 1775 announcing a new fund 'to encourage evangelizing, or itinerant preaching, in those places where it might be judged necessary and advisable'. The Northampton Association records its support for village itinerancy in 1779. The Essex Baptist Association bought a property in Rayleigh in 1796 to house its first itinerant. A decade later Shropshire followed suit.[83]

The other main stream of Baptist life, the New Connexion of General Baptists, had been, as its name indicates, both evangelistic and connexional in nature from the start, owing to the influence of Methodism in its origins. They worked regionally in village preaching and planting new churches, as seen above in the work of the Barton-in-the-Beans church and the Midlands Group.

---

79 Full details are found in Tidball, 'Nonconformist Home Missions', pp. 138-54.

80 These developments were paralleled among Independent churches. See Lovegrove, *Established Church*, pp. 31-33.

81 Ward, 'Baptists and Transformation of the Church', p. 172.

82 Douglas, *History of Baptist Churches in the North of England*, p. 241.

83 The details here rely on Lovegrove, *Established Church*, pp. 32-33.

In 1828 they employed Thomas Cook, later to become known as the first 'travel agent', as their special agent.[84]

The role of the academy

Closely allied to the work of associations in the encouragement of itinerancy was the role of the Dissenting Academies. Older academies were committed to fulfilling an educational role but they could not be unaffected by the transformation churches were undergoing in their re-discovery of an evangelistic mandate. Tensions between educational and evangelistic training were worked out in complex and varying ways, but some academies took their role not only in the training of itinerants but in the training of a new kind of missionary minister seriously.[85] New efforts were put into providing training in the reasoned defence of the faith and in evangelistic preaching. While some academies looked for in-coming students to have experience in village preaching, others enshrined the practice of it in their training.

Bristol Baptist Academy came into being as a result of a legacy left by Edward Terrill in 1679, although the establishment of the academy itself took some years to come fruition. As an older academy, the official records indicate it were primarily committed to education and consolidating the work of ministry among established churches. Lovegrove's research, however, suggests that whatever the official position, during this period 'Bristol students actively promoted itinerant evangelism'.[86] Among the newer academies that were facing the challenge of the growth of new industrial towns, however, there can be no doubt about their commitment. Students from the Bradford and Idle Academies were regularly sent to preach in the surrounding area, rural as well as urban, sometimes into virgin territory and sometimes to revive flagging village churches. When their work bore fruit, as it did, this put pressure on the academies to train more regular ministers and so the consolidation agenda began to supplant the evangelistic one once more.[87]

Baptist Tract Society

Itinerant preachers needed resources to aid them in their work. To that end, and in view of growing literacy rates, Baptists were involved in the founding of the Religious Tract Society in 1799 and many itinerants used its publications and subsequently those of the British and Foreign Bible Society (founded in 1804) and other non-sectarian agencies.

---

84 G. Jackson, 'The Evangelical Work of the Baptists in Leicestershire 1740-1820' (MA thesis, University of London, 1955), *passim*, but esp. p. 193.

85 For a general overview see Lovegrove, *Established Church*, pp. 66-87.

86 Lovegrove, *Established Church*, p. 79, and 'Particular Baptist itinerant preachers', pp. 130-31.

87 Lovegrove, *Established Church*, p. 79.

But, consistent with the growth of distinct denominational identities generally, a more denominationally conscious and sectarian Baptist Tract Society was established in 1841 with the aim not so much of preaching the gospel as disseminating Strict [Particular] Baptist principles.[88] Its sectarian character was evident in that it encouraged the distribution of tracts at events such as Confirmation services.[89] Its strategy was to divide a district into groups of twenty or twenty-five houses and loan tracts to their occupiers for two weeks. They believed the loan system ensured a higher reading rate than if the tract had just been left or sold. A fortnight later, the tracts would be collected and redistributed elsewhere.[90] Among the first twelve tracts published, most had to do with distinctive Baptist doctrines and the differences between Baptists and other denominations. Within five years they had published eighty-nine titles, eight of which were for children, twenty-seven aimed at believers and eighteen aimed at unbelievers.[91] By 1872 they had published 454 tracts, several of which had been translated into French, Spanish and German. They also issued large print tracts for the aged.[92] Rather than rejoicing over their readers having an evangelical conversion experience, they celebrated when their readers became convinced of believers' baptism, like the woman who had 'long known the joyful sound' but after twenty years as a Christian had become convinced of the need for immersion.[93]

The pan-evangelicalism of newly revived Dissent was giving way to a hardening of the boundaries and a desire to recruit to a particular denomination rather than to win converts for Christ.

Individual initiatives

If it is true that the BHMS, at least during the phase we have examined, neglected the more ordinary means of evangelism, the same is not true of other areas of Baptist church life. J. Howard Hinton may be taken as an example, although others could be chosen. Hinton trained at the Bristol Academy and Edinburgh University and held pastorates in Wales, Reading and Devonshire Square, London before a second spell in Reading. He served as General Secretary of the Baptist Union from 1841-1866. All his life he was committed to evangelism at home, balanced with a strong commitment to the Anti-Corn Law League and the anti-slavery cause.[94]

---

88 *Annual Report of the Baptist Tract Society* (1849), p. 4.

89 *Annual Report BTS* (1842), p. 9.

90 *Annual Report BTS* (1842), p. 9. The *Annual Report* for 1847 (p. 5) seems less strategic in its thinking in suggesting tracts should be dropped in fields so that 'the winds of heaven [may] carry them where the providence of God may direct'.

91 *Annual Report BTS* (1846), pp. 23-24.

92 *Annual Report BTS* (1872), pp. 61-62.

93 *Annual Report BTS* (1844), p. 8.

94 Ian Sellars, 'John Howard Hinton, Theologian', *BQ* 33 (1989), pp. 19-32.

In his early days, Hinton participated in the excitement of revival, preaching a sermon, which was then published, to encourage his church members at Hosiers' Street, Reading to join in 'the day of extraordinary prayer' for revival on 10 December 1828.[95] The 'vast slumbering body' of the church needed arousing and every member urged to bend their energies to seek divine blessing, since simply exerting themselves more in the labours in which they had been engaged would not bear fruit in conversions.[96] He was critical of the way in which the pastoral and edification task of the church had relegated the preaching of the gospel to a 'secondary and less important' role.[97] Recognizing that past efforts had not always been productive he sought to instil a sense of optimism in his hearers.

Preaching on Matthew 5:13, he claimed, 'The language of our Lord encourages a confident expectation of success.'[98] His theme, which was also to mark Hinton's later contribution to the discussion of home mission, was the need for every ordinary Christian to work for the conversion of their ungodly neighbours. It was a mistake to rely on professional clergy to accomplish the task since 'how much more good has unlettered and individual piety achieved in every age than all this magnificent and showy apparatus'.[99] Individual Christians might feel insignificant, but individual grains of sand, when combined with others, had the power to stop the sea.[100] Refuting other objections, Hinton pointed out that God had ample resources with which to convert the world without human instrumentality but even so had given Christians the honour of being a link in the chain of second causes through which he accomplished his purposes. He urged his hearers to ask what they had done for the unconverted, and starting with their wives or husbands, then their children and servants, he detailed the increasing circle where they might exert influence.[101] Working towards his climax, Hinton reminded them both of the spiritual privileges that were theirs and of their obligation in view of future judgment to seek to convert the lost, but, he concluded, he had not set these things before them to excite their feelings but to lead them to 'a material change of character' since the text concerned the character of Christ's disciples being brought into contact with ungodly men and women.[102]

A year after *The Means of a Religious Revival* was published, Hinton published a second volume on *The Work of the Holy Spirit in Conversion.* The book had limited objectives and did not set out to be a complete doctrine of the Holy Spirit but rather to examine his role in the conversion of sinners, since

---

[95] J.H. Hinton, *The Means of a Religious Revival: A Sermon* (London: 1829).
[96] Hinton, *Means of Religious Revival*, p. x.
[97] Hinton, *Means of Religious Revival*, p. xiii.
[98] Hinton, *Means of Religious Revival*, p. 23.
[99] Hinton, *Means of Religious Revival*, p. 27. See also pp. ix, 68.
[100] Hinton, *Means of Religious Revival*, pp. 28-29.
[101] Hinton, *Means of Religious Revival*, pp. 48-52.
[102] Hinton, *Means of Religious Revival*, p. 73, drawing also on pp. 30-31

some had considered his previous opinions to be 'derogatory' to the Holy Spirit in their emphasis laid on the activity of men and women in seeking conversions and in the unconverted having in themselves the ability to repent.[103] The old ghosts of hyper-Calvinism still stalked the churches.

On the absolute necessity of the Holy Spirit's role in conversion, he had no doubt, since the evidence of scripture was decisive, various and uniform. The unconverted state was one where the Holy Spirit was absent; the converted state one where he was present and the Spirit's role in bringing about the change of heart was essential and effective.[104] But there was much more to be said that this. In a detailed and carefully nuanced argument Hinton seeks to identify with but also lend clarity to the earlier work of Andrew Fuller.[105] The main body of the work is a lengthy refutation of those who believe men and women had neither the power in themselves to repent, nor to resist the Spirit's work. The Holy Spirit's role is to alter a person's disposition towards God, which in its natural state, is opposed to God,[106] but not to bypass a person's will. Since men and women had the power to turn to God he urged them to do so, and could equally legitimately encourage the work of preaching the gospel to the unconverted with integrity.

It is Hinton's third published work, *Individual Effort and the Active Christian*, that most fully sets out his aspirations for every Christian to be zealous in the work of seeking to convert others. Although published in 1859, the work came from the much earlier period of 1831-32. The Preface explains that people had looked to revival as the means by which God would bring many unconverted to faith, but that when this did not happen, disillusion set in. This, however, was a misunderstanding of revival and, when it was realised that revival meant God would bring about transformation in the church, Christians were less enthusiastic about it.[107] The essence of his argument was that what the church needed was an out-pouring of the Holy Spirit so that the church would diligently adopt the use of means for the conversion of others. Individual conversation was the best method of effective home mission.

Using a series of texts and employing a series of different arguments, Hinton stressed the responsibility of every Christian for the condition of his fellow human beings. In summary:

1. He first spoke of the privilege of being used by God: 'It is entrusted to us, not to be hoarded as treasure but to be used as a sword; and with a view to lead us to engage in the great warfare which God is waging against the enemy of mankind.'[108]

---

[103] Hinton, *The Work of the Holy Spirit in Conversion*, pp. ix-vii.
[104] Hinton, *Work of the Holy Spirit*, pp. 3-9.
[105] E.g. Hinton, *Work of the Holy Spirit*, pp. 287-93.
[106] E.g. Hinton, *Work of the Holy Spirit*, pp. 78-85, 308-09.
[107] Hinton, *Individual Effort*, p. xvi.
[108] Hinton, *Individual Effort*, pp. 40-41.

2. He next spoke of facing those whom they had allowed to die unconverted and face an angry God: 'There is nothing for which they will reproach us [on the great day of judgment] but our silence and for this their reproaches will be bitter indeed.'[109]

3. He then spoke of compassion for the lost sheep: 'Ought we not also to feel as Jesus did?'[110]

4. He argued that efforts to convert sinners were 'a principal source of Christian happiness and of the glory of God': 'A miserable Christian may be taken as a synonym for an idle one; and the only prescription for this malady is hard labour in the service of the Lord. Only enter into truly Christian labours and the greater part of your complaints will be speedily forgotten...'[111]

5. He pointed to the conditions of the present time which were favourable to the advancement of the kingdom of God, such as the extension of religious liberty and the increase of education and literacy. In this he partook of some of the postmillennial optimism of earlier evangelicalism believing that there was very little prophecy still to be fulfilled and what was left 'cannot be expected to occupy a long period of time': 'At what a magnificent and soul-stirring period do we live.'[112]

6. Then he turned to the pragmatic advantages of individuals exerting themselves for the conversion of others and the way in which this would greatly increase both the exploitation of opportunities and the impact of Christian influence. In fact, were individual Christians to engage in this work he believed the vast machinery of missionary endeavour, such as seen in the Christian Instruction Society,[113] would become unnecessary, concluding:

> For my own part, I have no other expectation but that they present system of pecuniary collection [for voluntary societies] to whatever extent it may be carried, will ultimately fall to pieces, and be succeeded by the comparatively unexpensive [sic], but far more effective method of every man saying to his neighbour, 'Know the Lord![114]

In the remaining lectures in the series on 'Individual Efforts' he was more practical, addressing those who felt themselves unfit to witness, setting out the

---

[109] Hinton, *Individual Effort*, p. 67.
[110] Hinton, *Individual Effort*, pp. 73-74.
[111] Hinton, *Individual Effort*, p. 112.
[112] Hinton, *Individual Effort*, pp. 133-34.
[113] The Christian Instruction Society was formed in 1825 primarily to work among the poor in the Metropolis. Although having its origins among the Independents and being an offshoot of their Home Missionary Society, it was supported by Baptists like Hinton and while the initial emphasis was on visiting after the pattern of Thomas Chalmers, became known for the lectures it sponsored for mechanics. Its supporters believed it to be a convincing example and argument in favour of the voluntary principle. See Tidball, 'Nonconformist Home Missions', pp. 233-42.
[114] Hinton, *Individual Effort*, p. 156.

means which could be used, from private conversations and the writing of letters to recommending profitable reading, and discussing the relationship between prayer, human labour and success.

In the second volume, published in the combined volume, *The Active Christian*, Hinton sought to move beyond awakening people's consciousness to directing their activity.[115] It served both as a manual for the cultivation of personal spiritual discipline in those who were seeking to convert others and a manual showing how conversations should be directed and how to handle various particular cases they would meet.[116] While stating realistically that personal evangelistic endeavours would lead to situations of conflict, he nonetheless argued that success should not only be desired but expected.[117] Equally realistically, he discussed how to interpret it if their efforts met with a lack of success.[118] He does not conclude on the negative point, however, and examines how when success was granted a person should act with joy, gratitude and humility remembering that success was not due to their own labours or the means they had chosen but to God's blessing on them.[119]

Hinton's advocacy of 'the individualising system', as it came to be called, was the logical outworking of the individualism characteristic of the enlightenment age. Already evident in the emphasis on personal conversion and assurance, it was a short step from that to it becoming a prominent method of evangelism. Hinton's approach was subject to criticism at first, but then came gradually to commend itself and be widely adopted by Baptists as a primary approach to home missions.[120]

Conclusion

Lacking a strong central organisation, most Baptist efforts were channelled through local or regional associations, which in themselves were shaped by their historic connexions as Particular or New General Baptists. Even more was left to individual initiative. The New Connexion churches experienced some success in planting new churches, especially in the Midlands and Yorkshire. Among Particular Baptists a national work did exist and some attempt was made to undertake preaching in the unevangelised villages and towns of England and the neglected areas of the country. But the BHMS was always the poor relation of the Baptist Missionary Society that worked overseas. Constantly under-resourced, it was subject to the various currents of excitement about revival rather than demonstrating any strategic thinking about the way to evangelise England effectively. Later Baptists became more denominationally con-

[115] Hinton, *Individual Effort*, p. 291.
[116] Hinton, *Individual Effort*, pp. 295-364, 439-60.
[117] Hinton, *Individual Effort*, pp. 511-19.
[118] Hinton, *Individual Effort*, pp. 523-56.
[119] Hinton, *Individual Effort*, p. 572.
[120] Sellars, 'John Howard Hinton', p. 127.

scious and the agenda shifted to emphasise the need for people to be won to the Baptist cause instead of to Christ. As is shown in the preaching of Howard Hinton, the Baptist approach to home missions often depended on outstanding individual pastors and leaders who characteristically emphasised the importance of the continuous and ordinary work of local congregations and, above all, the obligation of every individual Christian to be an active worker in witnessing for Christ to their circle of influence.

The contribution of Baptists to the cause of home missions in the late eighteenth and first half of the nineteenth century was typically activist, varied, complex and even confused. If any pattern emerges, it may be said to have progressed through a phase in which the pan-evangelical methods of itinerant gospel preaching were temporarily side-lined by an emphasis on revival, only to give way in turn to a focus on individual witnessing and soul winning. But the reality was far messier than any simplistic scheme would suggest.

CHAPTER 3

'The active duties . . . proper to her station': Women and Mission(s) in Wesleyan Methodism, 1813-1858

Margaret Jones

On 20 December 1858 'A Committee of Ladies Resident in London' met to set up 'The Ladies' Committee for the Amelioration of the Condition of Women in Heathen Countries, and for Education etc.' This was the first institution to formalise at national level women's involvement in the overseas missions of the Wesleyan Methodist Missionary Society (WMMS). Its successor bodies continued under changing titles, and with ever-closer integration into the general structures and funds of the Methodist Missionary Society (MMS),[1] until in 1987 all women's groups were merged in 'The Women's Network of the Methodist Church', now in its turn transmogrified in 2010 into 'Methodist Women in Britain.'

The Ladies' Committee had a pre-history. Women had been involved in the support of overseas missions since the beginning of the century. Their activity in preaching, leading classes, and setting up and running female benevolent societies in the period up to John Wesley's death in 1791 has been extensively described[2] and their spirituality well analysed.[3] Their role in the first half of the nineteenth century is less well known despite some significant work.[4]

This chapter aims to explore two related questions: 'In what ways and why did (Wesleyan) Methodist women support overseas mission in the period 1800

---

1 The name given to the merged societies of the various branches of Methodism after Union in 1932.

2 See especially Paul Chilcote, *John Wesley and the Women Preachers of Early Methodism* (Metuchen, NJ: Scarecrow, 1991); idem, *She offered them Christ: The Legacy of Women Preachers in Early Methodism* (Nashville, TN: Abingdon, 1993); idem, *Her Own Story: Autobiographical Portraits of Early Methodist Women* (Nashville, TN: Abingdon, 2001).

3 Notably in Phyllis Mack, *Heart Religion in the British Enlightenment. Gender and Emotion in Early Methodism* (Cambridge: CUP, 2008).

4 Linda Wilson, *Constrained by Zeal: Female Spirituality Amongst Nonconformists, 1825-1875* (Carlisle: Paternoster, 2000); Gareth Lloyd, 'Repression and resistance: Wesleyan female public ministry in the generation after 1791', in *Angels and Impudent Women: Women in Methodism* (Wesley Historical Society, 2007); Jennifer M. Lloyd, *Women and the Shaping of British Methodism: Persistent Preachers 1807-1907* (Manchester: Manchester University Press, 2009).

– 1850?' and 'In what ways did this activity affect the nature of their Christian discipleship?'

Preliminary questions: mission and Methodism

The establishment of the Ladies Committee in 1858 and the ending of the independent 'Women's Work' in 1987 'book-end' a period characterised, notably by David Bosch, by a distanced relationship between the 'doers' of mission in Western Europe and the 'done-to' elsewhere.[5] He identifies institutionalisation, colonialism and professionalisation as key features of this period, which is characterised by the devolution of mission activity to specialised societies.

The history of overseas mission in British Methodism does not entirely fit this pattern. In 2010 the Revd Stephen Poxon, Secretary of the Methodist Missionary Society, reminded the Methodist Conference that, '(The MMS) is not an agency: our Church is a missionary movement'.[6] The MMS is not a separate voluntary organisation: every member of the British Methodist Church belongs to it. Until at least the 1970s some service overseas was commonplace for British Methodist ministers.

John Wesley looked forward to 'The General Spread of the Gospel'[7] throughout the world by means of 'the leaven of pure and undefiled religion'.[8] Methodism was established in British colonies in his lifetime in the same way as in Britain: lay settlers in Nova Scotia, Newfoundland, the British colonies in the West Indies and North America preached and set up Methodist societies, and preachers under Wesley's direction visited occasionally. Preachers were regularly stationed in the colonies from 1786 on, but it is clear from the correspondence of Francis and Nathaniel Gilbert that, contrary to Allen Birtwhistle's assertion that mission to slaves in the West Indies also began at this date,[9] work across the racial and religious divide was on the agenda from the 1750s.[10]

After Wesley's death in 1791 institutional change was rapid. An increasingly professionalised ministry needed financial support. A distinction thus arose

5 David Bosch, *Transforming Mission and Paradigm Shifts in the Theology of Mission* (Maryknoll, NY: Orbis, 1991).

6 *Methodist Recorder*, 8 July 2010, quoting the Rev. Stephen Poxon, Secretary of the MMS.

7 The title of one of Wesley's sermons, written in 1783 and published in the *Arminian Magazine* in July and August of the same year.

8 Albert Outler (ed.), *The Works of John Wesley: Sermons 2 (34-70)* (Nashville, TN: Abingdon, 1985), p.493.

9 N. Allen Birtwhistle, 'Methodist Missions', in Rupert Davies, A. Raymond George and Gordon Rupp (eds), *A History of the Methodist Church in Great Britain* (London: Epworth, 1983), vol. 3, p. 2.

10 'A Letter from Mr Francis Gilbert, June 18th 1764', *Arminian Magazine* (hereafter *AM*) vol. 5 (1782), p. 384; John Neal, 'Methodist Missions 250th Anniversary: Oral traditions and historical aberrations', *Proceedings of the Wesley Historical Society* 58:5 (May 2012).

between work that could (in theory at least) be supported by those among whom it was exercised and that which could not. The latter, wherever located, was designated as 'mission', not only overseas but also within Britain and Ireland. Nevertheless the disproportion in the overseas work between local needs and local resources necessitated special financial structures in Britain. These were regularised, not by Thomas Coke, the leading advocate of overseas work, who greatly increased its public profile, but by arch-administrator Jabez Bunting who set up a central Committee of Finance and Advice in 1804. Finally in 1813 anxiety about the perceived 'diversion' of Methodist money into the London Missionary Society (via its wide network of local committees) led to the formation of the Leeds District Missionary Society. This local response, masterminded by influential Methodists (Bunting included), was widely copied and led to the foundation of the Wesleyan Methodist Missionary Society in 1817.

This blurring of home/overseas boundaries and relatively late centralisation arguably created a peculiarly Methodist context for the institutionalisation of overseas mission. This in its turn created a distinctive context for women's support of such mission and gave it a distinctive character.

Preliminary questions: mission and women

Leonore Davidoff and Catherine Hall set the agenda for the study of women's lives and roles in the first half of the nineteenth century by their focus on the question of 'public' and 'private' spheres. They themselves nuanced their basic thesis – that women's public roles were limited, and that the ideal of female identity centred on home, family and the virtues of delicacy and refinement.[11] Subsequent writers have critiqued the framework while acknowledging its continuing validity.[12] 'The evidence suggests that many people did think in terms of separate spheres, and that the nineteenth century saw new attitudes to the home and to women's role within it.'[13]

The setting up of the Ladies' Committee illustrates these points. It originated with the wife of a Wesleyan Methodist missionary, herself formerly a missionary teacher. Mary Batchelor suggested that the British Wesleyan Methodist Church should set up a committee 'not only to provide goods and money, but also to recruit and support women to work in "Female Education".'[14] The Committee's members were, in Methodist terms, extremely well-connected. They were wives and daughters (and mothers!) of both ministerial and lay male leaders of the Connexion, including Treasurers of the Missionary Society and

[11] Leonore Davidoff and Catherine Hall, *Family Fortunes: Men and Women of the English Middle Class, 1780-1850* (London: Routledge, 1987).

[12] Wilson, *Constrained by Zeal*; Lloyd, *Women and the Shaping of British Methodism*.

[13] Wilson, *Constrained by Zeal*, p. 226.

[14] Cyril Davey and Hugh Thomas, *Together Travel On: A History of Women's Work* (London: Cargate Press, 1984), p. 2.

members of its Committee.[15] While their sphere of work may have been limited, and defined by their marital status, the structures of church life thus gave them both informal access to the seats of power and the possibility of creating a protected space for their operations. Porous boundaries between 'public' and 'private' within the church enabled 'private' status to have 'public' implications. Wider social change also had an impact: a specifically Methodist training route into the developing profession of teaching was available from 1851 through the Westminster Normal College, to which the Ladies' Committee's first 'agent', Susannah Gooding Beale, was sent for training.

Wesleyan women were significantly engaged with overseas mission before 1858. In-depth study of the denominational magazine between 1800 and 1850, together with some separately-published 'Lives' of exemplary women, reveals much detail. The *Methodist Magazine*,[16] distributed by the preachers and extensively read across the Connexion, was the official organ of Methodism (later Wesleyan Methodism), published under the authority first of John Wesley and later of the Conference. From 1800 'Missionary Intelligence' was one of the two main areas of content, 'Lives' and obituaries of both women and men being the other.

The *Magazine* played a key role in developing a corporate identity of Methodist discipleship. Descriptions of pious lives and deaths were given particular weight by the *Magazine's* status and by the sheer volume of material (ranging from thirty three individuals in 1810 to 389 in 1845). The almost equally voluminous material about overseas mission both informed readers and contributed to their self-understanding.[17] Women's voices may have been very rarely directly heard at this period, but 'Lives' and obituaries, making due allowance for the bias of the narrator, can still provide indirect evidence of what they were thinking.

Separately published 'Lives' constitute the other category of evidence examined here: the same methodological considerations apply to them as to the shorter accounts in the *Magazine*. Their subjects would have been even more strongly selected for their exemplary character and by means of their influential connections. The telling of their stories is controlled by the didactic aims of the writer; their own writings may be quoted extensively but they are always used selectively. Despite these caveats (fully addressed by, *inter alia*, Brown and Wilson)[18] they provide a rich resource for the historian.

---

15 Davey and Thomas, *Together Travel On*, p. 3.

16 Variously titled *The Arminian Magazine* (1778-1798) *The Methodist Magazine* (1798-1822) and *The Wesleyan Methodist Magazine* (after 1822) [hereafter *WMM*].

17 Wilson, *Constrained by Zeal*, p. 22.

18 Callum Brown, *The Death of Christian Britain* (London: Routledge, 1983); Wilson, *Constrained by Zeal*.

Some exemplary(?) women

I have chosen accounts of five women's lives in order to explore some themes which occur more widely in the material.

Jane Gibson: going from house to house

Francis West introduces the life of Mrs Jane Gibson in 1837 with the disclaimer:

> The biography of a female moving in comparatively private life, furnishes little incident ... The writer can hardly expect that the volume will have influence or circulation much beyond the circle of her own friends . . .[19]
>
> That which is chiefly designed in the following pages, is nothing more than to present an example of practical piety, in the life of a retired female . . .[20]

As the story unfolds, however, we discover that

> In 1819 the Ladies' Branch Bible Association was formed in Newcastle, and Miss Gibson was appointed Secretary. In the management of its affairs she took a prominent part, and generally drew up the Report. . . . She bore her part also in the drudgery of charity, and for many years collected for the Society in the districts of Ouseburn and Sandgate, the latter in a district notorious for its wretchedness, moral and temporal. . . . She was also a Collector for the Society for promoting the Conversion of the Jews, and afforded the same help to the Church Missionary Society.[21]

She was connected with the Methodist societies in Newcastle-upon-Tyne and with the Established Church until marriage to a sea-captain took her to Rio de Janeiro. Both in her birthplace of Newcastle and in places where her private life took her, she built on contacts established within the safety of religious institutions to go to the edges of respectable society: not entirely the expected narrative of the 'life of a retired female'.

The use of the rhetoric of delicacy and retirement was important for narrators in establishing the respectability of their subjects, however much it might be subverted by the content of the story. The Rev. John Angell James, the influential minister of Carr's Lane Independent Chapel in Birmingham from 1805 to 1859, inveighed against 'young women . . . sent out with what are called "collecting cards", to wander over a town knocking on the doors of anybody and everybody for the sake of collecting money . . .'[22] Evidence from Wesleyan Methodist sources indicates that, within the confines of a denomination that

---

[19] Francis West, *Memoirs of Mrs Jane Gibson, of Newcastle-upon-Tyne, including selections from her correspondence* (London: Hamilton, Adams, 1837), p. iv.

[20] West, *Mrs Jane Gibson*, p. 3.

[21] West, *Mrs Jane Gibson*, p. 51.

[22] Cited in Davidoff and Hall, *Family Fortunes*, p. 430.

was becoming more respectably institutionalised, while random 'knocking on doors' might have been frowned on, a more limited 'going from house to house' was approved of and encouraged as part of women's active spirituality. Individual women were able to push the boundaries in their visiting, evidencing the mismatch between the rhetoric of female 'retirement' and the reality of their lives.

Sick visiting, a well-established part of respectable women's activities in the eighteenth and early nineteenth centuries could, under the stimulus of evangelical religion, lead to less acceptable behaviour. Dorothy Hincksman (née Hobson, subsequently Jones) as a young woman in the early 1820s visited the sick, apparently not in any organised way but following the example of her mother and sister. After her experience of 'perfect love' (sanctification), however, things changed:

> *[H]er* chief object was to do their souls good. She used to set off with her prayer-book, and some little present, and tried, as she says, to do the best she could. . . . But after a while she proceeded to pray without a book, and was much assisted and prospered in the attempt. She then began to distribute tracts in the village, and prevailed upon some of the local preachers to come and deliver their message in a good man's house once a month.[23]

Spiritual experience was thus a stimulus not only to visiting *per se*, but to a greater degree of self-reliance and autonomy in the practice of extempore prayer, and to her taking the initiative in the organisation of religious practice. Collecting for missions seemed a natural addition to her other activities:

> Shortly, she became a collector for the Missions; and indeed, for a considerable time, she sought to lay herself out for usefulness in every way she could devise.[24]

When her father forbade her 'praying in private and public, all attendance at Methodist meetings, visiting the sick, and begging for "those blacks" . . .'[25] and turned her out of the house, she took refuge with a classmate. This person was a widow and was thus able, without domestic opposition, to give refuge to a young woman who had put herself outside the bounds of respectability. The class meeting, with its bonds of godly friendship, thus supported Dorothy's transgressive behaviour and gave her a means of subverting parental authority. (Her father eventually gave in and allowed her to return home, agreeing that 'he would not interfere with her on religious subjects'.[26])

---

[23] John Hannah, *The Story of the wreck of the 'Maria' Mailboat, with a Memoir of Mrs Hincksman, the only survivor* (London: C.H. Kelly, n.d.), p. 19.
[24] Hannah, *Memoir of Mrs Hincksman*, p. 19.
[25] Hannah, *Memoir of Mrs Hincksman*, p. 20.
[26] Hannah, *Memoir of Mrs Hincksman*, p. 24.

Other female activities that necessitated visiting other people's houses included visiting the sick,[27] working with the Wesleyan Female Benevolent Society[28] and collecting for the Bible Society.[29] Collecting could be carried out entirely within a woman's immediate circle of friends and family, but it could also enable her to extend the boundaries of that circle without necessarily incurring censure.

Christian 'usefulness' not only motivated women to undertake, within a rhetoric of diffidence and 'retirement', the role described by Helsinger *et al.* as 'The Angel out of the House'.[30] Wesleyan Methodism in particular expected practical activism of its women members at this date. It also created religious and philanthropic structures which empowered and supported them in their work. The class meeting (which might be a women-only group) affirmed collectors and visitors in their work. Collecting for missions formed part of a portfolio of activities which might lead women into social adventure.

Evidence from obituaries suggests that the support of overseas mission was slow to impact on longer-established areas of women's religious activity. In the 'Lives' and obituaries in the *Magazine* so far analysed (every five years between 1800 and 1850) visiting the sick and/or helping the poor constitutes the most common type of religious activity (with one exception). The role of missionary collector does not appear at all before the early 1820s, and never exceeds half the frequency of the largest category thereafter. The role of collector for the Missionary Society (and/or the Bible Society) is never named as the sole activity undertaken by a woman.

	1820	1825	1830	1835	1840	1845	1850
Total women memorialised	23	26	47	20	75	195	150
Visiting the sick and poor	5	5	9	4	16	17	21
Class leader	3	5	8	6	10	17	20
Sunday School (or equivalent)	0	4	4	5	7	9	9
Hospitality to preachers	0	3	8	2	7	5	11
Tract distributor	0	1	0	2	3	3	7
Missionary wife	0	1	1	1	3	6	1
Missionary collector	0	2	4	2	4	6	6

For these women at least, support of overseas missions was not taking them away from other areas of work. They were simply adding another page to their portfolio of Christian service.

27 *WMM* (3rd series) vol. 17 (1838), p. 42 and vol. 4 (1825), p. 79.

28 *WMM* (3rd series) vol. 21 (1842), p. 734 and vol. 14 (1835), p. 655.

29 *WMM* (3rd series) vol. 17 (1838), p. 807.

30 Cited in Wilson, *Constrained by Zeal*, p. 9.

They were however encountering a field of activity which, although disqualified from undertaking and experiencing directly, they might respond to with particular excitement and commitment. Mary Cryer (née Burton) wrote to her aunt in 1836 describing:

> . . . our most delightful missionary services. . . . The good Chief of the Chippeway tribe of Indians interested and delighted us beyond measure. . . . Oh you would have been astonished and delighted, if you could have heard this once wild man of the woods, in his broken English, with such humility, simplicity and power, telling us of the miracles of saving grace. . . . Our collections have amazed everybody. Last year was an increase, but last year is far more than doubled . . .[31]

She followed up her astonishment and delight by marrying a missionary.

Margaret Clough, Dorothy Hincksman and Mary Cryer: marrying the vocation

In the early days of the missionary revival among evangelicals in Great Britain, Melvill Horne was adamant that a missionary ought not to be married:

> . . . the incumbrances of a wife and family must lay insuperable obstacles in the way of their acting, with that energy and decision we may expect from single men.[32]

Adam Clarke, however, writing in 1829, commends

> . . . a spirit and deportment which richly deserved to be better recommended to the imitation of every religious woman, and especially to those who are, or may be, the consorts of Missionaries. This, by the way, is a subject of vast importance; for on the wife of the Missionary not only all his own comforts, but much of his success in his ministry, depend . . .[33]

Margaret Morley met the Rev. Benjamin Clough in 1824 when he was expecting to go to India. His embarkation being delayed, he wrote to her parents.

> Mr and Mrs Morley, having seriously weighed the subject, communicated to their daughter the interesting and important contents of Mr Clough's letter, prudently reminding her of the difficulties and dangers she would necessarily have to encounter and, without expressing any opinion, left the matter to her own consideration and choice. In a few days she expressed her decided conviction that it was her duty to go to India, if her honoured and beloved parents, and her aged grandmoth-

---

[31] Alfred Barrett, *Holy Living: Exemplified in the life of Mrs Mary Cryer, wife of the Rev. Thomas Cryer, Wesleyan Missionary in the south of India. With extracts from her papers and correspondence* (London: John Mason, 1849), pp. 95, 96, 97.

[32] Melvill Horne, *Letters on Missions, addressed to the Protestant Ministers of the British Churches* (Bristol: Bulgin and Rosser, 1794), p. 66.

[33] Benjamin Clough, *Extracts from the Journal and Correspondence of the late Mrs M.M. Clough, wife of the Rev. Benjamin Clough, Missionary in Ceylon* (London: John Mason, 1829), citing 1840 ed. at p. 7.

> er, would give their consent. . . . Mr Morley then wrote to Mr Clough, candidly stating, that dearly as he loved Margaret, and great as would be the sacrifice in surrendering her, yet he could not oppose her views on so important a subject . . .

Dorothy Hobson's father (who we have already met, turning her out of the house for, *inter alia*, collecting for 'those blacks') opposed her marriage to the Rev. Thomas Jones:

> He intercepted letters, and even threatened personal violence if Mr Jones should appear on his premises. All this arose in part, or at least received strength, from an apprehension that Mr Jones would enter into the Mission work . . . a work which Dorothy herself loved beyond all others.[34]

Despite this, Dorothy would not agree to be married without her father's consent. 'Dorothy always felt, that if she were called to the work, her way would be made plain.'[35] After a calm discussion her father's conclusion was, 'Well, I neither say yes or no; please yourself.' 'Father, I shall think it my duty to go, as you do not forbid.'[36]

Mary Cryer's biographer interprets her earlier life as a preparation for being the wife of a missionary. In commenting on her acceptance of the Rev. Thomas Cryer's proposal of marriage he observes:

> The event stood linked with others in the all-wise scheme of Divine Providence. The Christian cannot help but look back, and see the little girl, sitting at her mother's feet in Darlington, and weeping over the 'Missionary Notices;' the pardoned penitent . . . giving herself up, if need be, to the dangers of the trackless deep; the happy believer, devoting herself . . . to a fresh performance of her covenant engagement with God . . . the toiling Secretary . . . sweetly urging on a band of frequently-discouraged Collectors: and then he will see in all this unity of design.[37]

Evangelical faith and practice nurtured a spirituality of personal commitment and enterprise. This informs contemporary biographers' view of women's acceptance of the proposals of marriage which actually took them into work overseas. Thomas Cryer's relationship with Mary Burton is portrayed as inseparable from the missionary calling.

> He saw qualifications eminently commending her as suitable to be the wife of a Christian Missionary, and beheld in her the very helpmeet that he wanted.[38]

At the same time Mary's decision was bound up with her existing family relationships – the locus of those 'relative duties' which played such an important part in the outward expression of a woman's faith:

---

34 Hannah, *Memoir of Mrs Hincksman*, pp. 25-26.
35 Hannah, *Memoir of Mrs Hincksman*, p. 26.
36 Hannah, *Memoir of Mrs Hincksman*, p. 27.
37 Barrett, *Holy Living*, pp. 150-51.
38 Barrett, *Holy Living*, p. 150.

> Many sympathies were now set at work in Mary's mind with reference to leaving her country, her brother and sister, and beloved friends and kindred; but, after much prayer and consultation with her nearest relatives, she decided in Mr Cryer's favour, believing it to be the will of God respecting her that she should thus act.[39]

Dorothy Hincksman's marriage is also interpreted as the fulfilment of her personal vocation: 'Dorothy always felt, that *if she were called to the work . . .*' (my italics). This understanding of marriage as the means of fulfilling a personal calling is far removed from present-day sensibility. (It is perhaps not surprising, but still worth noting, that Pauline Webb, writing in 1958, interprets Mary Fowler's decision in 1838 to marry James Calvert as the triumph of romantic love.)[40]

The role of parents in these weighty decisions is also worthy of note. Both Mr Morley and Mr Hobson, while having very different views about their daughters' inclinations, ultimately left the decision to them. Expectations about marriage at this period comprised a sometimes difficult mixture of family obligation and romantic love: the possibility of ministry through marriage added the obligations of religious calling to the mix.

E.W.: the Ladies in the Gallery

In November 1820 the *Methodist Magazine* published a letter identified only as 'from E.W. to M.C'. Internal evidence shows E.W. to be a woman: the gender of her correspondent is not revealed. The fact that the letter was published in the *Magazine* suggests that she had good Methodist connections. She described to her 'dear friend' the missionary meeting (again unidentified) that she had recently attended, which was

> in every respect what a Missionary meeting should be, except on one account. . . . But shall I mar your pleasure? Shall I tell you that Mr.__, unhappily towards the close of the meeting, came forward in such a comic strain, as to divert, and, I fear, dissipate much of that intense and devout interest which had so generally pervaded the meeting. He complimented the female collectors in such exaggerated terms of commendation as could not fail to disgust every intelligent mind.[41]

She went on to argue that not only was such flattery destructive of 'the delicate sensibility of the more discerning and humble' among the women hearers, and not only did it 'tend to detract from the injunction, "Do all for the glory of God",'[42] it was also demeaning to the women themselves:

---

39 Barrett, *Holy Living*, p. 151.

40 Pauline Webb, *Women of our Company* (London: Cargate Press, 1958), p. 15.

41 Webb, *Women of our Company*.

42 Webb, *Women of our Company*.

> Only let Mr.__ ask himself how *he* should feel if he were addressed in the same adulatory strain? Indignant and disgusted he would say, 'Is it imagined that my feebleness of understanding can approve, my excess of simplicity admit, or my vitiated taste relish a lavish compliment?' Now as Mr. __ is not the only person in the world who has discernment enough to reject this mischievous flattery, let him be more sparing in his distribution of it to others.[43]

This public outburst from a strong-minded woman prompts questions about the nature of her participation in this meeting.

Specifically Methodist 'Missionary meetings' were a relatively new phenomenon in 1820. The meeting which set up the Methodist Missionary Society for the Leeds District in 1813 provided a model which spread quickly across the Connexion. It was '(n)ot only . . . the first Methodist Missionary meeting; it was the first meeting of any kind, other than those for worship, prayer, Bible study or testimony, ever to be held by Methodists'.[44] Public meetings were new and anxious territory for Methodists, the legality of whose religious worship had only recently been confirmed by the Toleration Act of 1811. In the social and political context of 1813 – the Conventicle Act repealed only the previous year, economic distress and continuing war with Napoleonic France, government nervous about linked societies and public meetings – the presence of 'ladies' might function as one more guarantee of respectability.

The impact of their presence should not be underestimated. They might not be able to speak at public meetings, and they might have been segregated: if the chapel boasted a gallery (as at Leeds in 1813) its seating would be reserved for ladies.[45] (A gallery running round three sides of a chapel (such as the one in Wesley's Chapel, City Road) can provide around 75%, and a rear gallery up to 50%, of the ground floor capacity.)

The Revd Jabez Bunting singled out the women at the Leeds meeting for particular mention:

> Permit me, sir, to offer to the Meeting my congratulations on the public and avowed accession to the Missionary cause of those valuable *Female* Auxiliaries, who crowd the galleries this day. . . . They deliver no speeches in *public:* but they will both speak and act in *private* life. They do not *make* or *second Motions* in assemblies like this; but they will do what is better, they will *make subscriptions* for our Fund in their several domestic and social circles, and thus show themselves ready to *second all our efforts* for the honour of God, and the evangelization of the world.[46]

---

43 *MM*, vol.43 (1820), p. 861.

44 Birtwhistle, 'Methodist Missions', p. 25.

45 E.g. the report of the Leeds meeting of 1813 in *MM*, vol. 36 (1813), pp. 952-53.

46 James Nichols, *A Report of the Principal Speeches delivered at the Formation of the Methodist Missionary Society for the Leeds District ...1813* (London: Simpkin and Marshall,1840) [fifth edition], p. 38.

At the similar meeting in Dublin in 1814 Dr D'Olier made special reference to the presence and role of women:

> But it appears that women were present, and filled with the Holy Ghost on the day of Pentecost. . . . Women may indeed imbibe, and retain, a missionary spirit. . . . They may soften the asperity of the Missionary's labours, by soothing his cares, elevating his hopes, cheering his despondencies, and reminding him of God's promises. The seed sown by the Missionary in public they can water by their prayers; and cherish the growth of by their advice in private; their sex and tenderness will often gain them access and influence where the other sex would only meet with repulse . . .[47]

Greater numbers would have been involved in local meetings at circuit level than in large gatherings. This would be particularly the case for women, who were less free to travel. Such meetings would only achieve wider publicity in special circumstances as when Mrs Martha Thompson 'Died suddenly, from an attack of apoplexy . . . (at) a public Missionary Meeting in our Great-Bentley Chapel . . .',[48] or when the excitement of the Annual Meeting of the Wesleyan Methodist Missionary Society at the City Road Chapel proved too much for Mrs Mary Kruse in 1817: '(she) was seized with a paralytic affection. . . . From the effect of this alarming attack she never recovered . . .'[49]

Modern sensibility may read speeches as patronising which in their original context were heard as empowering. Modern interpretation can describe women's attendance either as an example of limitation (present but not allowed to speak) or as a step towards a public role (present with an identified and valued role). Given that the public meeting itself was a new phenomenon, the ability to be present and to observe was not insignificant. The 'ladies in the gallery' were honing skills both for the women-only organisations in which they were already involved and for the future.

E.W.'s indignation at the 'flattering unction' bestowed by the anonymous speaker can be read as an argument for Christian humility specifically for women. But E.W. is clear that her argument applies to women and men alike: 'Only let Mr __ ask himself how *he* should feel . . .'[50] Yet she immediately goes on to advocate humility in terms which appear to apply especially to women.

> Let not Christian diffidence so often be made to shrink from an admiration which it disclaims. Its loveliness consists in its retiredness. That would be deemed a rude hand which should venture to tear off the veil worn as a defence from the publick

---

[47] William Crook (ed.), *Report of the Speeches at the Formation of the Hibernian Branch of the Methodist Missionary Society ... 1814* (London: Hamilton, Adams and Co., 1863), p. 29.

[48] *MM*, vol. 44 (1821), p. 933.

[49] *MM*, vol. 41 (1818), p. 365.

[50] *MM*, vol. 43 (1820), p. 861.

> gaze. Let goodness work in her silent, unobtrusive way: to her, privacy is as grateful as human observation is irksome. Do not drag her forth to view, but contemplate her useful, unvarying, quiet course, with awful respect.[51]

Nevertheless a twenty-first century reader must interrogate the nature of the language. Perhaps we have here an example of the general feminisation of religious sensibility at this time posited by Callum Brown.[52] Is E.W. encouraging men and women alike to practise a spirituality that is particularly associated with women, with Christian diffidence itself characterized as female? Or does her personification of a veiled, female diffidence position her as speaking both for and to women alone? Dr D'Olier, unsurprisingly, is less ambiguous about the distinctive private nature of women's role and influence, and their endowment with the softer virtues. The characterisation of private prayers, private advice and the ministry of tenderness could itself have distanced British Wesleyan Methodist women from the overseas mission enterprise in the way that Bosch describes.

Elizabeth Wood: The Secretary

The 'Memoir of Miss Elizabeth Wood, of Bradford, Yorkshire', written by her sister, occupies nearly seven pages in the *Wesleyan Methodist Magazine* for January 1825. (The dates, the location and, I believe, the personality, lead me to conclude that she is 'E.W'.) Most of the material concerns her inner spiritual experience from childhood on with its somewhat contrived evidence of sin: 'her feelings were acute, and her temper was irritable: she was sometimes rather overbearing, and was tenacious of what she considered to be her rights.'[53] Thus her younger sister . . . The account of her conversion leads immediately to her activities:

> This entire change of principle was accompanied by a corresponding change of conduct ... She was an active Teacher in the Sunday-School, and devoted much of her time to visiting the sick and poor at their own habitations. She became a collector for the Missions, and frequently assisted in the Prayer-meetings . . .[54]

After the obligatory episode of backsliding and renewal,

> She was now ready for every good work; and whatever her hand found to do, she did it with all her might. She took much pleasure in distributing Tracts, and often gave a word of advice to the receivers of them. To the Juvenile Missionary Society she devoted much of her time and influence, and laboured assiduously both as Secretary and Collector. She obtained, in one year, forty subscribers by her own personal solicitation; and while under her care, the Society prospered greatly.

---

51 *MM*, vol. 43 (18200, p. 861.
52 Brown, *Death of Christian Britain*, pp. 58-87.
53 *WMM* (3rd series) vol. 4 (1825), p. 78.
54 *WMM* (1825), p. 78.

She visited the sick and poor, usually alone, 'because she knew the sick cannot bear much company . . . she always came to instruct and to pray'.[55] Not long after writing in her diary that 'I hope I shall not rest, till the work of sanctification be fully wrought . . .',[56] after nursing her dying sister for six weeks, she herself died of consumption, 'aged twenty-eight years and eighteen days'.[57]

This account is typical in its structure and content, and typical also in compressing a wealth of activity into a few sentences. All the activities mentioned are those which women habitually undertook, together with Sunday School teaching, leading classes and both visiting on behalf of and collecting for benevolent societies. In the year in which this Memoir appeared, of twenty six 'Memoirs' or (shorter) 'Obituaries' of women, eighteen mention this kind of activity, and of the eleven 'Memoirs' only one does not. One can only speculate as to the scope that organizing the Juvenile Missionary Society (an appropriate sphere of work for women) and recruiting subscribers gave to Elizabeth Wood's active, 'rather overbearing' temperament, transformed (one trusts) by grace.

The recruitment of collectors and subscribers for missionary funds both secured a steady income and stimulated and maintained enthusiasm, commitment and knowledge. Mr W.G. Scarth, speaking at the Leeds meeting of 1813 noted that the practice of weekly contributions:

> . . . affords to persons in the lower ranks of society an opportunity of uniting in this good work. . . . Only let a man contribute, though in a small degree, to the Missionary cause, and it will excite an interest in his mind which he would never have felt without such a contribution. Only let him *regularly* contribute, and it will keep that interest alive in his mind.[58]

The need to track and maintain such contributions generated a kind of church bureaucracy in which women could participate. Supporting paperwork was obtainable from the Mission House:

> the annual subscribers should be solicited to pay their subscriptions quarterly, in advance. There are books published for this purpose, called the ladies' collecting-books.[59]

The lady collectors were urged to enter everything in the correct books, to 'number the collectors' books progressively, irrespective of sex'[60] and to do everything by the due date.

55 *WMM* (3rd series), vol. 4 (1825), p. 81.
56 *WMM* (1825), p. 82.
57 *WMM* (1825), p. 82.
58 Nichols, *A Report*, p. 22.
59 Joseph Blake, *The Day of Small Things; or, incitement to Juvenile Activity and Usefulness, founded on practical effort in connection with Christian missions* (London: J. Mason, 1849), p. 52.
60 Blake, *The Day of Small Things*, p. 10.

Women were confined to the Committees of the separate Ladies' Associations, despite being listed (as widows, spinsters or married women of independent means) among the Contributors (of half a guinea or upwards) to local societies.[61] Nevertheless, the Rev. Thomas Vasey's comment at the Leeds meeting, that

> A number of individuals will be employed, as Collectors and members of Local Committees, who, for want of such appointments, have not, hitherto, thought themselves able to serve the public[62]

would apply to women's involvement in local administration. Just as participation in Methodist organisations is held to have prepared working people for participation in Trades Unions in the second half of the nineteenth century, so women's participation in Methodist organizations in its first half would have prepared them for wider public roles at a later date.

But perhaps the last word may be given to Charles Dickens, caricaturist but fiendishly accurate observer, portraying in *The Pickwick Papers* a woman's involvement in religious organisation through the eyes of her disillusioned husband, Sam Weller's father:

> What do you think they does, t'other day, Sammy? . . . Goes and gets up a grand tea-drinkin' for a feller they calls their shepherd . . . I sees a little bill about it: 'tickets half-a-crown. All applications to be made to the Committee, Secretary Mrs Weller;' and when I got home there was the committee a sittin' in our back parlour. Fourteen women; I wish you could ha' heard 'em, Sammy. There they was, a passin' resolutions, and wotin' supplies, an' all sorts o' games . . .[63]

Conclusion

What, then, of my opening questions? (1) *In what ways and why did (Wesleyan) Methodist women support overseas mission in the period 1800 – 1850?* The answer to the first part of this question is clear. Attendance at meetings, participation in the committees of Ladies' Missionary Associations, acting not merely as subscribers but as proactive collectors – all are well attested in the sources. The advocacy that doubtless went on in formal and informal settings remains largely unrecorded, although conversation at class meetings, before and after missionary meetings and in informal contexts is implied. For a few individuals, marriage provided the means of fulfilling or discovering a personal vocation.

At the same time the numbers actively involved must not be exaggerated. At no time in this period did the number of women named as 'collectors for the missions' exceed half of those named as either 'visitors of the sick and/or poor'

[61] *MM*, vol. 36 (1813), p. 951.

[62] Nichols, *A Report*, p. 35.

[63] Charles Dickens, *The Pickwick Papers* (London: 1836-37), citing 1907 edition at pp. 297-98.

or ‘class leaders’. Given the *Magazine*’s editorial bias towards overseas mission, this small proportion is significant.

As to ‘why?’ There can be no doubt that support of overseas mission formed part of a varied, active discipleship. ‘Support’ is not mentioned without ‘collecting’, and ‘collecting for the missions’ is very rarely the only activity listed in an obituary. They were indeed ‘constrained by zeal’ in active discipleship.[64] But the appeal of the exotic clearly played a part, not only through meetings such as that with the Chippeway chief which inspired Mary Burton, but through the ‘Missionary Notices’ in the *Magazine* over which she regularly wept. Personal fulfilment must also have been a factor, although it would not have been acknowledged in such terms. Elizabeth Wood’s obituarist implies that her active temperament was well suited to advocacy and administration.

Answers to the ‘why?’ question do not however lie solely with the women themselves. The sheer volume of missionary information regularly available through the ‘Missionary Notices’, the provision of ‘ladies’ collecting-books’ and other administrative support from Mission House, the existence of circuit structures ready to organize significant missionary meetings at local level – all these features of Wesleyan Methodist polity (even, dare one say, bureaucracy) gave support to women in their support of overseas mission.

(2) *In what ways did this activity affect the nature of women’s Christian discipleship?* As already noted, the evidence (albeit from a particular and limited section of the Church) does not support Bosch’s contention that support of professionalized overseas mission detracted from a holistic view of mission at this period. (The wider organizational and financial implications of the women’s success in attracting missionary contributions are outside the scope of this chapter.) The evidence suggests that Methodism’s well-established offices of class-leader and sick visitor continued to be regarded as of prime importance both in terms of numbers and in the assessment of their spiritual and mission significance. The model of discipleship presented in the *Magazine* is shaped by Methodism’s particular theology and practice of mission: comparison with other denominations may assess its distinctiveness.

The exclusion of women from the direct work of mission, other than through marriage, stands alongside their exclusion from preaching. But their confinement to ‘women-only’ spaces gave them some new opportunities. The importance of ‘women’s work’ in supporting overseas mission – itself a valued activity within the Connexion – gave them opportunities for direct advocacy, in class or (ladies’) missionary meetings, as well as experience of administration and the development of associated skills. Women were not excluded from the processes of institutionalisation at work in church and society, and their contribution in these spheres was publicly valued.

Present-day interpretation of these women’s lives hangs suspended between the poles of our title phrase – the opportunities offered by ‘active duties’ and

64 Wilson, *Constrained by Zeal*, p. 226.

the restriction implied by 'proper to her station'.[65] We hear E.W.'s chafing at the tension between them: she was surely not the only one.

[65] 'Memoir of Mrs Susanna Whitton', *WMM* (3rd series), vol. 14 (1835), p. 654.

CHAPTER 4

Brethren Mission in Spain: Planting British-style Churches Abroad?

Tim Grass

The contribution of the Brethren movement to world mission has been widely recognized. It is probable that in Britain the Brethren sent a higher proportion of their membership overseas as missionaries than did any other Protestant denomination. Spain was, for some time, the country which most attracted them. But why were they attracted? And what do we know about the movement called 'Brethren' and the churches called 'assemblies'?[1] This chapter attempts to tell the story of British Brethren mission to Spain, with special reference to the nineteenth century because it was during this period that the foundations of the work were laid.

Who were the Brethren?

The Brethren movement itself came into being in Ireland and England around 1830, when evangelicals in various denominations began meeting together in several places, including Dublin and Plymouth. They sought to transcend denominational barriers in order to study the Scriptures, pray and break bread together. They wanted to be known as 'Christians', and not as members of a particular denomination or sect. Their aim was to meet according to the New Testament pattern, abandoning the centuries of human traditions which had developed. Among them were clergy, but Brethren became known as a movement which appointed no ministers; every male believer was free to speak or pray in the meetings of their local congregations, which were called 'assemblies'.

Over the years Brethren have become known for their lack of ordained ministers and for their commitment to evangelism, but also for the high level of Bible knowledge found among their members. One of the aspects of Scripture which traditionally has interested them most is biblical prophecy, and their interpretative scheme is known as dispensationalism, because it divides history into several dispensations, periods in which God relates to humanity in a par-

---

1 For more information, see my history of Open Brethren in the British Isles, *Gathering to His Name* (Bletchley: Paternoster, 2006).

ticular way. It enabled Brethren to withdraw from the world of biblical scholarship and so to avoid much of the impact of nineteenth-century biblical criticism. Withdrawal from the world was evident in another way, too: British Brethren usually did not get involved in public life, and they viewed contemporary society with disfavour. Often they regarded social change as foreshadowing what would happen under the Antichrist. Similarly, Brethren spiritual experience and corporate worship focused on being seated with Christ in heavenly places, apart from the world.

In the 1840s the movement split into Open and Exclusive Brethren. The latter are often known as Darbyites / Darbistas. But there are few of them in Spain, and so this chapter focusses on the former, Open Brethren.

The main Brethren missionary agency in Britain was (and is) known as 'Echoes of Service'. It was founded in 1872 and is based in Bath, in the West of England. *Echoes of Service* was also the title from 1885 of its monthly magazine (previously known as the *Missionary Echo*). The agency was headed by the editors of the magazine, who also exercised oversight of the work and the workers. Echoes of Service still functions today. Assemblies and individuals who wish to support mission work may give by sending money to Echoes and indicating that it is to go towards the support of particular workers; Echoes also divides up other money it receives among the workers. But it does not guarantee to send a regular amount to each worker, and workers are not sent out or 'employed' by it. They are sent out by their home assemblies, who are expected to maintain interest and pastoral care. The key idea here is that God's primary agency for mission is the local church, and Echoes exists solely to assist assemblies in fulfilling their God-given responsibilities.

Nineteenth-century missionary work is often criticized nowadays because of the reluctance of many missions and missionaries to hand over control to local Christians. This is certainly so with regard to Brethren mission to Spain. The most important expression of this criticism came in 1933: two evangelicals, the Spaniard Carlos Araujo García (who had often spoken at Brethren gatherings and knew them well) and the Englishman Kenneth Grubb, published their *Religion in the Republic of Spain*. This offered a frank assessment of the reasons why Protestant communities had seen so little growth. Brethren came in for particular criticism, because the authors felt that the dominance of foreigners hindered the development of Spanish leadership.[2] García and Grubb also asserted that Spanish Protestantism had become introverted as a result of opposition, and that it was living in the past rather than engaging with the world of public discourse.[3] This may have been due in part to the world-denying influence of Brethren piety on Spanish evangelicalism generally. A third criticism

---

2 C. Araujo García and Kenneth Grubb, *Religion in the Republic of Spain* (London: World Dominion Press, 1933), pp. 65, 72-73.

3 García and Grubb, *Religion in the Republic of Spain*, p. 84.

was that Spanish evangelicalism was rarely self-supporting.[4] All these criticisms have since been repeated by others.

More recently, Kent Eaton in his doctoral research on Brethren work in Spain to 1936 has asserted that 'the thesis that runs through the Brethren missionary story in Spain is that when the controlling reins are held too tightly by the missionary community, a truly national movement will neither prosper nor be embraced to any significant degree'.[5] The missionaries who are in view here were almost all British; Spain was very much the preserve of British Brethren. Although new workers from other English-speaking countries were frequently listed in *Echoes of Service*, until the 1970s almost all new workers in the Spanish field were from the UK. Only in recent decades has this changed, so that most Brethren missionaries in Spain are now from North America.

When we evaluate what British Brethren did in Spain, we need to remember that external factors, most notably the severe and sustained opposition experienced from the Roman Catholic Church, made it difficult for Spanish assemblies to follow the usual process of developing independence. Without foreign involvement the work might not have survived, certainly in its early decades. Moreover, although Protestantism generally may have suffered through being seen as funded by foreign money, it also benefited from the diplomatic pressure which foreign powers could exert.[6] (An example of this came during the period 1945-65, when Brethren sought help from the British Foreign Office to put pressure on the Spanish authorities to allow the reopening of a number of their halls.) Although dependence on outside input hindered the process of indigenization, it could be claimed that apart from the measure of nourishment, support and protection provided by these links, there would have been little or no Brethren movement in Spain to become indigenous.

In saying this I am not trying to exonerate the missionaries; their work had plenty of faults, and some of them were indeed reluctant to hand over control. But the quality of their work may be inferred from the fact that when they were forced to withdraw after 1936, assemblies proved able to stand on their own, and indeed to grow, as they applied what they had been taught.

How did Brethren Interest in Spain begin?

It is often said that the father of Spanish Brethrenism was Robert Cleaver Chapman (1803-1902) of Barnstaple, who was also one of the major leaders in early British Brethrenism. Although others may have been active in Spain during the 1830s, Chapman was by far the most significant. He visited Spain in 1834 (briefly), 1838, 1863-65 and 1871; he preached about the need for mis-

4 García and Grubb, *Religion in the Republic of Spain*, p. 85.

5 Kent A. Eaton, 'The Implantation of the Plymouth Brethren in Spain, 1869-1936' (Ph.D. thesis, University of Wales, Lampeter, 2000), p. 7.

6 Raymond Carr, *Spain, 1808-1975*, Oxford History of Modern Europe, 2nd edn (Oxford: Clarendon, 1982), p. 351.

sion to Spain; he kept in constant touch with missionaries once they arrived there; and the movement's establishment has been regarded as an answer to his prayers. Writers often told the story of how in 1838 Chapman had stood on a hill overlooking Vigo and asserted that an assembly would one day be planted there.

Chapman's first two visits were part of a wave of British Protestant activity between 1833 and 1843. During these years the political climate was somewhat less hostile towards Protestantism, and so missionaries could enter the country.[7] However, Brethren work really began with the 'Glorious Revolution' in 1868, which led to the proclamation of a republic and the consequent declaration of religious freedom. This period lasted until the monarchy was restored in 1875 and a new constitution renewed the restrictions on public manifestations of non-Catholic faith.

In 1868 some of Chapman's co-workers in Spain from 1863-5 returned to the country. His advocacy of the needs of Spain bore more fruit as about eighty other missionaries followed them over the three following decades. Indeed, for several years during the 1880s Spain was the field receiving the largest amount of donation income through Echoes of Service. And apart from those who gave their whole time to the work, there were the 'tent makers', believers who went out as engineers and railway workers and who did evangelism in their free time. They are difficult to trace because they are only referred to occasionally in the magazines, but some of them did a great deal of work.

Whilst wider evangelical interest in the Spanish field declined from the 1880s, partly because it was overtaken by a new awareness of 'heathen' fields,[8] Brethren continued to send numbers of missionaries to the country until the 1930s. The lack of results had caused most other agencies to downsize both their expectations and their missionary force, but the Brethren missionary force remained large until the outbreak of civil war in 1936, numbering sixty or seventy workers from the Edwardian period onwards – about half of all foreign Protestant workers in the country. The sheer number of missionaries, in relation to the small size of the Brethren community, must have been one of the main factors hindering the indigenization of Brethrenism. This is ironic, given that British Open Brethren have traditionally regarded the autonomy of each local assembly as a fundamental principle. So if British missionaries were guilty of exporting British Brethrenism, it could be argued that they were inconsistent in not always allowing congregations to become autonomous.

---

7 C.J. Bartlett, 'The Question of Religious Toleration in Spain in the Nineteenth Century', *Journal of Ecclesiastical History* 8 (1957), pp. 205-16 (at p. 207); Frances Lannon, *Privilege, Persecution, and Prophecy: The Catholic Church in Spain 1875-1975* (Oxford: Clarendon, 1987), p. 4.

8 T. Valentino S. Sitoy Jr, 'British Evangelical Missions to Spain in the Nineteenth Century' (Ph.D. thesis, University of Edinburgh, 1971), p. vii.

What was the ethos of early Brethren work in Spain?

Unsectarian

Chapman, along with his wife's brother George Müller of Bristol, was the most open-minded of all the first generation of British Brethren.[9] Müller founded the Scriptural Knowledge Society (later the Scriptural Knowledge Institution) in 1834. This is best known for the large orphanages which were established in Bristol and funded by prayer, but it soon began to support overseas work. The family and fellowship connections between the two men doubtless influenced Müller to offer considerable support to Spanish work.

The openness of these two makes it likely that the type of Brethrenism exported by missionaries with whom they were in fellowship would also have been open and unsectarian, and that is what we find, certainly during the 1870s and 1880s. I want to illustrate this by talking about two influential workers who arrived from C.H. Spurgeon's Pastors' College in 1873, Thomas Blamire and J.P. Wigstone. Reports from these men appeared in both the Brethren monthly *Missionary Echo* (from 1885 *Echoes of Service*) and Spurgeon's monthly, *The Sword and the Trowel*. Wigstone said nothing to his Brethren audience about his receiving support from Spurgeon's church, and he never mentioned to his Baptist readers that his co-workers were Brethren.[10] In *The Sword and the Trowel*, he was happy to use the word 'pastor' of some of his fellow workers, which British Brethren of the time would have rejected if used in a formal sense.[11] He was also more direct in appealing for financial support than he was in *Echoes of Service*: as he once wrote, 'If you think the work we are doing is good, help us with your money.'[12] I have been unable to establish how these two came to be associated with Brethren. They had gone to college from Congregational churches, but by the time they went to Spain they could probably best be described as 'undenominational', i.e. not owing allegiance to any one denominational tradition. Spurgeon himself was in constant contact with a number of Christian leaders who did not belong to any denomination (and by

---

9 On the openness of Chapman and Müller, see Grass, *Gathering to His Name*, pp. 44-45.

10 In a survey of their work, Wigstone makes no reference to any Brethren co-workers: 'A Review of our Gospel Work in North-West Spain', *The Sword and the Trowel* [hereafter *ST*], April 1882, pp. 167-72.

11 Cf. the reference to a group meeting in Corunna 'with its own native pastor', whom Wigstone and Blamire had taught for two years: 'Letter from our Brethren in Spain', *ST*, January 1879, pp. 19-23 (at p. 22). Even Lydia Brooks de Wirtz (1852-1945), who served as a Brethren missionary for many years, referred to Blamire as 'Pastor Blamire', and to another missionary as 'Padré Faithful': Lydia B. de Wirtz and Winifred M. Pearce, *Spanish Harvest* (London: Marshall, Morgan & Scott, [1938]), pp. 12, 117.

12 J.P. Wigstone, 'The Gospel in Spain – Pontevedra', *ST*, August 1880, pp. 409-12 (at p. 412).

the end of his life I think he felt more at home with them than with leading Baptists). Blamire had been converted through an undenominational evangelist, Gordon Forlong, who was in frequent contact with Brethren. From Spain, Blamire and Wigstone corresponded with Forlong, who commended their work in an undenominational paper, the *Christian Standard*.[13]

It has to be said that in late nineteenth-century England it is often hard to tell who was Brethren and who was undenominational, because their local congregations often looked very similar, except that undenominational churches sometimes had pastors. Müller, whose Scriptural Knowledge Institution funded the day schools operated by Brethren missionaries in Spain from 1870 until forced by financial constraints to withdraw in 1892, could be seen as an undenominational figure, especially from the 1860s onwards. He functioned as a kind of pastor in the Brethren assembly to which he belonged in Bristol, but when touring abroad he preached in churches of all denominations. His Scriptural Knowledge Institution also received support from Christians in all denominations.

There is further evidence that Brethren in Spain were not narrowly denominational. George Lawrence, who had worked in Spain with Chapman from 1863 to 1865 and returned from 1868, served as an agent in Barcelona for the interdenominational Trinitarian Bible Society;[14] he ceased to be listed as a Brethren missionary after 1877, although he continued to work in Spain until his death in 1894. Another Brethren missionary, George Chesterman, was an agent for the National Bible Society of Scotland, which was also interdenominational.[15]

I believe that in Spain, as in Britain, the earliest phase of the Brethren movement's existence could be described as 'pre-sectarian'. In the early days in England and Ireland, they did not always constitute a distinct quasi-denominational body. Believers did not always leave their existing denominations when they began meeting with Brethren. And after the revival of 1858-62 which affected much of Britain and North America, a lack of concern with denominational boundaries reappeared among many British Brethren, especially in the Open wing of the movement. This probably influenced the outlook of the earliest Brethren missionaries to Spain, who often co-operated with workers of other persuasions. To that extent, their claim in Spain to be 'unsectarian evangelists' was justified.

---

13 *Christian Standard* 2 (1873), p. 105; 3 (1873-4), pp. 99-100, 167; 4 (1874), p. 115; 6 (1875), pp. 22-23. The paper's editor, James Grant, was the author of an anti-Brethren work, which was serialized in its pages.

14 He too received support from the Metropolitan Tabernacle: *ST*, January 1874, p. 44. This fluidity regarding identity may also explain why I have seen two influential Brethren missionaries, G.J. Chesterman and Henry Payne Sr, referred to as Baptists: Sitoy, 'British Evangelical Missions to Spain', p. 307 n. 95.

15 *Edificacion Cristiana*, no. 130 (November-December 1988), p. 8.

Having said that, some Brethren appear to have been uneasy about Wigstone and Blamire, and in 1881 an editorial note had to be inserted in the *Missionary Echo*:

> To remove misunderstanding, our brethren BLAMIRE and WIGSTONE ask us to mention that they are under no society or committee, nor is any one responsible for their work in a pecuniary way; that they take no denominational designation; that their custom is to baptize converts and teach them to remember the Lord's death each Lord's-day, and to recognize any spiritual gifts among them; and when gifted persons are manifested in any place they leave to them the care of the work, and take the gospel elsewhere.[16]

In other words, they were doing exactly what good Brethren missionaries should! But by the 1890s British Open Brethren were being divided by calls for a clearer definition of what it meant to be Brethren and a more consistent separation from all ideas and individuals which did not form part of that. This was to result in the so-called 'Needed Truth' division, which called itself the Churches of God. The Editors of *Echoes of Service* began making occasional comments in connection with reports received regarding evangelical work in Spain about the desirability of following the Scriptures in all things, which for them meant adopting a more distinctively 'Brethren' identity.[17]

Brethren and faith missions

Apart from the initially unsectarian ethos of work in Spain, we should also note that to some extent it reflected the ethos of contemporary faith mission work. Faith missions were so called because they did not guarantee their workers a regular income; instead, everybody prayed for God to provide what was needed. This has often been known as 'living by faith'. Among the pioneers of the faith mission movement were Brethren such as Müller, and its greatest spokesman was Hudson Taylor, who had spent a few years in assembly fellowship. Faith missions placed less emphasis on theological training for missionaries, and were often suspicious of contemporary theological trends and professional theologians.

It is clear that Brethren missionaries fitted this pattern. This lack of training was typical of contemporary British Brethren; the first generation of the movement had been led by ex-clergy, but after the revival of 1858-62, leadership tended to pass into the hands of the evangelists. Following the revival, great efforts were made in many denominations to continue the outreach which had begun then, so that the blessing might continue. Missions and gospel halls were set up all over Britain. Existing churches found that the focus of their weekly activities shifted from deepening the spiritual life of members to evangelizing those who were not saved. British Brethren shared in this, and they became a

---

16 *Missionary Echo* 10 (1881), p. 126.

17 E.g. *Echoes of Service* [hereafter *EOS*] 22 (1893), pp. 78, 92.

revivalist movement, often suspicious of theology and of theological colleges. This was the climate which produced the first Brethren missionaries to Spain. It is also important to note that the areas where the missionaries came from were marked by intensive evangelistic and church-planting activity. Devon and Suffolk were the two rural counties in England with the highest concentration of assemblies; and lowland Scotland was an urban area which also had a high concentration of assemblies.

Furthermore, faith missions accepted candidates from a variety of socio-economic backgrounds. Many Brethren missionaries to Spain during this period had previously been skilled manual workers; this reflected the strength of British Brethren among the skilled working classes. I wonder whether the lack of education meant that most of the missionaries did less strategic thinking about the shape their mission should take, and the principles on which it should be based. Rather, they were likely to begin with the assumption that British Brethren practices were in fact universally valid. It was probably hard at times for them to distinguish between being biblical and being British.

What did the missionaries do?

Evangelism

As with Brethren at home, evangelism was the first priority for workers in Spain, and other aspects of the work had on occasion to be justified in terms of their evangelistic potential, or the readers of *Echoes of Service* reminded that donations to them must not abstract from the support of direct evangelism. (Faith missions feared that older missionary societies were being diverted from evangelism into medical and educational work.) One of the chief methods of outreach was colportage, the itinerant selling or distribution of Bibles, Gospels, tracts and other literature: this was undoubtedly influenced by the example of George Borrow, who toured Spain during the late 1830s as an agent of the British and Foreign Bible Society. His immensely popular account, *The Bible in Spain*, was widely read in Britain. The copies owned by several early Brethren missionaries still survive, and most had probably read the book.

Colportage was successful in gaining the missionaries a hearing during the period of freedom from 1868 to 1875. Brethren missionaries and Spanish colporteurs distributed literature from market stalls, on trains, in visiting, and even placed gospels in the folds of the dresses of ladies hearing mass! Moreover, it appears that a focus on distribution of the Scriptures was, as one veteran recalled, 'thought wise by the leading brethren' – probably a reference to the editors at Echoes of Service exercising guidance regarding the development of the work.[18] The down side of colportage was that it did not aim to plant churches: Borrow worked for the Bible Society, and as such his brief did not include any-

[18] Henry Payne Sr, 'Surveys of Service: Reminiscences of Early Days in Spain', *Believer's Magazine* n.s.35 (1934), pp. 210-12 (at p. 211).

thing beyond Scripture distribution. So when Brethren adopted this approach, they were liable to neglect church planting, let alone longer-term objectives such as leadership development. But by the end of the nineteenth century they had established sizeable assemblies in Madrid, Barcelona and the north-western province of Galicia.

Once the brief period of freedom ended in 1875, and public manifestations of Protestantism were prohibited once more, one of the few opportunities for Brethren or other evangelicals to demonstrate their existence in public was, curiously, the funeral. By the 1890s *Echoes of Service* was often reporting such events in great detail. Certain features were common in these accounts. There was the struggle with the priest for the right of the dying or deceased person to a Protestant burial, the petitioning of the authorities for somewhere to bury non-Catholic dead (a legal right but one which was not always granted by local authorities), and the remarkable transformation of the funeral service into a preaching festival, to which missionaries would travel considerable distances in order to participate and large crowds would often be drawn. In an article on the phenomenon, Eaton argues that it was unsuccessful as an evangelistic strategy, but I do not think that such a conclusive verdict can be justified.[19] If nothing else, people would have been made aware that Protestants existed and would have heard something of what they believed, probably for the first time.

Why the focus on funerals? Well, the right of Protestants in Spain to a decent burial had already been the subject of diplomatic representations, but in Britain burial was a topic about which late nineteenth-century Nonconformists felt passionately because of their struggle for the right to hold non-Anglican burial services in churchyards. Also, among British Brethren funerals were seen as evangelistic opportunities. So, Brethren missionaries were probably predisposed to see it as an evangelistic opportunity by previous experience at home. Thirdly, a dignified burial was most important for many Spaniards; priests used the threat of being buried like a dog to dissuade people from leaving the Catholic Church. Therefore Protestants would have sought to ensure the provision of a proper funeral and burial for their people in order to lessen the force of such threats and as an important pastoral provision for the bereaved.

Schools

Missionary reports sometimes referred to the high rate of illiteracy in Spain; literacy was seen as important because it enabled individuals to read the Scriptures for themselves. Literacy was thus twinned with Scripture distribution, the two together being seen as the only way to undermine the dominance of Roman Catholic ideas. Brethren missionaries in Spain ran as many as sixteen day schools during this period, and a number of workers were occupied as schoolteachers. As with Brethren schools in the UK, they had two objectives: to evan-

[19] Kent Eaton, '"Go, Tell It in the . . . Cemetery?" Protestant Funerals in Victorian Spain', *Missiology* 31 (2003), pp. 431-48, accessed online.

gelize, and to protect children of believers from exposure to the religious teaching of the established church. The schools work was more prominent in Spain than in Britain because there was so little other opportunity for public evangelism. Missionaries therefore made much of demonstrations in which pupils sang hymns and recited passages of Scripture to an audience composed of parents and other relatives. I cannot judge how far the Spanish schools were culturally adapted, but it does appear that Protestant schools generally were seen as pioneering new educational methods, and the quality of their education was recognized.[20]

Medical Work

Medical work and other 'works of mercy' formed a third aspect of Brethren missionary practice, as in the outreach of assemblies in some British cities, but they received a much lower profile than the first two and were less extensively reported. This was mainly because Brethren saw direct evangelism as more important. There was an orphanage in Madrid from 1876-80, and medical work at times of epidemic helped to win the missionaries a hearing as their care for the needy was recognized, but it never became as significant as it did for Brethren in parts of the world such as central Africa.

How did the missionaries relate to Spanish assemblies and to British supporters?

Once assemblies began to be formed, missionaries often assumed the role of pastor. Whilst the theory of Brethren mission was egalitarian, stressing the priesthood of all (male) believers and the absence of a clerical caste, the practice was somewhat different. So why were missionaries slow to develop national gift? The Editors would have liked to see a quicker transition to local leadership, in line with their understanding of biblical missiological principles, and from time to time they offered advice to workers, often in an attempt to encourage them to hand over increasing responsibility to local converts. But their advice was not necessarily accepted. For example, in 1874 Blamire and Wigstone wrote: 'In reference to what you wrote as to dividing, and each taking a Spaniard to the villages [for open air work etc.], we only say we would be glad were it possible; but it is not so for several reasons. This is a difficult work, and exposes to great persecution. It therefore needs more moral courage than any of the Spaniards seem to possess.'[21] And there are frequent references in *Echoes of Service* to the reasons why the missionaries themselves saw this as impracticable: the immaturity and low educational level of converts, their proneness to relapse morally or religiously, and the lack of time to engage in church work

20 Eaton, 'Implantation', p. 227. Further research is needed on Brethren and schools work, both in Spain and elsewhere.

21 *ME* 3 (1874), p. 93.

because they had to work all hours to earn enough to stay alive. Failure to foster local leadership was evident in most Brethren fields of mission at this time, and it reflected British assembly life, which in the eyes of some was marked by a failure to bring out younger leaders.

The missionaries' reluctance to hand over leadership was reinforced by diplomatic considerations. As Blamire explained, Spanish brothers could preach, but pastors were needed; foreign workers were well placed to take such responsibility, as it involved dealing with the civil authorities, and they commanded more respect as having the UK government to back them up.[22] Brethren at home may have been rigidly apolitical, but they were not averse to seeking diplomatic assistance or protection abroad; Spain was not the only field where this was the case. Having said that, we may wonder why the Reformed churches in Spain (who would have had a higher conception of the pastoral office) found it quite possible to appoint national pastors from an early stage, when the Brethren did not.

Incidentally, the Brethren in Spain, as in Britain, were ardent royalists. This aspect of their thought has never been explored. But in Spain they used this to try and become more inculturated in a society in which it was asserted that to be Spanish was to be Roman Catholic; the myth that Protestants were mostly foreigners has proved remarkably persistent, even among scholars, aided until recent decades by (mis)information put out by the Spanish authorities.[23] In response to anti-British feeling around 1898, the following years show missionaries as keen to demonstrate their loyalty to Spain; in this way they responded to a Spanish problem by adopting a thoroughly British attitude. Enrique Turrall reported on a royal visit to Marín in 1900: 'We showed our sympathy in the general rejoicing, and our loyalty to the powers that be (which is so often denied by the enemies of the gospel) by the display of the Spanish and British flags, and by an inscription in large letters, "God preserve the King."' The Brethren demonstration was referred to in the Spanish newspapers, and Turrall was pleased to record that the King and Queen Regent 'cordially acknowledged our salutations'. All this is in line with contemporary British Brethren royalism, which was at its most pronounced during the period between 1900 and World War I.[24]

Another area where foreign involvement was vital was that of property. If an effective assembly was to be planted and to stand any reasonable chance of survival, it needed its own building in which to worship. Many landlords refused to let property to evangelicals, often under pressure from the local priest. The Continental Lands Company was therefore founded in 1895 to hold property on behalf of assemblies, because it was thought to be safer for a body based

[22] *EOS* 17 (1888), p. 205.

[23] *The Protestant Church in Spain* (*Six Reports on an anti-Spanish Campaign of Defamation*) (Madrid: Diplomatic Information Office, 1950).

[24] *EOS* 29 (1900), p. 309.

outside the country to do so. Some missionaries found themselves spending considerable amounts of time as *de facto* property consultants. Later, Brethren sought the application of discreet international pressure through the Foreign Office during the twenty years after 1945. As a result, a number of halls owned by the Continental Lands Company were reopened. In this respect, the slow pace of indigenization may have helped rather than hindered the work.

From the 1910s onwards the focus gradually switched to planting churches and not merely winning individuals. This paralleled the growth of an increased ecclesiological awareness among British Brethren, but it also reflected the fact that enough converts had now been won for such a step to become feasible. But as assemblies began to be established and the work grew, some missionaries found themselves tied to pastoring and preaching. Not all found it easy to justify a more settled role. Thomas Berkley wrote from Vigo in 1904: ‘It may be that our methods of work are faulty in not leaving the already established churches to themselves for more protracted periods, but it seems to be a fact, explain it as we may, that no Spanish church can be left long without suffering much in consequence.’[25] And developing local gift was not was straightforward as some might think. B.L. White wrote from San Tomé in 1905,

> we hear of other doors open or opening, and would gladly enter, but have not the power to do so unless home work is dropped, which would not be justifiable. Where are the men? The churches here are too poor to send forth their own men, though they might aid them, and would; the men cannot lose their days of labour, so the service on the Lord’s-day must be circumscribed, and the people are perishing without the gospel.[26]

It would be wrong, therefore, to accuse the missionaries of failing to develop local gift without acknowledging the very real problems which they saw as hindering this.

The move towards a more indigenous leadership probably began after the First World War. As the generation of missionaries which had come to Spain retired or died, they were replaced by new workers whose approach reflected developments in British Brethrenism. They began to see the need for the work to become truly indigenous and not to remain an exotic import from Britain.

What happened once the missionaries were forced to withdraw in 1936?

The Spanish Civil War lasted from 1936 to 1939. By its end, almost all Brethren halls had closed, and Protestantism was once again severely repressed under General Franco. Brethren were tainted by the association of all forms of Protestantism with the political liberalism of the Second Republic, which had lasted from 1931 to 1936. Many missionaries had left; others would leave dur-

25 *EOS* 33 (1904), p. 169.
26 *EOS* 34 (1905), p. 365.

ing the Second World War. Just four would remain, yet considerable growth occurred. Even though public meetings became very difficult, assemblies in Barcelona, for example, found that dividing into a number of home-based gatherings proved extremely effective evangelistically.[27] The success of such local initiative demonstrates to my mind that in some places at least assemblies had been taught principles of church life which they were able to apply creatively for themselves. Apologists for Brethren ways of doing mission and church sometimes argue that the principles can be applied absolutely anywhere and in any conditions – which some would say was what happened here. This growth and its roots in the work of the missionaries make it misleading, therefore, to end the story of Brethren mission in Spain in 1936.

From 1945 some missionaries returned, but to a situation which had changed remarkably. It would be impossible to turn the clock back, and Spanish Brethren were now well on the road to maturity as an independent community of churches. The Editors wrote in *Echoes of Service*:

> The effect of greater responsibility being thrown on the local elders, after the long years of careful preparation, is seen now in sturdy and well-balanced churches whose vitality, gifts and expansion have set an example to the other groups and led to the conversion of a number of people in nearly all the centres. The return of the workers as teachers and counsellors has been welcomed, and has helped consolidate the growth of the war years.[28]

The number of missionaries declined, but by contrast the number of Spanish workers began to grow. Gradually, and inevitably, the focus of cohesion among Spanish assemblies shifted from conferences for English workers to gatherings which were primarily for Spanish full-time workers and local elders.[29] But British missionaries had one further contribution to make. Assemblies frequently wanted the missionaries to return to the position of pastor, partly because of the esteem in which they were held and partly because few Spanish brothers had the time or money to devote themselves to pastoral work. But this was not the contribution; it was rather the establishment of a more disciplined pattern of leadership training. The assemblies were seen as passionate about the gospel and godly living, but it was felt that the teaching on offer was not of the depth needed to produce well-grounded leaders. The Spanish full-time workers were almost all evangelists. In 1947, therefore, Ernest Trenchard returned to Spain in order to begin conducting correspondence courses and offering oral instruction.[30] Although support was patchy the courses prospered, evidently meeting a felt need. Such a development reflected trends in British Brethrenism: whereas

---

[27] Paul W. Marsh, 'Selections from Westminster', *Echoes Quarterly Review* 10.1 (January-March 1958), pp. 8-18.

[28] 'Spain', *EOS* 76 (1947), p. 126.

[29] E.H. Trenchard, 'Madrid Conference', *EOS* 94 (1965), p. 4.

[30] *EOS* 76 (1947), p. 34.

before 1914 Brethren almost always decried theological training, they were now aware of the need to provide solid food for potential leaders. It was also paralleled among Spanish Baptists.

But how long did the missionaries need to stay during this period of developing national leadership? One of the key differences of opinion among them during the post-war years was that some saw their presence as essential in order to prevent congregations affiliating with denominations such as the Baptists or with other missions, while others were confident that that this would not be a serious problem because assemblies were well enough taught and Brethren church principles had been proved to be effective. Most British missionaries did eventually retire from the work, and few have replaced them. Now most Brethren missionaries in Spain are from North America; it is not clear, however, how far they and the British workers co-operate. Therein lies a topic for further research!

And what has all this work produced? In 2001, the Brethren community in Spain numbered about 140 assemblies and 11,000 members – they were no longer the largest Protestant community, as the Filadelfia church, a Pentecostal denomination working mainly among the Roma but also attracting many immigrants from Latin America, had over 600 congregations and 30,000 members.[31] Nevertheless, Brethren are still growing, even if their growth has not been without problems, and the leadership of the movement is very clearly in the hands of Spanish nationals. I would therefore disagree with the assessment by Eaton which I quoted at the beginning. Spanish Brethren have prospered, remarkably so when you consider that for most of their history they were persecuted. The challenge facing them now is to maintain their spiritual dynamism and to adapt to a more visible and public mode of existence, as well as coping with the impact of severe rural depopulation and a measure of internal division.

Conclusion

We have surveyed the main features of Brethren work in Spain, focusing mostly on the period before 1914 but noting significant later developments. Much of it seems quite similar to work undertaken by other missions. I would suggest, though, that in two respects developments among Brethren reflected what had happened several decades earlier among many other missions in Spain. (1) The withdrawal of British workers, which Valentino Sitoy in his doctoral research sees as evident among most groups by about 1900, did not happen among Brethren until they were compelled to do so by the events of 1936. (2) The focus on preparing churches for self-determination, which he sees as a result of the enforced inward turn evident in most Spanish Protestant communities after

[31] *Operation World* (2001 edn), <http://www.operationworld.org/country/spai/owtext.html>, accessed 14 May 2010.

1875,[32] was not really evident among Brethren until after the Second World War. By that time, Spanish assemblies had proved themselves able to cope surprisingly effectively in the enforced absence of missionary leadership. However, I would argue that the leadership provided by the missionaries, whilst inevitably hindering moves towards indigenization and certainly not beyond criticism, provided a measure of protection which allowed a fragile plant to survive ferocious storms.

[32] Sitoy, 'British Evangelical Missions to Spain', pp. 295-96.

CHAPTER 5

The Wesleyan Methodist Mission to Soldiers

John Handby Thompson

The beginnings of the Wesleyan Methodist mission to soldiers in the nineteenth century are not unrecorded but seem nowadays to be largely overlooked. A modern, definitive four-volume history of the Methodist Church in Great Britain, for example, makes no mention of soldiers. It offers one reference to William Harris Rule, the enthusiast who originally inspired the mission, but it is in a foot-note on the use of alcohol in Communion wine.[1] Rule's entry in the *Oxford Dictionary of National Biography* gives two sentences to his army work, though it covers his other enthusiasm, the conversion of Spain to Protestantism, more generously.[2] To be fair, this might reflect Rule's own view of his life-work, based on his autobiography,[3] but the Wesleyan army chaplaincy tradition, unique among Nonconformists before the Great War, was his more enduring achievement and brought much honour to the Connexion. It was the subject of a separate book of recollections.[4]

Rule's first encounter with soldiers was his appointment in 1832 as minister of the Wesleyan church in Gibraltar. It followed two years spent as a missionary in St Vincent. His intended first assignment had been a mission to the Druze in the Lebanon, but this was cancelled when he had reached Malta. Here he had observed the Roman Catholic Church in full pomp and noted, and deplored, its social hold on the poor. In Gibraltar he found Spanish political and religious refugees in his congregation. In keeping with his missionary calling he undertook a number of hazardous journeys in southern Spain and founded a mission station in Cadiz which was later suppressed. He compiled a hymn book in Spanish and translated other religious works into the language.

Immediately in Gibraltar, however, the freedom of soldiers to worship as they chose gripped his attention. The compulsory church parade on Sundays

---

1 Rupert Davies, A. Raymond George and Gordon Rupp (eds), *A History of the Methodist Church in Great Britain* (London: Epworth, 1965-88), four volumes, vol. 2, p. 224, note 22.

2 *Oxford Dictionary of National Biography* (Oxford: OUP, 2004), vol. 48, p. 104.

3 W.H. Rule, *Recollections of my Life* (London: T. Woolmer, 1886).

4 W.H. Rule, *Wesleyan Methodism in the British Army* (London: T. Woolmer, 1883).

followed the drum to the Anglican church as was the custom, but when the Highland Regiment was marched to it, and its officer said they had neither orders nor desire to enter it, Rule allowed them the use of the Wesleyan church for a Presbyterian parade service the following week.[5] After the Governor refused to quash punishments imposed on two soldiers, one for attending Wesleyan services and the other for supporting him, Rule appealed successfully to the Commander-in-Chief, General Lord Hill.[6]

In his appeal, Rule invoked Lord Hill's own General Order of 1839. This instructed commanding officers

> to be particularly attentive that no soldier being a Roman Catholic, or of any religious persuasion differing from the Established Church, is to be compelled to attend Divine Worship of the Church of England, but that every soldier is to be at full liberty to attend the worship of Almighty God according to the form prescribed by his own religion when military duty does not interfere.

Military orders need parsing, and the last six words made this one permissive rather than mandatory, and subject to local decision. Nor was it an exercisable liberty unless the soldier's religion had a church within reach to which he could be marched (but at least this was the case in Gibraltar). When the Governor declined to publish the General Order, Rule read it out in church.

Later, meeting the Governor, General Houston, for the first time – Rule had been arrested for trespass while seeking out Wesleyan soldiers in their barracks – he found to his surprise that they got on and he succeeded in receiving the Governor's permission for Wesleyan soldiers to be marched to the Wesleyan church on Sundays.[7] Indignation, challenge and argument came naturally to Rule, and he had a short fuse, but he was never to forget the value of clearing his lines with commanding officers through a personal approach.

On Rule's return to England in 1842 he bore circuit work in the country with diminishing patience and after a particularly explosive spell in Kent, when his chapel trustees locked him out, he was taken into the Wesleyan Book Room. But he had not forgotten soldiers. Working in the Conference Office, he had been able to draft a resolution passed at the Wesleyan Conference of 1848 which urged superintendent ministers, where there was a local garrison or military establishment, to take steps to gather Wesleyan soldiers into their congregations 'as military regulations allowed'.[8] There was no immediate response to the resolution. Soldiers were unpopular. Evangelical ministers and army officers had nothing in common.

---

5 Rule, *Wesleyan Methodism*, p. 32.

6 Rule, *Wesleyan Methodism*, p. 28.

7 Rule, *Wesleyan Methodism*, p. 30.

8 *Minutes of [the Wesleyan Methodist] Conference* (London: Wesleyan Methodist Book Room, 1848), p. 111.

The Crimean War (1854-56) presented Rule, still in the Book Room, with another opportunity to help Wesleyan soldiers. He persuaded his friends in the Wesleyan Missionary Committee to volunteer a missionary as chaplain to the British forces in the Crimea and they selected Peter Batchelor, who was returning on furlough from Mysore. He was granted free passage by Lord Panmure, Secretary of State for War, to Scutari where the Anglican chaplain found him accommodation. Given that Anglicans had had to advertise in the newspapers to recruit their body of chaplains for the war, whereas Catholics had delighted the authorities by quickly volunteering a number of priests, offering Batchelor might well have helped secure official War Office recognition of the Wesleyan Church. In the result, in Rule's (not altogether kindly) words,

> The change from the exhaustion of an Indian mission to the horrid grandeur of a campaign was too violent for our impoverished chaplain to sustain. Happily for him, the war ended soon after he landed and he returned forthwith without fairly coming into use . . .[9]

The reform of the army after the Crimean War, and in particular the construction of a large training camp on marsh-land near the hamlet of Aldershot, and well away from any existing town, moved the Wesleyan Home Mission Committee to extend their work to include soldiers. In a report to Conference in 1856 they said they had appointed Batchelor to meet and pray with Wesleyan soldiers in the Aldershot camp. His work would be overseen by London ministers on the Committee and a small Aldershot sub-committee would organise an appeal for public funds to erect a Wesleyan place of worship adjacent to the south camp.

Aside from these practicalities, and a brief reminder of the 1848 resolution, the report can be read as the first formal recognition of the Connexion's duty to soldiers.

> The British Army is itself a class. Separated almost entirely from civil society, the soldier occupies a position of his own. Ordinarily he is under extremely demoralising influences which the utmost efforts of discipline are insufficient to counteract; but . . . when the grace of God possesses the soldier's heart [it] generally constrains him to present a decision and earnestness of demeanour which is worthy of the highest admiration. The lukewarm inevitably fall away but the man who has fully consecrated himself to his way boldly advocates his Master's cause and pursues his way steadfastly through good report and evil. Towards this class of men, many of whom are Wesleyans, we have an imperative duty to discharge.

The report goes on to claim that the church's duty is also to those with more tenuous links:

---

9 Rule, *Wesleyan Methodism*, pp. 33-34.

> Besides these, there are multitudes in the army of various ranks who have been baptised by our ministers, taught in our schools and assembled in our congregations during their childhood and youth. Many of them cherish the remembrance of their early lessons, and of the examples, prayers, and instructions of their parents. Many of them, unsupported by the continuance of such example, have sunk into the depths of ungodliness. Yet, if the care of these souls devolves on any, it must devolve on us . . .[10]

Rule was working behind the scenes. He had little confidence in Batchelor and thought he could use his own experience in Gibraltar to good effect. In March 1856 he had already been down to Aldershot, called on General William Knollys, the commanding officer, secured his permission to visit soldiers in their tents and afterwards sent Knollys a report. Rule said he had found several Wesleyan Methodists who had expressed an interest in a service of their own on Sundays and he asked if a minister might come and preach to them. He undertook to respect regulations and 'to place our proceedings under the direct cognizance of the Officer Commanding'. This was punctilious, but disingenuous, as a Wesleyan service within a military camp would have been without precedent; and, indeed, Knollys refused the request on those grounds.[11]

Though Rule must have expected such a reply, he saw a risk that Knollys might refuse to march troops to a church built outside the camp. In such a locality, without soldiers, there would be no congregation. Rule, still acting alone, decided to seek the help of Lord Panmure, the Secretary of State for War, to whom, he had 'a private channel of access' through Arthur Kinnaird, the MP for Perth.[12] How Rule knew Kinnaird, a banker, he does not reveal, but both Kinnaird and his wife were supporters of a large number of evangelical causes and their house off Pall Mall was a well-known meeting place for them.[13] Moreover, both Kinnaird and Panmure were Free Church of Scotland men and Panmure, as Fox Maule MP, had played a part in the Disruption of the Church of Scotland in 1843. It is not hard to understand them giving ear to Rule and the mission to soldiers. Indeed, one wonders if Rule had used the same route to secure Batchelor's passage to Scutari though there is no evidence that he did.

Kinnaird told Rule by letter, that

> Lord Panmure cannot actually grant you a site within the camp, yet he will have much satisfaction in seeing you in its close vicinity and be ready to support you to allow the Wesleyan soldiers to frequent your services.[14]

---

[10] Wesleyan Home Mission Committee Report to Conference, 1856, p. 22.

[11] Rule, *Wesleyan Methodism*, pp. 35-38.

[12] Rule, *Wesleyan Methodism*, p. 38.

[13] See Kinnaird's entry in the *Oxford Dictionary of National Biography*, vol. 31, pp. 731-32.

[14] John Rylands University Library, Manchester, Methodist Archives [hereafter MAM], PLP 64.47.2.

Arrangements for marching were for the local commander, but the Secretary of State could let it be known it was his wish, and Rule understood that he had done so.[15] Rule's letter to Knollys in September 1856 formally requesting that Wesleyan troops be marched, however, seems to have been unanswered.

An iron church – in fact a wooden frame covered externally in iron and lined with matching boards internally – was erected with phenomenal speed on rented land near an entrance to the South Camp. It was opened on 10 July 1857. The President of Conference preached and a bandsman provided the music. On 18 July, there was a break-through: following the issue of orders in the camp, Wesleyan soldiers were marched to the iron church for the first time, and officers came with them. Rule, now appointed in place of Batchelor, conducted the service.

Rule was no more than five feet in height, and had a long beard. But he was still a presence, standing in front of a sea of men in their regimentals, dressed in gown and bands, and donning a white surplice for Communion at noon. His style of clerical dress, as well as his use of the liturgy, did not endear him to his superiors, but unlike them he proved well able to preach to soldiers and maintain discipline in the service.[16]

Rule reported all this to Prest, secretary of the Home Mission Committee, no doubt with a sense of relief as well as achievement.[17] The same letter notes that Queen Victoria and the Court had driven round from Windsor to survey the iron structure which, despite its unusual composition, was of conventional design with a tower. A year later Rule reported 400 to 500 Wesleyans in the camp out of 20,000, substantial as the basis for a mission, but an early indication of the limited attraction of the military life to nineteenth-century Nonconformists.

The Wesleyan Connexion had now formally recognised soldiers as a part of its home mission and local arrangements had been worked out, acceptable to the military, for the conduct of that mission in Aldershot which it was hoped might be copied elsewhere. But, when soldiers declared their religion, as they were required to do, there were only three columns in the army returns, Church of England, Presbyterian and Roman Catholic. Wesleyans were usually returned as Church of England. This meant that their right to be fallen out for their own parade service could always be questioned. The Wesleyan authorities, however, had still to consider how to gain the status of a 'recognised Church' in Army Regulations.

In 1858 the reform of the army extended to the Chaplains' Department. Increased complements of Presbyterian and Roman Catholic chaplains were announced. The reform also introduced standard payments to local clergy receiv-

---

15 Rule, *Wesleyan Methodism*, p. 42.

16 C.H. Kelly, *Memories* (London: Robert Culley, 1910), pp. 110-30 for an appraisal of Rule as minister at Aldershot.

17 MAM, PLP 93.22.3.

ing soldiers in their churches on Sundays.[18] That 'local clergy' meant those of the three recognised churches went without saying. Rule's only forum for mounting a protest at the exclusion of Wesleyans was the Aldershot sub-committee. It decided to do nothing. Once more on his own authority Rule decided to act. He wrote to the War Office seeking 'favourable consideration of any application for the appointment of a Wesleyan chaplaincy at [Aldershot] and for any application for head money which may come in regular form from Wesleyan ministers elsewhere'.

The War Office rejected the request, as usual on grounds of precedent: 'Recent regulations' – Hill's General Order had entered Army Regulations in 1844 – 'do not affect the system which has always prevailed of paying for their services to the troops only the clergy of the Church of England and of the Presbyterian and Roman Catholic Churches . . .'[19]

Rule had more success locally through Knollys's increasing respect for his work and influence among the troops. He was given the right to work within the camp, including permission to visit the sick in hospital. This was challenged by the Anglican senior chaplain who was upheld by the War Office. Rule appealed directly to the Commander-in-Chief, now HRH the Duke of Cambridge, who decided in 'the spirit of Christian Charity and toleration which marks the Regulations of the Army' that Dissenting ministers might be admitted to hospitals at the discretion of military commanders.[20] Rule thus ended at least one precedent, as 'sectarians' had been refused entry to military hospitals from the time of the Peninsular Wars, even when the patients asked for them.[21]

Rule's right to officiate in the camp cemetery was also supported by Knollys against the Anglican chaplains' objection. A Wesleyan section of the graveyard was secured and Rule was even allowed to use the adjacent garrison chapel for the service.[22] The War Office, however, denied him use of a school-room in the camp for religious or social use, though Knollys would have been happy to allow it. Rule tried to use this as a pretext for a formal complaint of religious discrimination but the President of Conference, to whom he appealed, was not to be moved.[23]

One can understand Dr Waddy's hesitation. At the Wesleyan Conference of 1859 objections from the floor were raised to the term 'Wesleyan soldier' – to be precise, at 'the application of 'Wesleyan', this honoured name, to the red-coated drunkard whose very presence in our towns is pestilential'. Others thought 'Wesleyan Soldier' should be confined to soldiers who were members

---

[18] *Hansard's Parliamentary Debates* (London: Hansard), House of Commons, 14 June 1858, col. 2014.
[19] Rule, *Wesleyan Methodism*, pp. 54-55.
[20] MAM, PLP 93.21.42.
[21] A.E.C Jarvis, in *Royal Army Chaplains' Department Journal*, January 1931.
[22] MAM, PLP 93.23.23, 24.
[23] MAM, PLP 93.22.12, 20, 21.

of a society or class meeting. If army returns of Wesleyans were to be sought on this narrow basis it would of course be disastrous in terms of numbers and clout.[24]

The 1859 Conference did however disband the Aldershot sub-committee and appoint an Army Committee 'for counsel and direction on affairs relating to Wesleyans in the Army'.[25] These brief terms of reference are important as they distinguish the Army Committee's remit from that of the Home Mission Committee, a body which funded evangelism and sought to proselytise. Nevertheless, Army Committee reports appeared as a section of the Home Mission Committee reports, Prest was secretary of both committees and there was other double membership. (Rule was appointed a member of the Army Committee.) The Home Mission Committee's contingency fund was used to pay for Rule's work at Aldershot, the work of C.H. Kelly, Rule's assistant at Chatham, and in due course the ministers appointed full-time at other military establishments.

Within twelve months the new Army Committee had drawn up a dignified and carefully worded Memorial addressed to the Secretary of State for War in which they sought to clarify and settle the status of Wesleyans in the army. The Memorial begins by claiming that

> The recognition by Her Majesty's Government of the Church of England, the Presbyterians, and Roman Catholics in the British Army, professedly to the exclusion of all others, but practically to the exclusion of Wesleyans, presses heavily on large numbers of Wesleyans throughout the Service.

It then notes that members of the three recognised communions are provided with the means of public worship and religious instruction, from which provision the Wesleyans are excluded. Some Dissenters may benefit from provision ostensibly made for the Church of Scotland by accepting the designation 'Presbyterian', but this is not open to Wesleyans.[26] The Memorial seeks no share of this public funding, but asks only for recognition of the religious rights of Wesleyan soldiers, complaining of the system which obliges them 'to be counted unjustly and untruly' as one of the three recognised religions.

> So long as there is no official return of Wesleyans in the Army it will be impossible for them to enjoy perfect freedom of worship or to be fully protected from intolerance. Your memorialists therefore earnestly and respectfully pray you to take such measures as shall enable Wesleyans serving in the Army to be at once re-

---

24 Rule, *Wesleyan Methodism*, p. 69.

25 *Minutes of Conference*, 1859, p. 297.

26 The army made no distinction between Presbyterians, established or free, Scottish, Irish or English. This meant, for example, that English Presbyterian soldiers had unquestioned freedom of worship and English Presbyterian ministers had the right to claim head money for any services they rendered to local troops: see J.H. Thompson, 'Army Chaplains and the English Presbyterians', *The Journal of the United Reformed Church History Society*, vol. 5, No.7, October 1995, pp. 383-92.

> turned under their proper religious designation, and effectually protected against the oppressing consequences of the system hitherto prevailing.[27]

By not seeking a share of the public funds which the recognised churches enjoyed, Wesleyan army work would remain voluntary; that is, it would be provided free by the church. This claim to the moral high ground was to prove in the long run greatly to the Wesleyans' benefit, though it came at considerable financial cost to the church as the work expanded. Rule's protest to the War Office over the reform of the Chaplains' Department in 1858, in which he had claimed head money, was therefore not endorsed. As he now accepted, 'many of our people would have disapproved of State help'.

Given this voluntary service, and the relatively straightforward administrative change needed to provide a fourth column for Wesleyans in the army returns, one wonders at the failure of the War Office to respond to the Memorial for nearly two years. It was presented to Sidney Herbert, Secretary of State, on 21 February 1860 by a deputation led by the President of Conference, Dr Waddy, and including Prest and Rule. Herbert was liberally inclined, religious, if a High Churchman, and a friend of Gladstone and Florence Nightingale. He was judged likely to be supportive and the hope was that the matter could be quickly settled, and by him. But Herbert was seriously ill and was forced to resign shortly after receiving the deputation. He died the following year. The appointment of a new Secretary of State provided some reason for delay.

Eventually, on 15 November 1861, Dr Waddy led essentially the same deputation as the previous year, to see the new Secretary of State, Sir George Lewis. A new document was provided which said in terms that commissions for chaplains or other forms of financial support were not sought. It asked for three specific changes: Wesleyan soldiers to be allowed to be returned as such, Wesleyan ministers to be allowed access to military camps and garrisons to conduct divine service, and Wesleyan ministers serving troops to be protected from interference by other chaplains. It was a down-to-earth document, drafted by Rule, and it was received coldly. In the discussion the deputation uttered a veiled threat: favourable consideration of the document would avoid further public action.[28] The meaning of this was left obscure.

On 3 January 1862 the Secretary of State wrote to Prest to say he had concluded that

> practical difficulties in the way of making the proposed alterations are such as to render it advisable to adhere to the existing arrangements in regard to the recognised denominations.[29]

---

[27] Rule, *Wesleyan Methodism*, p. 81, for the full text.

[28] Rule, *Wesleyan Methodism*, p.103. The full text of document is on preceding pages.

[29] Rule, *Wesleyan Methodism*, p.104.

This refusal to change existing arrangements was quickly followed by a determined attempt to end what concessions the Wesleyans had so far managed to achieve in Aldershot and Chatham. In March 1862, General Eyre, the commanding officer at Chatham, told Kelly, Rule's assistant there, that he had withdrawn permission for Wesleyan soldiers to be marched through the town for their Sunday parade service. Wesleyan soldiers would have to go instead to churches in Brompton or Rochester, neither easily reached on foot. The vicar of Chatham had objected to the marching, but Eyre's orders came from the War Office which also stopped Kelly's allowance which he had been (mistakenly) granted. In Aldershot, Knollys's successor, Sir John Pennefather, told Rule he was no longer permitted to recognise the word 'Wesleyan' in any official document, return or report, and this would affect the fall-out of men for his services. Rule was beside himself with indignation and frustration. He assumed it was a conspiracy, orchestrated by the Chaplain General, G.R. Gleig, son of an Episcopalian bishop, and a former officer in the Peninsular war. The simpler explanation is that the action flowed directly from the Secretary of State's apparently final decision on 3 January to confine recognition to the three churches. The privileges of recognition locally conceded to the Wesleyans had in consequence to be withdrawn. The only good outcome was that it brought matters to a head.

Rule wrote twice to the War Office without answer. He appealed to Lord Shaftesbury for his influential help over such blatant denial of religious freedom. Shaftesbury spoke to Lord de Grey, Under Secretary of State at the War Office, and assured Rule there would be no further trouble, but to tell him if there was.[30] Was this a portent of a change of mind already being considered, or early realisation that things had got out of hand? That was late March, but the War Office always moved slowly. Prest, now President-designate of Conference, wrote to Lewis on 1 May and was called to the War Office on 30 May. Waddy and Rule were also present. Lewis began the meeting by announcing a complete turnabout. The War Office were now minded to introduce a fourth column in the army returns for soldiers who were not of the persuasion of the three recognised churches and he went on to seek advice on what the column should be called. It would provide recognition of Wesleyan soldiers but a name like 'Nonconformist' would save separate concessions to other denominations. Rule's suggestion of 'Other Protestants' was accepted as causing less offence to the Church of England.[31]

In view of the result, what brought about the change of mind is perhaps unimportant. But the withdrawal of privileges had certainly been unpopular on the ground – the Marines' Colonel-Commandant in Chatham had asked for marching to be restarted for reasons of morale – and Pennefather, 'kindness itself,' said Rule, did not impede voluntary attendance at Wesleyan services in Alder-

---

[30] MAM, PLP 93.22.52.

[31] Rule, *Wesleyan Methodism*, pp. 111-14; Army Committee Report for 1862.

shot. The end of marching at Aldershot was out of public view but in Chatham people had crowded to watch the march and its ending was a very open demonstration of the Wesleyans' complaint of religious discrimination. The simple reintroduction of the concessions would have left the issue of recognition to fester on. The 'practical difficulties' of a fourth column foreseen by Lewis seem to have been very easily overcome.

The official letter following the meeting gave total satisfaction. Dated 17 June 1862, it confirmed that the marching of Wesleyan soldiers would be resumed and the classification of Wesleyan soldiers under existing denominations would end. A fourth class would be introduced named 'Other Protestants' for all who were not Episcopalians, Presbyterians or Roman Catholics, 'this class to be borne on the monthly regimental returns to the Horse Guards and over the beds of such soldiers in hospitals'.[32] The Duke of Cambridge was heard enquiring whether 'Dr Rule was now satisfied.' Perhaps the Duke, who had personally given satisfaction to Rule over hospital visiting 'out of Christian charity', had played a larger part in the change of policy than merely consenting to it formally as Commander-in-Chief. However it was achieved, recognition had been won, after a struggle nowadays barely credible, but important as a reminder of how hard it was in this period for Nonconformists to break through the crust of Establishment, whether military, ecclesiastical or social.

The fourth column was introduced in 1863. The army returns for 1864 show 5290 'Other Protestants'.[33] The Wesleyan church returns for the same base year from fourteen Districts show 4409 Wesleyans.[34] Both sets of figures exclude the Militia and the British Army in India. It appears that, outside India, Wesleyans represented at this time three to four per cent of the army and other Nonconformists under one per cent. But as the army grew, the number and proportion of Wesleyans also rose and was never less than five per cent. By the end of the century, but just before the South African War, there were (in round figures) 13,000 Nonconformists in the army, over 11,000 of them Wesleyans. The growth in ministry to match this growth in numbers has now to be traced.

Even before the fourth column, Rule was given an additional role as 'Corresponding Chaplain', routinely sending superintendent ministers in the country short notes of commendation on Wesleyan soldiers deploying from Aldershot to their area after training. He had also sent all circuit ministers advice on the procedure to be followed to secure the marching of Wesleyan soldiers to their churches on Sundays. The advice was both practical – not all local preachers can cope with soldiers – and political – stress to local commanders that Wesleyans are 'loyal' and not to be confused with Dissenters.[35] (He was very em-

[32] Army Committee Report, 1862.

[33] *Parliamentary Papers, House of Commons*, 1864.

[34] *Minutes of Conference*, 1863, pp. 605-06.

[35] MAM, PLP 93.21.9, 43, 52; PLP 93.22.9.

barrassed when members of the Peace Society, a body with mainly Quaker and Congregationalist members, stole into Aldershot camp and left pacifist tracts.)

After the fourth column was introduced Rule tried to encourage superintendent ministers to offer their services to Militia regiments in their area. There were 93 such regiments in England and Wales. New recruits had twenty eight days' training and each regiment had three weeks' annual training, so there were several Sunday church parades a year for each regiment. Potentially, this was a large field of ministry to largely local men.[36] Rule also started to train, advise and assess the performance of new appointments at Shorncliffe and Portsmouth, the first two military centres after Aldershot and Chatham to be served by full-time ministers without circuit duties.[37] The correspondence shows Rule had by now an invaluable understanding of the nature of military discipline and the necessity of respecting it, and also how hard it was for some new appointments to adapt. But Rule was often impatient and heavy handed in dealing with his fellow ministers and Prest had to counsel restraint.

Rule was now over sixty. He was still pushing boundaries, though somewhat frustrated by being forbidden by Prest to write to the War Office. He sought and was granted admission to the military prison at Aldershot in 1863 and advised other military establishments with prisons, Chatham, Gosport and the Curragh (where the Irish Wesleyan Methodist Conference provided ministers), of the agreement.[38] In 1864, urged on by Rule, Prest finally secured the War Office's agreement to the use of a room within the camp at Aldershot for Wesleyan weekday religious use. Rule hastened to advise other camps of this concession, a major one as it allowed routine Wesleyan religious work and church parades inside military establishments for the first time.[39]

A further example of the easier relations with the military was Pennefather's ready agreement to the building of a temporary Wesleyan church near the North Camp, where Rule's new assistant, Nehemiah Curnock ran the work. With the help of W.W. Pocock, a well-established London architect and member of the Home Mission and Army Committees, land for the new chapel was acquired at an advantageous price.[40] Pocock had a personal ambition to build up the Wesleyan presence in Surrey and saw Aldershot as a way of doing so. Ten years later he was to be the architect of the building which eventually emerged from this initiative of Rule's, the large Grosvenor Road Wesleyan church and the adjacent soldiers' home.[41] Both were very substantial Wesleyan

---

36 Army Committee Reports, 1863 and 1864; Rule, *Wesleyan Methodism*, pp. 117 *et seq*.

37 MAM, PLP 93.22.57, 78, 84.

38 Army Committee Report, 1864; Rule, *Wesleyan Methodism*, p. 120.

39 Army Committee Report, 1864.

40 MAM PLP 93.22.72, 74, 76, 77.

41 On Pocock's wider work and family relationships, see Clyde Binfield, 'Architects in Connexion: Four Methodist Generations', in Jane Garnett and Colin Matthew (eds),

presences in the army's principal military centre. In the intervening years, parade services, class meetings and Bible study for soldiers in the North Camp were held in the room now provided by the army and a small soldiers' home for recreational purposes was built next to the iron church which continued to serve soldiers in the South Camp.[42]

The Army Committee did not ask Conference to renew Rule's stationing at Aldershot in 1865. His service to Wesleyan soldiers was over. The Connexion had rules about length of stationing which had hitherto been creatively interpreted to keep Rule in Aldershot, but now the view was evidently taken that his determined mind-set and authoritarian manner had served their purpose. After recognition, consolidation of the work required a quieter spirit. Charles Kelly, twice President of Conference, who as a young minister worked closest to Rule in Aldershot and Chatham and knew him at the height of his powers, thought him 'the most remarkable man with whom I ever came in contact'. His view that 'practically, Dr Rule was not appointed to Army work; he initiated it', is borne out by the record. There was another side. Those who had suffered at Rule's hand perhaps called to mind the report of a church committee enquiring into his clerical dress and use of the liturgy which had concluded that 'Brother Rule's wisdom is pure but not peaceable.'[43]

The 1860s saw the army still retraining after the Crimean War. It was thus mainly a peace-time army and gave the Wesleyans time to extend the number of home stations served by ministers engaged full-time on army work. By 1866 these were Aldershot, Chelsea, Chatham (including Sheerness), Shorncliffe, Portsmouth (including Parkhurst), and Dublin (including the Curragh). The reports of the Army Committee and of the Home Mission Committee in this decade share a common evangelistic tone as if to emphasise the mission side of the work with soldiers. Letters of testimony from soldiers printed in the reports speak of the value of the religious work in home stations then carried to overseas postings.

When approached by the Army Committee in 1865, the Admiralty agreed to allow officers and seamen classed as Other Protestants to attend religious services ashore and to pay head money to ministers taking them. This was an early and straightforward benefit of the recognition given by the 'Other Protestants' column. Access of ministers to naval hospitals and prisons was also agreed later.[44] The Wesleyan Army Committee took the Navy into its title in 1866.[45]

The Cardwell reforms of the army in the 'seventies created sixty nine military centres in the British Isles for recruitment and initial training and intro-

---

Revival and Religion since 1700 (London: The Hambledon Press, 1993), esp. pp. 170-71.

42 Army and Navy Committee report, 1869.

43 Kelly, *Memories*, pp. 110, 111, 118.

44 Army and Navy Committee Report, 1869.

45 Army and Navy Committee Report, 1866.

duced shorter and improved terms of service. The Army and Navy Committee saw this development as helpful to their mission as it allowed local ministers to engage with local recruits and ensure that young Wesleyans declared themselves as 'Other Protestants' at the start of their army career. Better conditions also increased the likelihood that more recruits would come from Nonconformist homes.[46]

As the practice grew of posting one battalion of the new regiments abroad while keeping one at home, the need to supply ministerial cover overseas grew and explains the at first startling decision in 1878 to change the composition of the Army and Navy Committee by adding the officers of the Wesleyan Missionary Committee. This resulted from the advice of a special committee on which Rule and Kelly had served alongside Sir William M'Arthur and Sir George Hayter Chubb. The argument was that overseas army work might more sensibly fall to missionaries on the spot than to ministers despatched from home. This was already happening in India to some extent. No conflict was apparently envisaged between the missionaries' work with soldiers and among the native communities to whom they had been sent.

Missionary giving was an important part of church life. Two other developments began to draw the church as a whole into closer support for work with soldiers and sailors. First, through public appeals, Wesleyans started to provide reading or recreation rooms for Wesleyan soldiers and sailors (called 'homes') at a time when such provision from public funds was negligible and military accommodation itself poor. As in the first 'home' at Aldershot, the rooms might be used for religious services or simply as places to spend spare time away from worldlier temptations. Chubb became a prominent supporter of this work which over the years became an important public manifestation of the Wesleyans' concern for soldiers' welfare. By the end of the century 'Wesleyan soldiers' and sailors' homes' spanned the Empire, and those in London and in military and naval hubs like Malta were substantial buildings.[47]

Secondly, when Wesleyan ministers and missionaries started to be attached as chaplains on military campaigns, and their experiences came to be reported or published, those in the pews at home came to feel they had a share in it. And indeed they had, as this overseas service, like that at home, was still a form of voluntaryism. The chaplains were paid by the church, not by the army. That said, according to circumstances on individual campaigns, varying forms of support from public funds became inevitable. These are noted below. Though practically necessary, they also accustomed the Connexion to the notion of public subsidy.

John Laverack was the first Wesleyan minister working full-time with the troops at home to accompany an overseas expedition – the Ashanti war of 1873. His work was confined to the hospital ship as no transport could be found

---

46 Army and Navy Committee Report, 1873.

47 O.S. Watkins, *Soldiers and Preachers Too* (London: C.H. Kelly, 1906), pp. 155-81.

to allow him to accompany the fighting troops, but he was supplied with rations and other necessities.[48]

The first Wesleyan missionary to be involved in a fighting expedition – the second Afghan war (1878-79) – was Arthur Male. Based in Lucknow, and totally without military experience, he was gazetted by the Indian Government in Calcutta as chaplain to Presbyterian and Wesleyan troops in the expeditionary force. He messed with the officers, was provided with a horse, wore a Sam Browne, but was neither commissioned nor paid. He was nevertheless promoted Divisional Chaplain when an Anglican returned to India and was the only chaplain to survive the outbreak of cholera which ended the war. His main duty on the retreat until he lost consciousness was to conduct the burial of every soldier who fell. His work became in fact for all 'religions', in the army sense of the term, but the committee at home conscientiously noted that 'among the native troops he was not able to do much as they were Pathan, Sikh and Gurkha regiments'.[49]

In the Zulu War of 1879 four missionaries served as chaplains, one from each mission district in South Africa. They had to find their own horses and were unpaid, but were provided with rations and 'camp equipage'; and they were mentioned by name in the General Order at the end of the war. One of them, Theophilus Woolmer, was the first Wesleyan minister to be personally involved in action (at Kambula and then in the battle of Ulundi). 'I did not expect to come out alive, but left it all with God,' he told the committee at home. Another, T.H. Wilkins, was the first Wesleyan minister to receive a medal. Another, T.W. Pocock, was a nephew of Rule's Aldershot architect. The fourth was Owen Watkins, father of Owen Spencer Watkins, who was to become Methodism's greatest army chaplain. The committee said the four missionaries' appointment as chaplains 'was amply justified by the service rendered to the men in the field and in hospital and by the Christian steadfastness of many of our soldiers in the midst of severe hardship and temptation . . .'[50]

The first missionary to be mentioned in despatches was Henry Cotton who served with colonial forces in the Basuto uprisings of 1880-81. Owen Watkins served again in the short engagement in 1881 against the Boers, which resulted in Transvaal's independence. Another Wesleyan chaplain, Henry Weavkind, was in the siege of Pretoria and was used by the army in negotiations with the Boers.[51]

In this period of growing military action abroad, a new duty at home was to visit troop ships before they left. The purpose was to try to 'appoint class lead-

48 Army and Navy Committee Reports, 1874, 1875.

49 Army and Navy Report, 1880; A.H. Male, *Scenes through the Battle Smoke*, (London: Dean and Son, 1901).

50 Army and Navy Committee Reports, 1879, 1880; Watkins, *Soldiers and Preachers Too*, pp. 193-96.

51 Watkins, *Soldiers and Preachers Too*, pp. 196-97.

ers and in other ways to enable devout soldiers to help their comrades prepare to meet God'. This may be blunt, but using lay class leaders on board ship, ministers and missionaries in the field, and before all this ministers in the training camps at home engaged full-time on chaplaincy duties, the Wesleyan Connexion was now fulfilling the mission defined long ago in 1856, but in war as well as peace, and on a broader canvass than Rule could have conceived.[52]

Male's chaplaincy work continued in Egypt and the Sudan, a campaign for which he volunteered when on furlough in England, an indication of how much he liked the military life. He describes gathering up the wounded in the night desert after the battle of Tel-el-Kebir and accompanying them by train and boat to hospitals at base.[53] Earlier, in Afghanistan he had worked in hospital tents. But when the expedition was stationary in Jellulabad, he had also described parade services, voluntary evening services, the importance of short sermons and hymn singing, life in short much as at home. Chaplains remained ministers however caught up they became in the military campaign.

Nevertheless, a question must have been in the minds of many in the pews. Male asks it and answers it: 'And how comes it that I, a minister of religion, should be thrown into association with scenes of carnage such as I have attempted to depict?' His answer:

> Soldiers are not mere physical frames to be kept strong and fighting fit. . . . The British people, recognising the deeper needs of her soldier sons has her Chaplains Department ... and there are never wanting men who in this path of duty go forth ... to enhearten the men and keep them in touch with that higher duty of the soldier life.[54]

Male died on returning from Egypt aged only 52.

1881 was a watershed year in Wesleyan recognition by the army. Charles Prest, revered in the church, but who may only rarely have met a soldier, had retired in 1875. His successor as secretary of the Army and Navy committee, R.W. Allen, was a man of very different style. He had begun his ministry as chaplain at Chatham in 1870, then moved to Aldershot in 1872. He now doubled as Wesleyan chaplain to the Guards Regiments in London. He was the embodiment of the experienced Wesleyan chaplain at home; and he had the record of the church's service to the army at home and abroad to buttress his approach to the War Office for greater recognition.

It came, willingly enough, and in the form Rule had asked for in 1858, though now of course on a much greater scale. Wesleyan ministers serving troops locally were to receive head money. Wesleyan ministers working full-time in the military establishments at home were to receive subsistence pay-

---

52 Army and Navy Committee Report, 1881.

53 A.H. Male, *Through Two Campaigns, Afghanistan and the Soudan* (London: Robert Culley, 1903), an extension of his earlier book, *Scenes Through the Battle Smoke*.

54 Male, *Scenes through the Battle Smoke*, p.18.

ments. There was an even greater prize, a column in the army returns for Wesleyans alone. (The column 'Other Protestants' continued for other Nonconformists to whom Wesleyan chaplains continued to minister as they had none of their own.) A distinctive place for Wesleyan Methodism was to be accorded in Queen's Regulations. And there was also to be a free issue of Methodist hymn books to Wesleyan soldiers.[55]

Subsistence payments were a financial relief to the committee as there were now over twenty full-time chaplains in military establishments at home. It gave status to the Wesleyan chaplains, though they remained civilians, without uniforms. The chaplains themselves thought their lack of officer status helped their work with the men, though it meant they did not appear in the Army List alongside the other churches' chaplains. Some in the Connexion murmured about receiving State money, though chapel trustees had been pressing hard for it.

Rule was happily still alive, 'venerable and full of years', to witness this fuller recognition of his church's service to the army. Long ago a DD (from Dickenson College in the United States) for work on the Spanish Inquisition, in retirement he had published scholarly works on the Reformation, Savonarola and the Kararite Jews, among others. 'The Little Doctor', as the army nicknamed him, completed his account of army work and published it in 1883. He sent a copy to General Knollys, now Black Rod, as an affectionate reminder of their early sparring days in Aldershot. A recently completed report for the Wesleyan Conference on the religious state of affairs in Spain showed that he still retained his interest in his other enthusiasm. He died in 1890.

In terms of mission, 1881 marks the end of the beginning of a work which continues even today in Afghanistan. But some later high points may be briefly mentioned to show the direction followed. In 1883 the Indian Ecclesiastical Establishment started to pay a form of head money to Wesleyan missionaries conducting services for soldiers, though by 1897 Wesleyans numbered only 3711 (and 'Other Protestants' 495), the usual five per cent of the total force, but in India very widely scattered.[56]

Wesleyan chaplains served in all four campaigns in Egypt and the Sudan in the 'eighties and in Kitchener's march on Khartoum against the Mahdi. This was O.S. Watkins' first campaign as a young chaplain. He represented the Wesleyan Church at the memorial service for General Gordon in Khartoum in 1898 and took part in it.[57] Wesleyan chaplains also saw service in Bechuanaland, Upper Burma, the Northwest Frontier of India and in a bloodless but disease-ridden campaign against the Ashanti, near Kumasi.[58]

---

55 Army and Navy Committee Report, 1882.

56 Army and Navy Report, 1898.

57 O.S. Watkins, *With Kitchener's Army*, (London: S.W. Partridge and Co., 1899).

58 Watkins, *Soldiers and Preachers Too*, pp. 203-208.

No fewer than forty Wesleyan chaplains served in the South African War (1899-1902), several from Colonial Conferences, all now perforce uniformed in the new khaki and, although not commissioned, treated as Chaplains Fourth Class for rations. One who served with the Guards Brigade, E.P. Lowry, was promoted Chaplain Second Class, equivalent of Lt. Colonel. Watkins endured the siege of Ladysmith. Both wrote accounts of their experiences.[59]

In response to an approach by R.W. Allen after the South African War, the War Office offered the Wesleyans an establishment of five commissioned chaplains. Officials were encouraged by the Commander-in-Chief, Lord Wolseley, who had known Wesleyan chaplains in the field since the first Ashanti campaign, which he had commanded. He now minuted, 'none look after our soldiers better than the Wesleyans'.[60] (He would doubtless have the Wesleyan soldiers' homes in mind as well as the chaplains.) The Wesleyan Conference however declined the offer, even when temporary commissions were offered in place of permanent: they wanted their chaplains to remain civilians and to be answerable to the church, not the army.[61] The War Office was nevertheless determined to honour the church's work, and responded by adding to the Army List, as Assistant Chaplains, twenty Wesleyan ministers working full-time with soldiers. Assistant Chaplain was a civilian rank reserved in the other recognised churches for those awaiting a commission. In 1913, the Secretary of State recommended to King George V that two Wesleyan Assistant Chaplains with the longest service be made Honorary Chaplains to the Forces. (There were only four Honorary Chaplains and one of the other two was R.W. Allen.) One now honoured was E.P. Lowry, the other O.S. Watkins.[62]

The Wesleyan chaplains' service in military campaigns abroad must have added weight and colour to the denomination's well-remarked celebration of the Empire. No fewer than sixty two Wesleyan chaplains with war service are listed in the appendix to Watkins' record of Wesleyan service to the army up to 1906, and the list excludes Rule and Kelly and others with entirely peace-time service.[63] Other Nonconformists, Presbyterians apart, had a more guarded attitude to interventions abroad: as is evident from the figures of Other Protestants, their men felt little call to military service and their ministers none at this point to military or naval chaplaincy. Congregationalists and Baptists were riven by the South African War in particular, though did their utmost to conceal it in their Assemblies. The Wesleyans may have regretted the war, but they still supported it, and, as noted, provided forty chaplains.

---

59 E.P. Lowry (ed. H.K.), *Chaplains in Khaki, Methodist Soldiers in Camp, on the Field and on the March* (London: Marshall and Son, 1900); O.S. Watkins *Chaplains at the Front* (London, 1901).

60 The National Archive, WO 32/6441.

61 *Minutes of Conference*, 1903, pp. 50-51.

62 The National Archives, WO 5635.

63 Watkins, *Soldiers and Preachers Too*, pp. 239-47.

Books by Wesleyan chaplains were a further stimulus to the Imperial spirit. Male's is an astounding story of bravery, selflessness and religious duty to the soldier in lands then barely known. More stylistically written, and bound like Henty novels, making them ideal for Sunday School senior scholars at prize givings, are Watkins' two books detailing his battle experiences in the Sudan and then in the South African War. Lowry's book on South Africa was similarly bound and had a similar appeal. Though all these books show the work of chaplains among the men, inevitably campaigns and battles are the context and can be read as tales of British military endeavour.

Still excitingly written but, as befitted the times, simply bound, was Watkins' account of the retreat to the Marne after the Battle of Mons in the early months of the Great War when he was attached to a Field Ambulance.[64] This book was compiled from despatches sent to the *Methodist Recorder*, which (according to Watkins' obituary) so impressed King George V that he subscribed to the *Recorder* for the rest of the War. The book's importance in keeping alive the patriotic spirit among Nonconformists in the difficult second year of the War can be gauged by its five impressions between March and September 1915. Though books celebrating the glory of military endeavour continued to be written during and after the Great War, no more came from Watkins' pen.

256 Wesleyan chaplains, holding temporary commissions at the War Office's insistence, were serving by the end of the Great War and they were to be found in every theatre of the war. 170 were in France.[65] Three had been killed by enemy action; five died of other causes.[66] After the War, but with lingering reluctance, Conference accepted that Wesleyan chaplains serving in the much reduced Chaplains' Department should receive permanent commissions.[67] This was perhaps the final token of Wesleyan recognition.

In 1918, Watkins, the most senior Nonconformist chaplain abroad, had become Principal Chaplain, Italy, where a British Army was assisting the Italians against the Austrians. At this rank he commanded all chaplains whatever their religion. The Pope received him and thanked him for 'being a like a father to my priests' and added, 'I think it is a beautiful thing that Christians should thus work together.'[68] In 1924 Watkins was appointed Deputy Chaplain General, the first of only two Nonconformists to hold that rank. The other was a Primitive Methodist, George Standing, in 1929, a United Board appointment.

---

64 O.S. Watkins, *With French in France and Flanders* (London: C.H. Kelly, 1915).

65 *Statistics of the Military Effort of the British Empire during the Great War* (London; H.M. Stationery Office, 1922), p. 190.

66 P. Howson, 'Deaths among Army Chaplains, 1914-1920', *Journal of the Society for Army Historical Research* 83/333 (2008).

67 Methodist Forces Board papers, 15 January 1919.

68 Watkins' obituary in *Methodist Recorder*, January 1957.

The United Board had been formed in 1914 to recruit chaplains from the four main non-Wesleyan churches.[69] Whatever their attitude to the army before the War, they matched the Wesleyans in numbers of chaplains and losses during the War. On Methodist reunion the United Board lost its Primitive and United Methodist members and was confined henceforth to Congregationalists and Baptists. The old Wesleyan Army and Navy Committee had become a Board before the War and now was reborn as the Methodist Forces Board.

From the introduction of the fourth column, and particularly in the overseas campaigns which followed, and in the Great War, the Wesleyan chaplain's duty to the soldier – the mission – ceases to be a fight for his freedom to worship. Rather, Rule's determination to give the soldier far from home the chance to worship as a Wesleyan, and so have the comforts of the religion he knows best, is pursued by the chaplains abroad, in camp, on the march, in battle and with the wounded or dying. Also, from Male onwards, chaplains increasingly work in the hospital tents. This intensifies in the Great War. Wesleyan chaplains, like others, had a range of duties then but attachment to field ambulances, casualty clearing stations and field hospitals, just behind the lines, bandaging, consoling the wounded, writing letters for the dying, and conducting burials under fire, are what most remembered and found hardest. There were still church parades at Base, and sick visiting in Base hospitals, but at the front the chaplain's Christian duty to the soldier was personal and could be profound. It was also conducted largely free of religious difference among chaplains, giving vain hope of a more united church-life at home after the war.

---

[69] Neil E. Allison, *The Clash of Empires,* volume 1 of the Official History of the United Board (Didcot: United Navy, Army and Air Force Board, 2008).

CHAPTER 6

The 1857 Indian Rebellion and its Impact on the Wesleyan Mission

John Pritchard

In the old history books, written from a European perspective, it was the Indian Mutiny. From an Indian perspective, it is now usually called India's first War of Independence, though given that there was no insurrection in the south that is perhaps a claim too far. On the other hand to call it the sepoy revolt does not do justice to the extent to which the uprising involved civilians as well as troops.

It is well known that the spark that lit the conflagration was the new Pattern 1853 Enfield rifle. To load it, the infantryman – or sepoy in India-speak – had to bite the cartridge open, pour the gunpowder out into the muzzle and then stuff the cartridge case into the barrel as wadding before loading a ball. The standard issue paper cartridges had to be greased to make them waterproof, and the word went round that they were being greased with either lard or tallow. Lard – pork fat – was of course anathema to the Muslim soldiers and tallow – beef fat – just as unacceptable to the Hindus. In fact, over three months before the rebellion erupted, the East India Company's Military Secretary had ordered that when the new rounds were issued, they were to be ungreased. Each sepoy would have to grease his own cartridges with whichever grease he took no exception to. But the rumour was more potent than the truth.

At the time the Company kept three armies. Company rule did not extend to the whole sub-continent. There were numerous 'Princely States' where the writ of the nawab or nizam, raja or maharaja ran. The Company nevertheless controlled huge swathes of territory, divided for administrative purposes into three 'Presidencies', and each had its own army: Bombay, Madras and Bengal. In total the three armies in 1857 comprised 311,000 Indian troops, 40,000 European troops and 5,362 officers. There was no revolt in the Madras army and only three regiments out of twenty nine in Bombay mutinied. The rebellion began in the Bengal army, which had 74,000 Indian soldiers and 12,000 Europeans.

There were many reasons why the Bengal regiments were restive long before the Enfield rifles arrived. Whereas Madras and Bombay recruited caste-neutral armies with no special preference given to high-caste men, Bengal, from the time of Warren Hastings seventy five years before, had recruited men from the Brahmin caste who enjoyed considerable favours. For example, they were never posted overseas because they held that to be polluting. The Hindu festivals were officially recognized. They asserted their rights, and any suggestion that their principles were being overlooked was red rag to a sacred bull. Burma they regarded as overseas, and being dispatched to fight the Anglo-Burmese war in 1856 was a serious grievance.

Resentment of the British was not confined to the army. The East India Company was far more than a mercantile organization and Company rule was draconian. It inherited from the Mughal emperors a revenue collection system and among its officers in each district the Collector had the most important function. It steadily expanded the area under its direct rule, especially under Lord Dalhousie, the Governor-General from 1848 to 1856. He rode roughshod over the lesser traditional rulers, applying what was known as the Doctrine of Lapse, whereby the Company inherited their property and powers if a ruler died childless (and girls did not count). When the jewels of one 'royal family' were auctioned in Calcutta, the indigenous aristocracy were gravely insulted.

But not least among the underlying grievances was the fear that the Company was surreptitiously masterminding mass conversion to Christianity. To Europeans that was a laughable thought. There was a long-standing hostility in Company circles to missionaries. In the eighteenth century they were banned – the first Protestant missionaries were confined to the Danish enclaves. The activity of missionaries, the Directors held – and no doubt correctly – would threaten their commercial interests. They would allow no religious friction to complicate their activities. Almost to a man, they categorically resisted anything that might cause Indians to feel threatened and so foment unrest. Almost – but that man was Charles Grant, who went to India as a cadet in 1768 and rose to be Chairman of the Company. From 1776, when he found peace with God after a period of personal distress, Grant promoted a change of policy. Every twenty years the Company's charter had to be renewed by Parliament, and in 1793 he and his ally Wilberforce pressed for the inclusion of a 'Pious Clause' which would oblige the Company to make provision for the religious instruction of Indians and would have opened the way for missionaries. The dogmatism with which the Clause was opposed is indicated by the words of one Director, who had made a fortune in India: he was fully convinced 'that suffering clergymen . . . to overrun India, and penetrate the interior parts of it, would . . . prove utterly destructive of the Company's interests, if not wholly annihilate their power in Hindustan; that so far from wishing that they might make converts . . . he should lament such a circumstance as the most serious and fatal disaster that could happen.'[1] The Court of Directors rallied support and ensured that the clause was roundly defeated. A decade later, their attitude unchanged, they passed a resolution which declared 'The sending of Christian Missionaries into our Eastern possessions is the wildest, maddest, most expensive, and most

[1] Quoted in Stephen Neill, *Colonialism and Christian Missions* (London: Lutterworth Press, 1966), p. 85.

unwarranted plan that was ever proposed by a lunatic enthusiast.' Yet Grant was patient; and when the Charter next came up for renewal in 1813 there was a different result. Wilberforce and his allies lobbied hard. The parliamentary debates wound on from March to July. The 'Pious Clause' which was eventually enacted did not concede all they sought, but the Company undertook to support an Anglican bishop of Calcutta and three archdeaconries, while Nonconformists welcomed a clear statement that promoting 'the Interests and Happiness of the Native Inhabitants' involved 'religious and moral improvement' together with an undertaking to provide 'sufficient facilities . . . to persons desirous of going to and remaining in India, for the purpose of accomplishing these benevolent designs.'[2]

The year 1813 is a significant date in Methodist mission history. It was the year Wesleyans chose to mark as the foundation of their Missionary Society, though that was a strange choice. It was also the year when Thomas Coke, who had been promoting foreign missions for thirty years, set sail for Asia. With India hitherto closed, the destination of his party was Ceylon, but their ships were Bombay-bound. Coke himself died on the voyage; his companions had no knowledge of the provision he had made for funding the enterprise. What a relief to find that, with the new Charter in place, they were sympathetically received and bills of exchange were arranged. The Governor of Bombay had as a child known, or at any rate heard, John Wesley and, according to William Harvard who remained for some time in Bombay after his colleagues left for Ceylon, 'expressed the high sense which the British Government had ever entertained of Mr Wesley's principles and proceedings'.[3] The party continued to Ceylon as Coke intended, but it was not long before their activity extended to Madras. Over the next forty years Wesleyan mission stations, chapels and schools were established in Tamil Nadu and on the Mysore plateau. The attitude of Company officials to the missionaries' activities was one of non-interference and they were not on the whole incommoded. On the other hand a Hindu who became a Christian lost several rights: he could not inherit family property, he was debarred from holding any public office, and he was forbidden to remarry if he was deserted. These disabilities applied of course to male converts; women naturally had no such rights.

Indian suspicions of a dastardly plot to overthrow their religion and undermine their way of life were aroused during the governorship of Lord William Bentinck from 1827 to 1835. It was during his time that the first two disabilities were lifted, though the third, forbidding remarriage, was not removed until after the rebellion. But what Hindus found most offensive was that Bentinck tram-

---

2 See Eugene Stock, *History of the Church Missionary Society* (London: CMS, 1899), vol. 1, p. 103, and compare Penelope Carson, *The East India Company and Religion, 1698-1858* (Woodbridge: Boydell, 2012).

3 Quoted in G.G. Findlay and W.W. Holdsworth, *The History of the Wesleyan Methodist Missionary Society* (London: Epworth Press, 1921-24), vol. 5, p. 25.

pled on their customs by banning the practice of *sati* – burning widows on their husbands' pyres. He was of course supported by the missionaries, but he acted for reasons of humanity rather than Christian teaching; his motive was to civilise Indian society and he did not consider that he was imposing change on non-Christian people in the name of Christianity.

By the 1850s, however, there were more Company officials and army officers who wore their faith on their sleeve. The evangelical movement had taken hold in the Established Church, in which most had grown up, as well as in Nonconformity. Their manifestly earnest Christianity was observed and Indian antipathy grew in reaction. The suspicions of a plot in high places, however, were utterly misplaced. Even in 1859, when the uprising was over, the East India Company had been ousted and direct crown rule instituted, there was an episode when high places in Calcutta gave a sharp wrap on the knuckles of the Commissioner of Amritsar when with some colleagues he attended the baptism of six converts at the CMS mission.

Yet had Hindus and Muslims known of the manner in which they were regarded in Europe they would have had ample reason to re-act. Did any Indians know of Pope Pius IX's vigorous re-assertion of the *Extra ecclesiam nulla salus* doctrine? In 1856, in *Singulari quidem,* he re-iterated:

> Outside of the Church, nobody can hope for life or salvation unless he is excused through ignorance beyond his control.

The qualification is important. It was there two years earlier when he pronounced:

> It must be held by faith that outside the Apostolic Roman Church, no one can be saved; that this is the only ark of salvation; that he who shall not have entered therein will perish in the flood; but, on the other hand, it is necessary to hold for certain that they who labour in ignorance of the true religion, if this ignorance is invincible, will not be held guilty of this in the eyes of God.[4]

In the ears of Catholics and others alike, however, the whispered qualification was drowned out by the dogmatic exclusivism. The precise terms of the papal allocutions were doubtless unknown to all but a handful of people in India, but they were echoed in the attitudes of Protestant as well as Catholic missionaries.

Reginald Heber became Bishop of Calcutta in 1823. Four years earlier, in his vicarage in Wrexham, he had penned a hymn which became one of the anthems of the missionary movement, among nonconformists as well as Anglicans. I sang it in my youth. 'From Greenland's icy mountains' included lines like 'Can we, whose souls are lighted with wisdom from on high, Can we to men benighted the lamp of life deny?' and a verse which went

---

4 *Singulari quadam*, 1854.

> What though the spicy breezes
> Blow soft o'er Ceylon's isle;
> Though every prospect pleases,
> And only man is vile;
> In vain with lavish kindness
> The gifts of God are strown;
> The heathen in his blindness
> Bows down to wood and stone.

That language reflected the attitude of mission executives and shaped the thinking of their supporters. Wesleyans took a broader view of *ecclesiam* than Catholic teaching, yet their motivation, for many if not all, lay in a less nuanced view of *salus*: 'lest souls pass into eternity and the torment of hell-fire without even hearing of Jesus Christ'.[5] William Moister, a much-travelled missionary whose 500-page *History of Wesleyan Missions* was published in 1869, wrote in candid terms of both Muslims and Hindus. Of Muslims, that 'they required all, by the powerful arguments of fire and sword, to submit to the dogmas of the false prophet'. Of Hindus, that 'it is on the occasions of the great festivals, when the people congregate to the number of tens of thousands, that the sin and folly of these miserable idolaters are most apparent . . . Surely there never was a people on the face of the earth who stood in greater need of the Gospel than the dark, benighted Hindus.'[6] And that was saying a lot considering the way he wrote about other places: 'degraded', 'depraved', 'disgusting' and 'savage' are favourite Moister-words. But what would have given Hindus and Muslims alike the greatest cause to fear was the language of conquest and crusade with which the literature abounds. Another quotation, albeit from a later source, will illustrate the triumphal tones that were used in missionary meetings and writings:

> The overthrow of Hinduism was a task requiring sacrifices and efforts such as the Protestant Churches when they commenced the attack had little dreamed of – Methodism least of all. The host of Israel stood before walls which no trumpet-blowing, no seven days' perambulation, would bring to the ground.[7]

The military metaphors came home to roost in April 1857. Barracks and officers' bungalows were torched in several cantonments by disgruntled sepoys. At Meerut on 24 April an unsympathetic commanding officer ordered ninety of his men to practice firing drill. All except five refused to accept their cartridges. The other eighty five were court martialled, and most were sentenced to ten years' imprisonment with hard labour. The entire garrison was paraded, and watched as they were stripped of their uniforms and shackled. As they were

---

5 Hudson Taylor, quoted in Kenneth Cracknell, *In Good and Generous Faith* (London: Epworth Press, 2005), p. 159.

6 Cracknell, *In Good and Generous Faith*, pp. 420f.

7 G.G. Findlay and M.G. Findlay, *Wesley's World Parish* (London: Hodder & Stoughton, 1912), p. 122.

marched off to jail, the condemned soldiers berated their comrades for failing to support them. The next day revolt broke out. The prisoners were freed, the killings began.

It lasted for thirteen months, with atrocities on both sides. The story of the sieges, the massacres, the savage retaliation is not for telling in detail here. In terms of sheer numbers, there was far greater loss of Indian life, among the rebels and among the troops who remained loyal to their British commanders, than among Europeans. A letter published after the fall of Delhi in the *Bombay Telegraph* and reproduced in the British press demonstrates the brutal nature of the reprisals:

> All the city people found within the walls (of the city of Delhi) when our troops entered were bayoneted on the spot, and the number was considerable, as you may suppose, when I tell you that in some houses forty and fifty people were hiding. These were not mutineers but residents of the city, who trusted to our well-known mild rule for pardon. I am glad to say they were disappointed.[8]

One of the officers who witnessed the scene wrote in a letter to his brother 'With all my love for the army, I must confess, the conduct of professed Christians, on this occasion, was one of the most humiliating facts connected with the siege'.

Missionaries and members of their families were not specifically targeted in the uprising, though almost forty died, caught up in a tide of vitriolic animosity to all things western. But large tracts of the sub-continent were not directly affected. There was as yet no Wesleyan work in the north. Much of the south, where the Wesleyans had their mission stations, was not under direct British rule and the rebellion did not spread there, though it was at this time that the Madras Mission House was wrecked by a mob. A schoolboy made a confession of faith and sought baptism. When his parents failed to deter him, the manse, where he was staying, was stormed and both he and the missionaries had to clamber over the compound wall to escape. That sort of hostility was not exceptional and was unconnected to the insurrection. Indeed, it is unlikely that in the south as much was known as back in Britain – even in 1947, a missionary said of the horrific communal killings which followed partition, 'We in the South were told little, if anything, about them.'[9] The 1857 troubles themselves did not therefore endanger Wesleyan missionaries, but once the troubles died down they found themselves in a very different world.

The East India Company was always a strange beast, far more than a mercantile organization, effectively a quasi-sovereign power. Throughout the rebellion Disraeli, in opposition, had pressed for the abolition of the Company and in 1858 it was disbanded by Act of Parliament, an 'Act for the Better Government

---

[8] Quoted in William Dalrymple, *The Last Mughal* (London: Bloomsbury, 2006), p. 364.

[9] Ruth Anstey, in *Indo-British Review* (Madras), vol. XIV.

of India'. The Raj came into being. Signing the Act into law, the Queen proclaimed:

> Firmly relying ourselves on the truth of Christianity, and acknowledging with gratitude the solace of religion [these opening words being her own composition], We disclaim alike the right and the desire to impose Our convictions on any of Our subjects. We declare it to be Our royal will and pleasure that none be in anywise favoured, none molested or disquieted by reason of their religious faith or observance, but that all alike shall enjoy the equal and impartial protection of the law; and We do strictly charge and enjoin all those who may be in authority under Us that they abstain from all interference with the religious belief or worship of any of Our subjects, on pain of Our highest displeasure. And it is our further will that, so far as may be, Our subjects of whatever race or creed, be freely and impartially admitted to offices in Our service, the duties of which they may be qualified by their education, ability, and integrity, duly to discharge.[10]

It took some while for the fact of these liberties to be drilled into the heads of some civil servants, as the incident in Amritsar to which I referred well demonstrates. It was 1866 before the third of the civil disabilities was removed by an Act on the Re-marriage of Native Converts. Speaking in its support, Sir Henry Maine enunciated the basic principles which were now in place:

> We will not force any man to be a Christian; we will not even tempt any man to be a Christian but if he chooses to be a Christian, it would be shameful if we did not protect him and his in those rights of conscience which we have been the first to introduce into the country.[11]

In this new situation, the Wesleyan Missionary Society judged it opportune to re-open work in the north. Back in 1830 two young missionaries were sent to Calcutta. Both were to have distinguished careers, Peter Percival in Jaffna and William Hodson in Mysore, and it was not due to any shortcomings on their part that they were withdrawn after less than two years on the grounds that 'results had not come up to expectations'. They had devoted themselves assiduously to studying Bengali. They had found convenient premises. They had begun a school. But the Society was impatient for quick results. It was then still in its infancy, and the ambitions of its zealous Secretaries and Committee overstretched resources. Now, a quarter-century on, a new attempt was made. It began, as such Wesleyan initiatives often did, with the army. There were four hundred Wesleyan soldiers in the garrisons of the Bengal Presidency. In 1859 Daniel Pearson was sent to the Barrackpur cantonment to work among them. He was a missionary rather than a chaplain, and the distinction is significant. Under the new regime there were chaplains to the army and civil service who were appointed by the government and were much better paid. Pearson was

---

10 Quoted in Neill, *Colonialism*, p. 98.

11 George Smith, *Twelve Indian Statesmen* (London: John Murray, 1897), p. 267.

appointed by the WMMS and received the regular missionary allowances. He was soon joined by two others, who were posted to Calcutta. One was designated to minister to the English-speaking community, the other to work in Bengali, once he had acquired the language. Later Pearson was transferred to Lucknow, where he inherited from American Methodists a congregation of two hundred Europeans. Among Indians, results were no quicker than thirty years before, but this time there was no retreat and foundations were laid for a far more substantial ministry in the twentieth century.

Another development brought about by the new administration was the offer of grants-in-aid for educational purposes. There was no question of a national education service – there was nothing of the sort in Britain until 1902. India's rulers were products of public schools. However, before the transfer of power, the Company's Board of Control in London was already working on a scheme to extend educational provision. It took effect in 1859, and enabled any agency running schools or colleges to claim grants provided they followed government syllabuses and agreed to government inspections. Religious instruction would be allowed provided other subjects were taught satisfactorily. Wesleyans, along with almost every other Missionary Society, took up the offer, but not without debate. There were warnings that they would soon find themselves compromised, but there was no strong resistance. Before long two-thirds of the cost of education was borne by the government, and the missions were able to expand both their schools and their other activities. The number of institutions multiplied. Fed by a network of elementary schools, the Methodist High Schools in Madras, Negapatam, Bangalore and Mysore all expanded during the 1860s and 1870s to offer better qualifications to the most successful students.

Yet compromised they were. Opium 'is small in bulk, light, not quickly perishable, and very expensive. The revenue derived from opium, was an essential item in the Indian government's budget.' A long war was waged against the trade, with as much fervour and as little success as the campaigns against the slave trade in the eighteenth century and the arms trade much more recently. Ashley, the future Lord Shaftesbury, had moved a resolution in parliament in 1843, after the first Opium War,

> That it is the opinion of this House that the continuance of the trade in opium, and the monopoly of its growth in the territories of British India, are destructive of all relations of amity between England and China, injurious to the manufacturing interests of the country by the very serious diminution of legitimate commerce, and utterly inconsistent with the honour and duties of a Christian kingdom.

But to no effect: the trade 'continued for three generations to enrich individuals, to disgrace governments, and to perplex the Christian conscience of the world.'[12] In 1858, revenue from the opium trade amounted to one seventh of the East India Company's total income, and the rebellion had little or no impact

[12] Neill, *Colonialism*, p. 135.

on the traffic. The Raj's policy on opium was no different from the Company's. The missionary conscience was especially perplexed and lamentably divided. The most vociferous missionary apologists for the opium trade were found among those working in education, who feared the loss of opium revenue would mean cuts in government grants. In 1893, after a Missionary Conference in Bombay failed to condemn the trade the *Bombay Guardian*, a Christian weekly, thundered:

> When men who have been deputed to come to India by the Churches of Great Britain to work for the salvation of souls confess that they are silent on an official crime that is dragging millions down to perdition, through fear of having their grants diminished, it is time the home Churches should consider their relationship between the work of God and mammon.[13]

and Hugh Price Hughes, speaking in Exeter Hall, said that never in his life had he

> witnessed anything more deplorable than this exhibition of sane men, professing to represent the missionary societies in India, standing up to resist the protest that comes to us from the bleeding hearts of missionaries in China.

It was, he said, 'the most appalling proof of the demoralising effect of associating with Indian officialdom'.[14]

The most significant impact of the rebellion, however, was in Britain. The public had already been treated to a taste of India at the Great Exhibition of 1851. The art and artefacts on display included an Ivory Chair of State, presented to the Queen by the Maharaja of Travancore, and a stuffed elephant complete with howdah. The rebellion brought the realisation that exoticism was not all India had to offer. As one commentator (McCarthy) put it later:

> Never in our time, never probably in any time, came such news upon England as the first full story of the outbreak in India. It came with terrible, not unnatural, exaggeration. England was horrified by the stories of wholesale massacres of English women and children; of the most abominable tortures, the most degrading outrages inflicted upon English matrons and maidens.[15]

The press 'waxed hysterical in demands for more severe punitive measures to be taken, and the rituals of revenge-killing were enacted even in . . . nurseries and schools.' Flora Annie Steel, who years later became the Mrs Beeton of Anglo-India, recalled in her autobiography how she and her brothers played mutiny games in their large country house in Scotland and wrote, 'I hanged and burned and tortured the Nana Sahib in effigy many times'.[16] (The Nana Sahib

---

[13] *Bombay Guardian*, 7 January, 1893.
[14] *Bombay Guardian*, February, 1893.
[15] Justin McCarthy, *A History of our own Times* (London: Chatto and Windus, 1897).
[16] Pat Barr, *The Memsahibs* (London: Century, 1989), p. 142.

was the name by which the British scornfully knew the Maharajah of Bithur, whose siege of Cawnpore was the deadliest of the atrocities suffered by the British.)

Once the troubles were over and the new regime installed, the hysteria was forgotten. India, however, was not. Henceforth the sub-continent featured much more prominently in the public mind. For Wesleyans it was a wake-up call. In the past the Society's support for its personnel in India had often given them cause for complaint. The Committee failed to appreciate the expense entailed in opening new stations. When, in cases of dire need, those on the spot incurred unauthorized expenditure, they brought severe criticism down upon their heads. Fearful of further censure, it was easy to become paralysed, unwilling to risk any initiative. There were always too few missionaries for the work in hand. The letters they received from London not only failed to give any clear guidance, but lacked any words of sympathy for their privations, bereavements and frustrations. Now India attracted more serious attention. If the general public paid more attention to Indian affairs than ever before, Methodists prayed about India as never before. The Society sent funds to assist post-war relief. Sensitized to the circumstances of thousands of British soldiers, a chaplaincy service was given priority. With the new opportunities in education, more funds for plant and staff were released. The statistics tell the story. Between 1850 and 1870 the number of schools rose from forty five to seventy one, the scholars from 1780 to 4866. By comparison the growth in church membership was slow, from 388 to 646, but the number of ministers rose from twelve to twenty two, together with twelve assistants. The aftermath of the rebellion did more for education than for conversion, but the influence of the Wesleyan mission was much wider than the membership returns suggest.

A postscript

The endeavours of Wesleyan missionaries in India were without exception founded on love of God and of neighbour. Yet there was an underlying assumption of racial superiority, and the language of conquest persisted in the letters they wrote, the addresses and sermons they delivered on furlough, the articles which appeared in magazines, and the thinking of those at home who subscribed the funds. The Methodist sub-conscience has always been strongly influenced by hymns; their beliefs and attitudes are formed at least as much by what they sing as by the sermons they hear, and they sang Charles Wesley's hymns more than any other. Hymns like 'Jesus, the conqueror reigns', lines like 'till all his foes submit', verses like 'O let us still proceed in Jesus' work below; And following our triumphant head to further conquests go' left their mark. The theme of battle and conquest was developed by George Clayton in an account of *Methodism in Central China*, which he marred with a devastating – and, incidentally, wrongly directed – attack on Buddhists:

> Buddha's conquest has not been over Christianity, nor over the power of sin, but over all that is noble and pure, all that is honest and of good report. As his worship has spread in this land, purity has been vanquished, and in his train have come immorality, lust, murder, suicide, cruelty. And now a new strife has begun. The Galilean has thrown down the gage of battle. Day by day the armies of the Christ are battling against superstition.[17]

There was nothing peculiar to Wesleyans in such triumphalism; it was, with few exceptions, how Christendom had approached the regions beyond since the time of the crusades.

Yet it was not the only way in which the missionary task could be approached. In 2 Corinthians 5.20 Paul wrote (I quote the version invariably used in those days) 'Now then we are ambassadors for Christ, as though God did beseech you by us.' There is all the difference in the world between an ambassador and a conquistador. And embassies, after all, are otherwise known as diplomatic *missions.* A study of how often that text was used in missionary meetings and sermons would be revealing. Francis Asbury preached on it in a mid-Atlantic storm on 13 October 1771, on his way to America. But the military metaphors predominated. Indeed, the *History of the Wesleyan Missionary Society*, in the volume treating of India which was published in 1924, has a chapter entitled 'The Weapons of our Warfare'. Neither the savagery of the Rebellion and the distress of subsequent wars, not even the horrors of the Great European War, had led the authors to abandon such terminology. Of course they were speaking of the battle for hearts and minds, though that was a phrase that did not gain currency until the Vietnam War. It may be that there was a conscious effort to insist that the weapons of *our* warfare are not swords but ploughshares, instruments of peace not of destruction – but there is no internal evidence to support that defence. If it was as natural for children in Scotland to play mutiny games as for my generation to play cowboys and Indians, oblivious to the cruel realities we parodied, it was similarly natural for Holdsworth, steeped in the Pauline language of the whole armour of God and fighting the good fight, to use the language of war. The weapons he wrote about were 'The Preaching of the Gospel', 'Educational Missions', 'Industrial Schools', 'Literature and the Press', 'The Ministry of Healing' and 'The Training of the Ministry'. A preferable but unused metaphor springs to mind: could these 'weapons' not equally be labelled 'baskets' – baskets from which seeds of the gospel were being broadcast? And some, indubitably, 'fell on good ground, and did yield fruit that sprang up and increased.' The legacy of the Wesleyan mission, now found within the united Churches of South and North India, bears witness to that.

---

17 Barr, *The Memsahibs*, p. 128, quoting George Clayton, *Methodism in Central China* (London: C.H. Kelly, 1906).

CHAPTER 7

Turning the other cheek? The Use of Violence by Victorian Missionaries in the Tropics

John H. Darch

Missionaries are rarely, if ever, viewed in a positive light in postmodern popular culture. They are seen stereotypically either as purveyors of western spiritual and cultural values, riding roughshod over indigenous faiths and cultures, or as hapless victims, suffering (often stereotypically and comically in cannibal cooking pots) at the hands of violent indigenous tribes.[1]

This chapter will seek to address and to challenge the second of these stereotypes and, pointing to case studies from tropical Africa and the Pacific in the 1860-80s, it will be argued that, far from being passive victims of violence, missionaries were at times prepared to use targeted violence against indigenous peoples for their own ends. And, although these cases were small in number, they are significant in displaying a very different view of missionaries from that which is popularly held.

Providing the backcloth for this discussion are the underlying assumptions of British governments about appropriate and inappropriate responses to the death of British subjects at the hands of native peoples. Missionaries are often seen as direct or indirect agents of European imperialism, but when examined any direct link is seen to be tenuous or extremely rare. In giving instructions to the commissioner he was sending out to the Fiji Islands in 1860 the Colonial Secretary the Duke of Newcastle, after speaking favourably of the work of the Methodist mission, warned him against identifying too closely with them:

> I must caution you not to suffer your sympathy with the Missionaries or your admiration of their achievements, to affect your judgment. . . . Her Majesty's Government must continue to entrust the Gospel in the distant parts of the earth . . . to the piety and zeal of individuals.[2]

---

1 This negative interpretation was less apparent in the second half of the nineteenth century when the exploits of missionaries were frequently reported with a heroic and adventurous ring.

2 Newcastle's 'Instructions to Smythe', 23 December 1859, enc. in Sir F. Rogers to Lord Wodehouse, 31 July 1860. National Archives, Kew: Colonial Office (CO) papers, 83/1.

In official eyes the missionaries had a civilizing and Christianizing, but not an imperializing, purpose and that voluntary purpose was for them to carry out by their own means without any aid from the government.

Newcastle's successor, the Earl of Carnarvon, made a statement in the House of Lords following the murder of J.C. Patteson, missionary bishop of Melanesia in 1871. Disagreeing with the Bishop of Lichfield, who had stated that missionaries knew the risks they were taking and that retribution was a matter for God, Carnarvon argued that 'Murder required punishment and he did not think it well that in such a case the State should do nothing, but leave the matter to the vengeance of God.'[3] This was less a policy statement than an expression of outrage and no new machinery was put in place at a governmental level to implement Carnarvon's wish. Indeed, the bill[4] under discussion was designed to protect, not missionaries from indigenous peoples, but indigenous peoples from Europeans and white Australians.

Missionary life in the nineteenth century was undoubtedly hard and, as I have written elsewhere, death was an inexorable companion of the missionary and a common feature of missionary existence.[5] Some Victorian missionaries would, no doubt, have agreed with Tertullian that 'the blood of the martyrs is the seed of the church'.[6] But there were actually very few European missionary martyrs *per se* in the south-west Pacific in the Victorian period. Considering the opposition, threats and intimidation that they had to endure, remarkably few European missionaries suffered violent deaths at the hands of indigenous peoples. Disease and the unhealthy climate were the greatest enemies of European missionaries.

So this chapter will examine, through specific examples, not violence experienced by missionaries but the use of violence by missionaries or on their behalf and with their consent. In the Pacific and tropical Africa in this period of the nineteenth century there was a sufficient number of such cases to indicate that, though numerically small in total, the use of violent means was not insignificant.

Tanna

The first incident to be considered took place on the island of Tanna in the New Hebrides (present day Vanuatu) in 1865. The New Hebrides Mission, a transnational Presbyterian mission, whose missionaries were largely Scots or expatriate Scots, had been working quietly in the islands since 1848 when John Geddie arrived from Nova Scotia. Geddie worked alone until 1852 when the first of

3 *Hansard*, Third Series, CCXI, cols. 368-70.

4 Eventually passed as The Pacific Islanders' Protection Act, 1872.

5 See John H. Darch, 'Love and Death in the Mission Compound', *Anvil*, 17 (2000), pp. 22-39, and *Missionary Imperialists?: Missionaries, Government and the growth of Empire in the Tropics, 1860-1885* (Milton Keynes: Paternoster, 2009), pp. 35-46.

6 *Apol.* 50.13.

what were to be a number of missionary colleagues, mainly from Scotland or the Scottish diaspora, joined him.

Geddie and his colleagues found ministry to the often hostile Melanesians was difficult at the best of times, but also discovered that the work of the mission in promoting a gospel of love was frequently undermined by the depredations of the Australian labour traders who called at the islands on a regular basis seeking to exploit commercially the islands' benefits and in particular its reservoir of cheap, strong labour. This labour was in demand for the Queensland plantations and by the 1860s a sea-borne trade securing indentured labour on five-year contracts was in full swing. Often less than scrupulous in the way they worked, the labour traders frequently left behind death, destruction and anger towards Europeans on the islands they visited.

The island of Tanna was one of the more difficult postings for members of the New Hebrides Mission. John Paton lost his first wife and baby son there in 1859 and three years later he, and fellow missionary J.W. Mathieson, were driven off the island altogether. Though they continued to visit Tanna there was no missionary resident on the island when a violent incident took place in 1865, the exact details of which remain unclear.[7] What is highly significant is that the visit to the islands of the naval vessel HMS *Curaçoa* coincided with the temporary absence of the senior missionary, John Geddie. In all probability (though there is no extant evidence for this)[8] John Paton seized the opportunity of Geddie's absence to persuade Commodore Wiseman to teach the inhabitants of Tanna a lesson in European authority with a show of naval strength that would hopefully make the Tannese more tractable and amenable to the missionaries. The other missionaries would either have agreed with him or not felt strong enough to oppose him. Did the missionaries intend bloodshed? Almost certainly not, but whatever the actual sequence of events, matters quickly got out of hand. A seaman and a Tannese chief were killed in scuffles and the guns of HMS *Curaçoa* were turned on Port Resolution, the island's major settlement, in a two-hour bombardment. In the shocked aftermath of the escalation of violence John Paton denied any personal responsibility and pointed the finger at Commodore Wiseman.[9] Patton was later compelled to defend himself at the presbytery of Sydney.

---

7 W.P. Morrell, *Britain in the Pacific Islands* (Oxford: OUP, 1960), p. 99 and Jane Samson, *Imperial Benevolence: making British authority in the Pacific Islands* (Honolulu: University of Hawai'i Press, 1998), pp. 134-35, for example, give different sequences of events.

8 Dr Brenchley, the ship's naturalist, wrote an eye-witness account of the bombardment; he was not privy to Commodore Wiseman's decision making. Julius L. Brenchley, *Jottings during the Cruise of H.M.S. Curaçoa* (London: Longmans, Green & Co., 1873), pp. 201-204.

9 John G. Paton, *John G. Paton, Missionary to the New Hebrides. An Autobiography* [1889] (Edinburgh: Banner of Truth, 1965), pp. 297-302.

On his return to the islands, John Geddie carefully condemned the naval action without condemning his brother missionaries:

> I believe the punishment of the Tannese was a great but unintentional mistake. The weapons of our warfare . . . must be spiritual, and not carnal. We shall do far more to subdue, humanize and elevate these natives with Bibles in our hands than with the whole British navy at our backs. Natives walk by sight rather than by faith, and understand actions better than words. We may now tell these islanders that we come to them with a message of love, but the case of Tanna will raise doubts in their minds. The mission on these islands has now a character to redeem as well as a character to maintain.[10]

But Geddie was in the minority, and seven years after the event, in June 1872, the Foreign Missions Committee of the Reformed Presbyterian Church in Scotland officially endorsed the action as being 'of considerable advantage to the New Hebrides Mission'.[11] The committee's approval of the use of military force—when beneficial to the mission—was clear. But missions walked a tightrope over such issues. It was a matter of principle that they were voluntary societies supported by individual church members from the highest to the lowest in society.[12] Given the fact that there was a multiplicity of societies for mission-minded British Christians to support, a degree of competition was inevitable. The Anglo-Catholic UMCA, for example, suffered a slump in donations in the 1870s following a series of disasters which seriously undermined the confidence of their home supporters.[13]

Blanche Bay

Though probably instigated and certainly supported by the missionaries it was Royal Naval personnel who meted out violent retribution to the people of Tanna in 1865. In 1878 at Blanche Bay on the Pacific island of New Britain (today part of Papua New Guinea) it was the area's leading missionary who actually led the violence.

Born in County Durham before emigrating to New Zealand, George Brown had led the Australian Wesleyan Methodist mission in the Bismarck Archipela-

---

[10] Quoted in James W. Falconer, *John Geddie* (Toronto: Board of Foreign Missions, Presbyterian Church in Canada, 1915), pp. 98-99.

[11] Paper issued by the Foreign Missions Committee, 25 June 1872, printed as an appendix in A.H. Markham, *The Cruise of the 'Rosario' amongst the New Hebrides and Santa Cruz Islands* (London: S. Low, Marston, Low and Searle, 1873), pp. 268-72. For an impartial account of the events see Morrell, *Britain in the Pacific Islands*, pp. 99-100.

[12] The annual reports of most missions in this period give a detailed list of subscribers and the amount of their donations—from the wealthy mill-owner's largesse to the widow's mite.

[13] Darch, *Missionary Imperialists*, p. 24.

go (between New Guinea and the Solomon Islands) since 1877. In April 1878 a missionary and four teachers, all Fijians, were attacked, killed and eaten by Talili, a local chieftain on the Gazelle Peninsula. When he heard of the murders Brown sailed immediately for Blanche Bay from his base at Port Hunter on Duke of York Island. After ensuring the safety of the women and children of the mission he took charge of a punitive expedition of some sixty armed men. Over a period of six days three villages were burned, and two brief skirmishes were fought. Casualties were variously estimated between ten and a hundred. The native chiefs quickly sued for peace and Brown re-established good relations with them. No further trouble ensued on the Gazelle Peninsula and the local naval commander, Capt. Purvis RN, commented that, 'Mr Brown, having regard for the safety of those people entrusted to his care, could hardly have acted otherwise than he did.'[14]

Brown's actions did not receive universal plaudits, however. The Australian labour trader, W.T. Wawn, no lover of the missionaries who sought to disrupt and outlaw his livelihood, commented, not unreasonably, 'if such reprisals had been undertaken by a layman, a howl of indignation would have arisen from Exeter Hall. Likely enough, too, the leader of the expedition would have been hanged when he got home.'[15] Indeed, Chief Justice Gorrie of the Western Pacific High Commission tried to begin proceedings for manslaughter against Brown, but the High Commissioner Sir Arthur Gordon overruled him.[16]

Heinz Schütte describes Brown as both 'a European imperialist' and 'a conqueror, albeit of the missionary variety'.[17] In her recent study of Brown, Helen Bethea Gardner asserts that, 'Such a large-scale attack, with so many deaths, all led by a Christian missionary, was without precedent in the modern missionary movement.'[18] Yet in the long term Brown's notoriety did not adversely affect his missionary career. As an influential writer and anthropologist, he wrote a regular column in the *Sydney Morning Herald* and from 1887-1908 he served as General Secretary of the WMMS in Australia.

Kalo

But not all Nonconformist missionaries agreed with the 'eye for an eye' philosophy of George Brown and John Paton. The London Missionary Society's mis-

---

14 Quoted in Morrell, *Britain in the Pacific Islands*, p. 247.

15 William T. Wawn, *The South Sea Islanders and the Queensland Labour Trade* (London: Swan Sonnenschein, 1893), pp. 169-70.

16 Morrell, *Britain in the Pacific Islands*, pp. 246-47; Gorrie to Hicks Beach, 11 November 1878. CO 225/1. For Brown, see also John Garrett, *To Live among the Stars: Christian Origins in Oceania* (Geneva and Suva: World Council of Churches, 1982), pp. 220-32

17 Heinz Schütte, 'The Six-Day War of 1878 in the Bismarck Archipelago', *Journal of Pacific History* 24 (1989), pp. 48, 51.

18 Helen Bethea Gardner, *Gathering for God* (Dunedin: Otago University Press, 2006), p. 65.

sionaries in Papua New Guinea were very progressive by Victorian missionary standards. Relaxed about native nudity and uncomfortable with imperialism, they opposed the use of punitive force. When in March 1881 four of the mission's Polynesian teachers and their families were murdered at Kalo, the missionaries stuck to their principles and did not report the incident to the authorities in order to prevent the further violence and bloodshed that punitive reprisals would entail. Indeed, rather than blaming the perpetrators James Chalmers reflected, 'I fear we are not altogether free from blame. The teachers are often very indiscreet in their dealings with the natives.'[19] But the secrecy was not maintained and, some months later, HMS *Wolverene* arrived to punish the village responsible for the murders. James Chalmers complained:

> [I]ndiscriminate shooting down of innocent natives, burning villages and cutting down cocoa-nut trees, I think [is] mere barbarism. It ought not to be done by our navy . . . is it right that a great nation should do such things to savages? Better far that we should suffer than that we should do wrong.[20]

It is significant that these views were expressed by members of a mission community who were themselves at risk from violence and, taken with the previous case studies, it provides clear evidence of a diversity of missionary opinion concerning the use of violence. Chalmers would have agreed with the *Sydney Morning Herald* that 'Christian missionaries undermine their own special force when they bear the sword'.[21] The irony is that Chalmers himself perished at the hands of a native assassin twenty years later in 1901.

Examples from outside Nonconformity

Though the focus of this volume is on missionaries from the Protestant Nonconformist denominations,[22] it would be a mistake to assume that issues arising from the use of violence in furthering their ends did not also apply to missionaries from other Christian denominations. This was a non-denominational phenomenon. The missions of the national churches of England and Scotland also experienced the same problems. At Mombasa in East Africa the Church Missionary Society, the largest mission agency of the Church of England, found itself running a settlement for freed slaves known as Frere Town. Here the real difficulty of keeping order among a large number of often unruly and unwilling ex-slaves led to the use of violent means to control them. Both the Lay Superintendents in the period 1876-1881 were brutal in their punishment regime,

---

19 Quoted in Cuthbert Lennox, *James Chalmers of New Guinea* (London: Melrose, 1902), p. 95.

20 Quoted in Lennox, *James Chalmers*, p. 97.

21 18 September 1878

22 Though the term is generally understood in a UK context the concept of Nonconformity was actually redundant on the mission field since there was no Established Church to which to conform.

though they had no legal jurisdiction over the ex-slaves. Reports from the British Vice-Consul and a Royal Naval Commander were both damning in their criticism. Similarly, in Central Africa the Church of Scotland mission at Blantyre, also caring for large numbers of former slaves, received adverse headlines in the British and colonial press when details of its even more brutal punishment regime including flogging (so severe in one case that the prisoner died) and even an execution, were reported to the UK press by a visiting journalist.[23]

The publicity given to missionary violence in the press meant that other missions now became more scrupulous in administering punishments, no doubt thankful that their punishment regimes had not been exposed in the media. In Zanzibar for example, Bishop Edward Steere of the UMCA wrote to his Archdeacon, Chauncey Maples: 'I have no choice but to forbid altogether all beating of women.'[24] Clearly he would not bother to forbid what was not already taking place, but equally clearly his prohibition did not extend to men. As in Freretown and Blantyre, routine violence was being used to keep order and it can be assumed that for every case that has come to light there are probably several others which have not.

Reflections

Missionaries were simultaneously people of faith and practical realists; they knew the risks they were taking and by and large did not feel that armed force would greatly help them in the long term. Yet there are too many examples of missionaries refusing to 'turn the other cheek' and approving the use of punitive measures by British forces against recalcitrant native peoples to be ignored. Sometimes they, or their mission staff, even used force themselves to maintain order and discipline in the mission community. It was clearly an area where there was real division of opinion in missionary ranks.

Danger of Anachronism and Political Correctness

In examining this issue care must be taken not to judge Victorian missionaries by the liberal Western European standards of the twenty-first century. After all, Britain was itself slow to renounce the institutional use of violence. Brutal floggings in the Army did not end until 1881, birching of young offenders continued until 1948, hanging was in regular use until 1964 and corporal punishment continued in schools until the 1980s. Missionaries were no plaster saints and they reflected many of the mores of the society and culture from which

---

[23] Andrew Chirnside, *The Blantyre Missionaries: Discreditable Disclosures* (London: William Ridgway, 1880). See also A.J. Hanna, *The Beginnings of Nyasaland and North-Eastern Rhodesia* (Oxford, 1956), pp. 28-34 and John McCracken, *Politics and Christianity in Malawi 1875-1940* (Cambridge, 1977), pp. 65-68.

[24] Steere to Maples, 10 May 1882, quoted in A.J. Temu, *British Protestant Missions* (London: Longman, 1972), p. 30n.

they came. This is illustrated in an 1869 letter from one of the General Secretaries of the Wesleyan Methodist Missionary Society, W.B. Boyce:

> I fear the French are on the whole better administrators than we are for colonies like ours in West Africa; [despite their] arbitrary acts. . . . the community gains the benefit of having only one master and matters are quickly settled . . . good national government in which the rulers *'bear not the sword in vain'* but are *'a terror to evil doers'* (Rom.13) is equally an ordinance of God.[25]

Though no imperialist European nation was guiltless of violence towards indigenous peoples, the British had a relatively better track record than the Germans, the Belgians or the French. It is therefore of some significance that the head of a British missionary society should speak so favourably of the harsher French methods of colonial administration

But as with missionaries in the field, there was more than one opinion amongst mission administrators on the 'home front' concerning the use of violence in mission circles. R.N. Cust, a progressive senior member of the Church Missionary Society, who served on its Home Committee, complained in 1889 about savage beatings administered by one missionary in East Africa and concluded:

> if it is agreed that an expedition cannot be carried on, unless the leader of it commits day by day acts of brute violence, the reply is, that *missionary expeditions had better not be undertaken.* If missions can only be worked by methods which no supporter of the mission would dare to state in detail on a mission-platform, then missions had better not be undertaken.[26]

Missionary Isolation

Elsewhere I have identified isolation and loneliness as perhaps the main determining factors of missionary life.[27] Isolation and loneliness bred fear in what was, after all, an alien minority who felt the need to protect themselves and their families and to keep control of their lives and their destinies. The paradox was that though they were on the mission field in order to proclaim the gospel of love that 'casts out fear' they often perceived themselves, and particularly their families, to be in danger, both moral and physical. This led to them separating themselves and their families from those they had come to serve. In some cases the mission compound became virtually a fortified redoubt, inaccessible to indigenous members of the mission. Both for educational reasons and to protect them from 'moral pollution' missionary children were sent far away to school in the UK and the white settler colonies.

---

[25] W.B. Boyce to Dr James Rigg, 17 September 1869. CO 87/98B.

[26] R.N. Cust, *Notes on Missionary Subjects* (London: Elliot Stock, 1889), pp. 29-30.

[27] *Anvil* 17 (2000), 22-39 and *Missionary Imperialists?,* pp. 35-46.

As has been outlined above this fear also led to harsh punishment regimes, punitive reprisals and making use of the armed services of the Royal Navy which often provided a lifeline to civilization for isolated missionaries. The aim was, as George Brown semi-humorously put it, to make indigenous people understand that 'roast missionary is too expensive a dish for them to indulge in'.[28]

The growing influence of Imperialism

It is important to be aware that missionaries were not only missionaries but also Europeans and their fate was inextricably bound up with that of other Europeans on the fringes of Empire in the nineteenth century. In particular they were (mainly) British subjects and as such, if their mission stations were in the south Pacific, came under the protection of the Royal Navy. Jane Samson has noted the strength of evangelical and humanitarian influences on naval officers of this period.[29] Naval officers were often natural allies of the missionaries but they were allies with power who, either proactively or as a result of missionary persuasion, could use that (often violent) power to missionary advantage. But as the nineteenth century progressed, missions and European imperialism became increasingly entwined in a way that can be difficult to unravel. As humanitarianism declined, imperialism grew and a *sine qua none* of imperialism was that indigenous peoples had to be put in their place when they challenged European supremacy; in many contexts that supremacy was in the hands of missionaries.

Only a few saw the irony and ultimate futility of using violent means to protect and uphold the supremacy of Christian missionaries. One of these was John Geddie, who remarked that the growing preoccupation with prestige 'sweeps away at one stroke the character for which we have been endeavoring for years to establish as ambassadors of the Prince of Peace'[30] and that 'The weapons of our warfare . . . must be spiritual, and not carnal. We shall do far more to subdue, humanize and elevate these natives with Bibles in our hands than with the whole British navy at our backs'.[31]

It should be remembered that these violent incidents were actually isolated ones, noted because of their rarity. More often missionaries steadfastly opposed violence and protested when it was unleashed on their behalf by the military. Missionaries, whether they liked it or not (and as the nineteenth century waned a small number liked it very much indeed), were representatives of European power and in an age of imperialism that power could not be seen to be flouted. A very small number of missionaries used or made use of violence on their behalf, but it had no wide support and it engendered a great deal of guilt.

---

28 Brown to Revd J. Wallis, 2 July 1878, quoted in Schütte, p. 44.

29 Samson, *Imperial Benevolence*, pp. 130-47.

30 Quoted in George Patterson, *Missionary Life among the Cannibals* (Toronto: J. Campbell, J. Bain and Hart, 1882), p. 482.

31 Quoted in James W. Falconer, *John Geddie* (Toronto: Board of Foreign Missions, Presbyterian Church in Canada, 1915), pp. 98-99.

CHAPTER 8

'Faithful unto Death': Christian Mission, Common Sense and Changing Attitudes: a Congregational Dimension.

Clyde Binfield

I

This chapter explores the relationship between mission, mindset, and denomination, each in constant evolution, each dependent on individual agency. The exploration is introduced by a vocation, an ordination, the career which followed from it, a friendship, and a sermon.

The vocation was to Congregational ministry. The ordination was at High Street Congregational Church, Lancaster, on 13 September 1859. The ordinand was in his early twenties. He was fresh from Cheshunt, the theological college in Hertfordshire which had originally been founded in mid-Wales by the Countess of Huntingdon for the service of all evangelical churches and especially those of her own Connexion. By the 1850s, however, Cheshunt chiefly prepared men for the Congregational ministry or for work with the London and Colonial Missionary Societies. This young man, Robert Dawson (1836-1906), was to serve with the London Missionary Society.

Dawson's missionary vocation was life-long but his service overseas was brief. He sailed for Shanghai on 21 October 1859 and reached Shanghai on 23 March 1860; he left Shanghai on 13 October 1861 and reached England on 8 March 1862.[1] Health had been the problem. Dawson had set himself to learn Chinese to such effect that after eighteen months he was able to preach in the language but it was also after eighteen months that his health collapsed: 'he was carried on board a ship with only slight hope of reaching England.'[2]

Long sea voyages were still kill or cure in the 1860s; this voyage cured Dawson. His commitment to overseas mission, however, remained unimpaired. Forty years after his ordination he guaranteed the salary of an unmarried medical missionary in China in addition to the doctor's salary for which he was already responsible.[3] His own mission was now to be exercised at home, first as minister of two contrasting Congregational churches, one in Devizes for seven

---

1 James Sibree, *London Missionary Society. A Register of Missionaries, Deputations, Etc. from 1796 to 1923* (4th edn., London: London Missionary Society, 1923), p. 74.

2 *Congregational Year Book* (1907), p. 151.

3 Undated cutting, of LMS Board Meeting, 11 July 1899.

years and the other in Nottingham (where he 'found four walls without a pulpit, a pew, or a congregation') for eleven, and then as the London City Mission's organising secretary. He directed that important operation for twenty-five years.[4]

Robert Dawson was the sort of minister for whom denominational strategists yearned. His call was undoubted, his views were evangelical, his intellect was sharp, his education was good, his denominational connections were impeccable, and he had a private income. His brother and father were public-spirited landowners near Lancaster. The family invested wisely in land and industry, cushioned by the fortune accumulated by Robert's maternal grandfather whose London firm had clothed the Household Cavalry during the Napoleonic Wars and—so family lore had it—the French Emperor's guard for good measure.[5] Robert's mother was one of that fortune's two co-heiresses. Robert himself was educated at Mill Hill School and he graduated from the University of London, benefitting from a scholarship endowed by his clothier grandfather.[6] Better yet, he had been baptised by a revered kinsman, George Clayton, one of the stateliest of metropolitan Dissenting ministers, and he married Sarah Rawson, daughter of the Leeds solicitor and hymn writer, George Rawson.[7] She too was related to the Claytons. It would be hard to imagine a more entrenched, long-lasting, or well-circumstanced Congregational cousinhood than that to which Robert and Sarah Dawson belonged. They had no children but there was no lack of kith or kin.

So to the friendship, which leads directly to the sermon. Henry Robert Reynolds was Sarah Rawson's minister.[8] He married Sarah Rawson and Robert Dawson and he gave the charge at Robert's ordination. Reynolds was eleven years older than Dawson and within a year of the latter's ordination he had left his outstanding ministry at East Parade, Leeds, for the presidency of Cheshunt, Dawson's old college. That is significant. It was Dawson, 'ardently attached to Cheshunt College and to his beloved friend Dr Reynolds', who founded its Old Students Union and organised its annual gatherings.[9] The fact of their enduring friendship is an encouragement to look more closely at Reynolds's charge to Dawson.

In 1865 Reynolds published *Notes on The Christian Life*, a selection of nineteen sermons of which one, 'Faithfulness unto Death', had been 'preached at

---

4 *Congregational Year Book* (1907), pp. 151-52.

5 I am indebted for this information to Mr G.A.H. Bousfield.

6 Ernest Hampden-Cook, *The Register of Mill Hill School 1807-1926* (London: Mill Hill School, 1926), p. 85.

7 I am indebted for information to the Revd Nigel Lemon; for George Clayton (1783-1862), see Thomas W. Aveling, *Memorials of the Clayton Family* (London: Jackson, Walford, and Hodder, 1867); for George Rawson (1807-1889), see *Oxford Dictionary of National Biography* [hereafter *ODNB*].

8 For Henry Robert Reynolds (1825-1896) see *ODNB*.

9 *Congregational Year Book* (1907), p. 152.

the dedication of a friend to foreign missionary service at Shanghai'. Robert Dawson was that friend.[10]

Who can tell from a sermon's printed version what was in fact said, and what was heard or misheard, any more than who can tell who, or how many, read what was printed and to what effect? Reynolds's sermons made few concessions in length or seriousness of content. He was, however, known for the beauty of his voice and the nobility of his bearing. He was made for the pulpit. He never travelled to the Far East but its cultures and its religions commanded his scholarly attention. In 1883, for example, he published a comparison of Buddhism and Christianity.[11] Within a year of his Lancaster sermon, Reynolds had begun to train successive generations of Congregational ministers and missionaries. This gives that sermon a particular interest. Its tone was orthodox, its foundation learned; it was also humane and it demonstrated an intelligent, strategic grasp of the Christian's missionary calling. It was a wise, moving, logical, shrewd, and loving address, pulling no punches, spoken directly by a pastor to a friend called to the other side of the world and yet also encompassing every other hearer, committing each one in a momentous, emotionally charged occasion.

Given that it 'is impossible to exaggerate the responsibilities of one who essays to become a messenger and apostle of Christ', 'Faithfulness unto Death' was a sensible, even inevitable title.[12] Reynolds described a scale of faithfulness – to the heart, to the conscience, to 'your Master and His Word', to 'the Society in England, by which you are recommended to the grace of God', and so indeed unto death.

'Faithfulness to the human heart' allowed for a powerful demonstration of the preacher's art as well as a ruggedly realistic prospect of the terrain ahead:

> Let me say to you my beloved brother, your heart will often tell you, when you are dealing with the Mahommedan, the Buddhist, or Confucianist, that there is a great deal of truth and goodness at the heart of these men; that there is what you call, in defiance of theology, good nature and kindness; that there is considerable development given to what is, in our country, described by even a wider name than Christianity—I mean humanity. You will find that men are even better than their religions; a thing, by the way, which can never be said of Christians; that there is filial reverence, and brotherly love, and patriotism, and care for the infirm and destitute; that there is, in fact, much recognition of the great moral laws, to which your own reason perpetually aspires. Be faithful, then, to what your heart

[10] Henry Robert Reynolds, *Notes on The Christian Life. A Selection of Sermons* (London and Cambridge: Macmillan and Co., 1865), pp. 353-85, esp. p. 353. The friend is not identified but I am indebted to the Revd. Nigel Lemon for confirmation that it was Dawson.

[11] H.R. Reynolds, *Buddhism: A Comparison and a Contrast between Buddhism and Christianity* (London: RTS, 1883).

[12] H.R. Reynolds, 'Faithfulness unto Death', in *Notes on The Christian Life*, p. 357.

> teaches you, what your simple humanity may reveal of brotherly feeling and of the common ground that you and they occupy together. Endeavour to find out what is really good in the Chinaman, and what are those eternal principles which he has not, with all his pride, materialism, and selfishness, contrived to conceal or obliterate. God is striving with China, and has been for all these thousands of years. Do not suppose that you take with you the Divine Being. He is there before you, in every heathen's soul, in every throb of conscience, in every laudable emotion, in every glimpse of truth, in every predisposition and susceptibility for the revelation of heaven, in all the structure and facilities of that marvellous language which He has fashioned for their thinking powers, in all the stupendous march of His providence, and in the wages of sin that He has imposed upon transgressors. Christ is there, . . . is there now, in China. . . . Your heart will tell you, more than any rules of logic, more than any human instructions, where He is working. Discover and use the leverage of good that there is in the heart of these men, and be faithful to this talent of judgment that God has given you.[13]

Was this orthodoxy? Or was it insight? Faithfulness to the heart was to be accompanied by faithfulness to the conscience. It was as dangerous 'to be blinded by theology or criticism to the proof that God is at work within the soul of man, irrespective of Church or creed', as it was dangerous 'to become indifferent to the systematic violation of God's eternal laws'.[14] Here Reynolds spoke from the heart of English Nonconformity, alerting his friend to 'that chill latitudinarianism about religious truth, which affects every class of Chinese society'.[15] 'As a Christian missionary in China . . . your whole life must be a testimony . . . ,' he told Dawson, 'your daily business a proclamation of dissent from all around you. . . . Heathen society is as the movement of a mighty wheel; you may make little progress in trying to stop it, but if you cease the effort it will crush you.'[16]

The third faithfulness—'to your Master and His word'—was the most intellectually demanding, or so Reynolds made it seem. Dawson would soon find that the 'Chinaman . . . has universally the notion of a Master and of the written word of that Master.'[17] It followed that Dawson's particular work must be 'a comparison of Masters, a comparison of Bibles'. That would demand a special faithfulness to Christ:

> Let no Chinaman whom you can influence be able to charge you when you stand together at His bar—when Confucius and Laotse, and Gautama and Mohammed will stand there with you—that you only represented Him as one of them. Be faithful to Him who is the Prince of all the kings of the earth . . .'[18]

---

[13] Reynolds, 'Faithfulness unto Death', pp. 366-68.
[14] Reynolds, 'Faithfulness unto Death', p. 368.
[15] Reynolds, 'Faithfulness unto Death', p. 369.
[16] Reynolds, 'Faithfulness unto Death', p. 370.
[17] Reynolds, 'Faithfulness unto Death', pp. 371-72.
[18] Reynolds, 'Faithfulness unto Death', pp. 372,373.

Such faithfulness entailed due recognition of Chinese religious insights and their strengths – the ethical power of Confucianism (which Reynolds summarised, in an up-to-date way, as a sort of Positivism), Taoism's recognition of the physical in man, and (most gripping of all, for Reynolds) metaphysical, intellectual Buddhism:

> Its asceticism, its ceremonial, its priestly life, its vast extent, its colossal promises, its conception of humanity as a whole, its supposed basis on truth, make it a fascinating study, as well as one of the most awful facts in the history of the world.[19]

Confucianism, Taoism, Buddhism – Dawson would have to face them all: 'Now you, my brother, have to bring the gospel of Christ to bear upon this dread trinity of misconception and delusion.'[20]

Reynolds had not quite finished. There remained Dawson's duty to the London Missionary Society: 'Be faithful to us; do not allow us to slumber or forget you.' Reynolds angled his advice sensitively: 'Be faithful to us in England. Your work will soon be stripped of its romance. . . . It will . . . be a . . . hand to hand encounter with ignorance, prejudice, and sin.'[21] Without word from Dawson how would the watchers' bands at home know how to help?

And so he came to the ultimate fidelity:

> Death is the sad, grim accompaniment of every one of our projects; he mingles with all our plans; we can in reality do nothing which does not bring us nearer to him. . . . Death is the term of our service, and nothing short of this.[22]

Did these words come to mind two years and a month later, when Dawson was carried aboard that home-bound ship in Shanghai? 'The condition of our service, my dear brother, is that it <u>must</u> include the hour when the overtaxed or exhausted human energies shall sink.'[23]

II

Neither Dawson nor Reynolds was, socially or materially, a run-of-the-mill Congregationalist, yet that missionary ordination was a truly representative Congregational occasion and Dawson and Reynolds could only have been Congregationalists. Dawson's denominational connections have already been noted; Reynolds could be added to them.[24] The Reynolds were connected by

---

19 Reynolds, 'Faithfulness unto Death', pp. 374,375.

20 Reynolds, 'Faithfulness unto Death', p. 375.

21 Reynolds, 'Faithfulness unto Death', p. 379.

22 Reynolds, 'Faithfulness unto Death', pp. 380,381.

23 Reynolds, 'Faithfulness unto Death', p. 382.

24 The Dawsons can be followed in Nigel Lemon, 'Missionaries to Lancashire and Beyond: The Dawsons of Aldcliffe', *The Journal of the United Reformed Church History Society*, 8.5 (November 2009), pp. 245-65. The Reynolds can be followed in Clyde Binfield, '"A Saint if ever there was one": Henry Robert Reynolds (1825-90)', in Pe-

marriage as well as friendship and pastoral responsibility to the second of the two military cloth heiresses. Such connections, expressing the promise of the nineteenth century in the context of evangelical revival, expressed no less a tradition that went back to earlier and differently stirring times. They serve to introduce this chapter's exploration of the evolving relationship between mission, mindset, and denomination.

The long nineteenth century (1789-1914) marked a transformation in Congregational polity and attitude. No doubt the same could be claimed for the long eighteenth century (1689-1815) or the long twentieth century (1914 to the present). It could certainly be claimed for the short twentieth century (1919-1972) and for the short seventeenth century (1649-1689). It was the long nineteenth century, however, which saw the evolution of a distinctive, national denomination, English-speaking, London-focused and headquartered, and appropriately serviced.

The operative words are 'distinctive' and 'appropriately'. Nineteenth-century Congregationalism's worshipping units – its organisational *raisons-d'être* – related to each other at differing levels, national, county, and individual. They were buttressed by schools (for the children of laypeople as well as those of ministers and missionaries), by colleges (for the training of ministers), and by a clutch of societies (to promote chapel-building, ministerial sustentation, every level of education, and the general needs of vulnerable individuals). Chief among the societies were those for overseas mission, the internationally respected London Missionary Society and the less known Colonial Missionary Society. Each of them, however, reflected Congregational Independency. They were the natural as well as convenient outworking of that apparent contradiction in terms. The worshipping unit was the Church. The society, the school, the college, the county union, the national union, were autonomous auxiliaries at the service of each church and of the federated churches. Each served the Church. Their evolution into a discrete Congregationalism may from time to time have seemed uncertain, even fraught. In retrospect it seems remarkably natural and it worked surprisingly well. The autonomous bodies were expressions of a recognisable mindset, however much they appeared to go their own way or develop their own life; such was the case with the London Missionary Society even if, in the later twentieth century, it did indeed go its own way. Robert Dawson's ordination and Henry Robert Reynolds's charge at High Street, Lancaster, in September 1859, illustrate all these points.

One reason for their natural evolution lies in the contribution of collaborating individuals, ministerial and lay, with more women among the latter than might appear from the archival record. These were people of ability and means. They were able to contribute financially to a host of causes, in consistent, cumulative, and intelligent generosity, knowing that the single guinea could be as

---

ter Clarke and Tony Claydon (eds), *Saints and Sanctity* (Studies in Church History. 47, Woodbridge: Boydell & Brewer, 2011), pp. 318-33.

fruitful as the tens or hundreds. They had the time to give to committee work or back-room organisation, and often spread that time across a host of committees. They also had the character – names were not enough – to make their committee service effective. Their names appeared repeatedly on overlapping lists. At a time when journalists were discovering that words were deeds and the cause of deeds, philanthropists found that to give was to act, and the cause of action; and philanthropy and journalism frequently joined forces. Such individuals achieved earlier in the century what a more structured organisation (run, it might be noted, by very similar individuals), designed to meet more complex needs, achieved at the century's end. They oiled the inevitability of change while providing continuity.

They also politicised a steadily enlarging nation, for they were natural stakeholders. Enough of the men among them had been county voters in unreformed England and some, where circumstances permitted, had been borough voters. They were certainly at the heart of the steadily reforming municipal world, learning how to run towns and cities. They knew that world and how it worked, and as evangelical Congregational Dissenters they applied their knowledge to the home and overseas mission of their churches. It was a task requiring expertise in specifics. Of course, it attracted one-idea-ed crotcheteers but, to a remarkable degree, it encouraged an integrated, indeed a catholic sense of what was meant by mission. Such people were to be found in Lancaster's High Street Congregational Church on 13 September 1859.

III

To illustrate the relationship between mission, mindset, and denomination, all in evolution and each dependent on individual agency, the focus turns to two Congregationalists, Thomas Thompson (1785-1865) and Jemima Luke (1813-1906), a father and daughter whose base, though chiefly London and the South-West, was effectively nationwide. Since their lives extended from 1785 to 1906 their service almost covered the long nineteenth century. Overseas mission was at the heart, but not solely at the heart, of their concern. They were undoubtedly evangelicals, of a conservative yet pragmatic and optimistic kind. They were the sort whose doctrinal conservatism accommodated liberal politics, an attitude perhaps determined by their temperament. Most obviously children of the Evangelical Revival's Whitefieldite wing, they also nurtured links with the Old Dissent. In them the seventeenth century met the twentieth. And they too could be linked, at least tangentially, to that Lancaster ordination: Robert Dawson's elder brother was shortly to marry, perhaps was already engaged to, a Stockport connection of this father and daughter.

The chief sources for their lives are two books, one an autobiography, the other a filial biography, both written by the daughter.[25] They can be read with

[25] Jemima Luke, *Sketches of The Life and Character of Thomas Thompson* (London: James Nisbet & Co., 1868); [Jemima Luke], *Early Years of My Life. By the Author of*

confidence and they deserve close reading. They also illustrate the integration in mindset of mission and denomination, the natural evolution of change in continuity, and the role of individuals, in this instance the Cheeryble role of an apparently archetypal evangelical layman and busybody and the pacesetting role of a woman who, as far as one can tell, never openly revolted in her life. Because the books are by the daughter, it is proper to begin with her, or rather with the hymn by which she became widely known. What might be gleaned from its words? How did it come to be written? What lies more generally behind it?

The hymn, to which its author gave the title 'Child's Desire', was written in 1841. It caught on at once and was widely sung into the 1970s. Congregationalists at large became aware of it through the popular *Leeds Hymn Book* (1853), edited by Henry Robert Reynolds, with George Rawson as coadjutor and contributor. It held the fort in *Congregational Praise* (1951) but was dropped from the United Reformed Church's *Rejoice and Sing* (1991). This version is taken from a card inserted in the Congregational Library's copy of the author's life of her father:

I think when I read that sweet story of old.
When Jesus was here among men,
How he call'd little children, as lambs to his fold,
I should like to have been with them then.
I wish that his hands had been placed on my head,
That his arm had been thrown around me,
And that I might have seen his kind look when he said,
'Let the little ones come unto me'.

Yet still to his footstool in prayer I may go
And ask for a share in his love;
And if I now earnestly seek him below,
I shall see him and hear him above:
In that beautiful place he is gone to prepare
For all that are wash'd and forgiven;
And many dear children are gathering there,
'For of such is the kingdom of heaven'.

But thousands and thousands who wander and fall,
Never heard of that heavenly home,
I should like them to know there is room for them all,
And that Jesus has bid them to come.
I long for the joy of that glorious time,

'I Think When I Read that Sweet Story of Old' (London: Hodder and Stoughton, 1900).

The sweetest, and brightest, and best;
When the dear little children of every clime,
Shall crowd to his arms and be blessed.
J.T. 1841

The reverse side of the card shows an engraving of Jesus, holding an infant, surrounded by mothers and children and with a quartet of bearded males behind him, in illustration of the text, 'He took them up in his arms, put his hands upon them, and blessed them' (Matt. 19:14).

Nearly fifty years later, William Garrett Horder, Congregational minister, theological liberal, and hymnologist, was sure that this hymn deserved 'to be reckoned classic' and wondered why its writer had failed to follow it up with others. He also noted its genesis: '. . . written in a stage coach, for a village school near Poundsford Park, Bath, where the writer's father resided'.[26] That, allowing for hazy geography (Poundsford is near Taunton, not Bath), is essentially correct. What, then, might be gleaned from this 'Child's Desire'?

At first sight here is a rural childhood idyll in which intimations of mortality might mingle with immortality. This is a child's world at a child's level. It introduces that autonomous dominion in the Evangelical Commonwealth, the Sunday School. It also introduces the far horizons – and therefore the imperatives – of Christian mission; it introduces that other autonomous dominion in the Evangelical Christian Commonwealth, the Missionary Auxiliary. So how, in fact, did it come to be written?

By the writer's own account, as published eleven years after Horder's short summation, it began one spring day in 1841.[27] Jemima Thompson, as she then was, had to visit Wellington, an hour's drive from Poundsford, to see a small branch auxiliary of the Female Education Society in the East. She travelled by two-horse carriage (not quite Garrett Horder's 'stage coach') and, since she was the only inside passenger, she got out a letter and on the back of its envelope wrote the first two verses of what became her hymn. Her intention was to teach it to the children at the school which had been started by her step-mother at Blagdon, a neighbouring village, Later she added a third verse, 'to make it a missionary hymn'. At this point her father took a hand. He superintended the Sunday School of a small chapel belonging to the Poundsford estate and liked to let the children choose the first hymn. When they struck up a hymn and tune that were new to him, and he learned from his younger daughters that 'Jemima made it', he asked her for words and tune and sent them to the *Sunday School Teachers' Magazine*. Not long after, she was invited to edit a children's missionary magazine which the son of a celebrated China missionary had recently

26 W. Garrett Horder, *The Hymn Lover. An Account of the Rise and Growth of English Hymnody* (London: J. Curwen & Sons, n.d. [1889]), p. 455.

27 This account is drawn from *Early Years of My Life*, *The Hymn Lover*, pp. 132-33.

started. The missionary dimension of 'Child's Desire' is inescapable. Did more lie behind it?

In 1841 Jemima Thompson was in her late twenties and unmarried. When, at the turn of the century and in her late eighties, she turned to autobiography, she was Jemima Luke and had been widowed for over thirty years. For the intervening twenty-five years she had been a minister's wife. Her husband, Samuel Luke (1809-1868), was a passably eligible catch for a gentlewoman approaching thirty. He was respectably born (his father was a deacon at an historic London church), well educated (there had been a session at Edinburgh University), and with an encouraging first pastorate in Chester (where Bishop Sumner unavailingly urged episcopal ordination on him and where H.R. Reynolds's maternal grandfather was one of his deacons). This was to be followed by pastorates in central London and Clifton which were as successful as his uncertain health allowed. His obituary drew attention to his clarity and sweetness of voice, his felicity of illustration, and – perhaps more revealingly than might at first sight appear – his ability to place old truths in fresh light and thus renew their power.[28] Jemima Thompson and Samuel Luke proved to be admirably matched. Jemima was a woman of parts, perhaps better prepared than most ministers' wives and certainly with more means than most ministers' widows; and she retained into old age an admirable clarity of intellect, as her memoir, *Early Years of My Life*, demonstrates.

Early Years has an immediate charm, not least for its crisp comparisons between then and now. It is also carefully angled. The life of a manse wife, 'with its round of Bible classes, mothers' meetings, societies, committees, visits to rich and poor, home duties, wifely and motherly cares' – in Mrs Luke's case a quarter-century's cutting-edge experience of back-room organisation – she tantalisingly dismissed as 'too well-known to be of public interest'.[29] Thus freed from any temptation to slip into anecdotage or sweetly relaxed tittle-tattle, she could concentrate on describing something of greater moment: how a young woman, Jemima Thompson, not yet Luke, found a role on terms as acceptable to herself as to her family and still kept within the bounds of general convention. Mission was the door to her narrative and foreign mission its key. *Early Years*, published at the dawn of a new century, was a call to modern mission.

IV

Jemima Thompson was fortunate in her family, which was loving, and its circumstances, which were affluent. She was reared in a succession of comfortable town and country houses, each of them unostentatiously reflecting her fami-

[28] *Congregational Year Book*, 1869, pp. 256-58; Frederick James Powicke, *A History of the Cheshire County Union of Congregational Churches* (Manchester: Thomas Griffiths & Co., 1907), pp. 129-31.

[29] *Early Years*, p. 147.

ly's position. They also reflected the state of its health. Two sisters and two brothers died in infancy, at least one of them a victim to best contemporary medical practice, and her mother was a chronic invalid; death and disease were ever-present realities in even the most sheltered households. Jemima's most important early relationship was with her father, with whom she shared her birthday. She was his eldest surviving child and her name – Jemima, 'in allusion to Job and his previous losses'[30] – expressed her place in his heart and his household, for whose smooth running she was by the 1830s increasingly responsible.

Had she been a daughter of the manse or, indeed, of a failed businessman, Jemima Thompson's future would have been as a governess, with matrimony as the prime escape route, but she was too fortunately placed for that. There came a point when she found the paradox of her situation hard to bear:

> To spend it in the luxurious care of a beautiful country house, reading interesting books, writing chatty letters to friends, receiving and paying calls, doing Berlin woolwork, and making wax or paper flowers as then in vogue, and knitting babies' socks and antimacassars for bazaars – was this, in the prime of life, with an excellent constitution, untiring energy, and years spent in mental cultivation, a satisfactory life for an immortal being, or a meet offering for Him to whom I owed my all?[31]

That is where she found herself in 1839 when her position in her father's household was unexpectedly (the word is hers) transformed. Since girlhood she had been her parents' confidante, encouraged by them to be usefully, intelligently, and self-reliantly lady-like. With her mother, she would listen to her father's accounts of philanthropic committee meetings, especially those of the London Missionary Society, whose board he joined in 1827. Her mother's steadily failing health in part left Jemima to her own devices, in part thrust household management upon her, and in part developed her aptitude for teaching since her younger sisters needed tuition. That entailed a morning tutor, a music mistress, and 'history with me in the afternoon'.[32] Her own preparation for such work had been thorough. Jemima had been a morning pupil of Caroline Fry, editor of *The Assistant of Education*, whom she found an admirable role-model, a woman of 'much originality and imagination, and a masculine vigour of thought such as seldom characterises a woman's writing'.[33] There was a strategic common sense about Miss Fry's evangelicalism, perhaps helped by having survived a youth 'warped by infidelity':

---

30 *Sketches of the Life and Character*, p. 19. Jemima was the eldest of Job's daughters, born after the restoration of his fortunes: Job 42:14.

31 *Early Years*, p. 107.

32 *Early Years*, p. 71.

33 *Early Years*, p. 65. For Caroline Fry (1787-1846) see *ODNB*.

> One of the incentives to diligence which she held out to her pupils was her conviction that according to their progress in mental cultivation here would be their intellectual expansion in the world to come, as one lesson to be gleaned from the parable of the talents.[34]

The strategic common sense of leading evangelicals is sometimes overlooked. In the 1830s Jemima Thompson enjoyed the ministrations of three leading metropolitan pulpit strategists. On Sunday mornings she sat under the Congregational James Stratten at Paddington Chapel; on Sunday evenings there was the Anglican Baptist Noel at St. John's, Bedford Row; and there were also Bible classes – with the Congregational John Leifchild at Craven Chapel and again with Baptist Noel.[35] The Noel link proved to be almost counter-productively providential.

Baptist Noel was a rising star in the evangelical firmament with an appeal which easily crossed denominational boundaries and regularly sparked missionary initiatives. In 1834 he had been behind the Society for Promoting Female Education in the East; in 1835 his concern led to the Female Aid Society. The latter's focus was on moral reformation in London. It was the former which attracted Jemima Thompson and particularly the opportunities offered by its Ladies Committee with its four stalwarts, Miss Braithwaite, an ex-Quaker burdened by a famous Quaker name, to whom, therefore, 'the idea of feminine agency was not a new one', Miss Webb, who devoted the next sixty years to the new society's administration, Miss Adam, and Miss Hope, 'a Scotch lady of great energy and perseverance, and much sound sense and executive ability'.[36]

Jemima prized executive ability; she too became a committee woman, meeting potential missionaries and helping to form local auxiliaries until, 'fostered by association with missionaries, by reading and lectures and public meetings, by Miss Braithwaite's influence, and by interviews with missionary candidates', she became convinced 'that there was a great field for Christian women to occupy, and that unmarried women, well qualified and with courage and prudence, could do more than missionaries' wives, whose hands were fully occupied with missionary duties'.[37] She was no less convinced that the New Testament was on her side, from the ministering women of Galilee to St. Paul's female fellow labourers in the Gospel: women, in fact, like herself.[38]

The crisis came in 1839, two years after her mother's death, when, as she expressed it without grievance or dislocation, 'our father's second marriage most unexpectedly set me free from home duties'.[39]

---

34 *Early Years*, pp. 65-66.

35 For James Stratten (1795-1872) see *Congregational Year Book* (1874), pp. 363-64; for John Leifchild (1780-1862) see *ODNB*; for Baptist Noel (1798-1873) see *ODNB*.

36 *Early Years*, p. 72.

37 *Early Years*, p. 85.

38 *Early Years*, pp. 85-86; cf. Phil. 4:3.

39 *Early Years*, p. 86.

The second Mrs. Thompson proved an understanding step-mother. Charlotte Welman was a widow in her late forties. She was a woman of birth and property. Her late husband, Thomas Welman, was a Somerset country gentleman, considerably older than herself, whose family had owned the Poundsford estate, near Taunton, since 1704. The Welmans were Dissenters; Philip Doddridge had been a family connection.[40] Charlotte's only child, and heir to the Welman estate, was now married and well settled the other side of Taunton leaving his mother, after ten years of widowhood, as mistress of Poundsford, a delectable and judiciously improved Elizabethan house. Thus, on her remarriage in 1839, Poundsford became the Thompson home but now Jemima Thompson no longer had charge.

Charlotte Welman, now Thompson, had continued the Dissenting tradition of her late husband's family uniting it with the distinctive tradition of her own family, the Noels. Four of her brothers were Anglican parsons; one of them, six years her junior, was Baptist Noel. Her eldest brother, whose first wife – by the sort of generational twist common to very large families – had been the only child of Charlotte's late husband's first marriage, was a leading evangelical peer. Since 1823 he had been the third Lord Barham; from 1841 he would be the first Earl of Gainsborough.[41] Their mother, Baroness Barham in her own right, had been second only to Lady Glenorchy and the Countess of Huntingdon as an evangelical church planter, in her case with a small connexion of chapels in the Gower Peninsula.[42] There Charlotte Welman continued her work. Like her mother she made no bones about speaking and praying in public. She too was an organiser of mission.

Jemima Thompson seized her opportunity. The middle-class Caroline Fry, Anna Braithwaite, Miss Hope, Miss Webb, and Miss Adam were capable, organising, educated women; so was the aristocratic Charlotte Welman. What should her own work be and where should it lie? England's poor and England's children were without number but England already had 'tens of thousands of Christian women' to see to their needs and the Female Education Society had alerted her to 'our miserable sisterhood in heathen lands'.[43] For too long,

> women especially had been content just to look on. At long intervals some member of the Society of Friends, or some Moravian sister had quietly stepped into the

---

[40] Brian Kirk, 'The Welmans of Poundisford Park', *Journal of the United Reformed Church History Society*, 6.6 (May 2000), pp. 404-407; see also *Burke's Landed Gentry*, 1937, 'Welman of Trewarthenick formerly of Poundisford Park and Norton Manor', pp. 2398-99. 'Poundsford', the usual spelling in the early nineteenth century, has more recently been spelt 'Poundisford'.

[41] Of the second creation; see *Burke's Peerage*; also Gerard Noel, *Sir Gerard Noel MP and the Noels of Chipping Campden and Exton* (Chipping Campden: Campden and District Historical and Archaeological Society, 2004).

[42] For Diana Noel, née Middleton, Baroness Barham (1782-1823), see *ODNB*.

[43] *Early Years*, p. 107.

> gap, but the Female Education Society had been the first to brave the prejudices and difficulties which stood in the way of women's mission.[44]

She determined to become a missionary overseas. She would set the pace for women of her background.

Her father's support was critical. His instincts were sound: she should go to India under the auspices of the London Missionary Society; he would cover all her costs and guarantee an annual income of £150.[45] She prepared accordingly. She met missionaries on furlough. She observed teaching methods, first at a British School in Taunton and then, more intensively, at the Normal Infant School in Gray's Inn Road. That was a culture shock, especially when it was her turn to take a demonstration class on the subject of 'Jesus in the Manger'. She found the children, who were attentive and responsive, in the gallery while her fellow trainee-teachers were ranged critically below. They were not really her fellows; the social gap was suddenly too wide; they criticized her 'with unmitigated severity':

> I had expected criticism and wished for it, but the animus displayed was a mystery. I had felt kindly, and, I think, spoken pleasantly when in brief contact with any one of the teachers and could only supposed that they thought me an intruder on their province.[46]

Jemima was philosophical, at least in long retrospect. She found the discipline of 'unspeakable value'. Indeed, she 'could never have written *The Child's Desire* or the *Missionary Stories* which followed but for the rough handling at Gray's Inn Road'.[47] Her reasoning was straightforward. One of the trainees' tests was to march up and down the schoolroom singing the marching songs that their future charges would have to learn. Among them was the tune which she later adapted for *Child's Desire*:

> The words set to it in the book of marching pieces were simple and pretty, but I thought the air would better adapt itself to a hymn, and subsequently tried in vain to find one to suit the measure for mamma's village school.[48]

She was now ready for India. It remained only to select the cabin on her ship. And there it stopped; she succumbed to 'a violent attack of erysipelas', head swollen, eyes closed, semi-conscious. She recovered, but now the doctors insisted that she would 'probably die of brain fever in a hot climate'. It was not only India which was now out of bounds, for her father vetoed its possible alternative: secretaryship of the Female Education Society. Jemima's faith in his support wavered: 'Perhaps he almost unconsciously sympathised with the prej-

---

44 *Early Years*, p. 108.
45 *Early Years*, p. 113.
46 *Early Years*, pp. 120-21.
47 *Early Years*, p. 121.
48 *Early Years*, p. 122.

udices against the Female Education Society, which in some quarters had been cynically called "the Bachelors' Aid Society".'[49]

She adapted herself to her lot; there was little option to do otherwise. That meant London for the season, though for her London was Blackheath and the season meant the May Meetings, with parties for missionary guests, on this occasion from Madagascar. She contributed to the art work for a book about missions in Madagascar; it was 'only the second specimen of coloured printing then published'.[50] Back at Poundsford there were classes to be taken at her step-mother's school, there were missionary stories to be written, and there was now the editorial work for her *Missionary Repository*, which she believed played a key role in popularising the missionary cause in Sunday Schools.[51] There was also some tactful secretarial work for her father, with his passion for issuing printed appeals for unfailingly good and occasionally quixotic causes. These 'had to be revised, condensed, possibly reconstructed'; only Jemima could get him to do that.[52] And there was the ordered life of a godly country house, with her room high on the morning-sun side, early morning tea brought to her at 7 am, family prayers at 8.45 am, dinner at 3 pm. This was the context for *Child's Desire*, 'the happiest and most useful portion of my life'.[53]

In 1843 she married. Twenty-five years as a Congregational minister's wife were followed by nearly forty as a Congregational minister's widow: 'what a blessed thing it is not to be a Hindoo widow!'[54]

V

Thus it was that the India which Jemima Thompson never saw remained Jemima Luke's prime concern as she turned her memories into a missionary appeal for a new age. H.R. Reynolds's warning to Robert Dawson, Shanghai-bound in 1859, applied no less to India in 1900: 'Heathen society is as the movement of a mighty wheel; you may make little progress in trying to stop it, but if you cease the effort it will crush you.'[55] The condition of Hindu women had improved little, the work of missionary agencies was infinitesimal when set against the need, 'Yet these have long been our fellow-subjects. God has placed them under English rule, and made us responsible for taking to them the blessings of Christian faith and hope, education and happiness'.[56] The opportunity for Christian Englishwomen was greater than ever, not least because now – so it was said – there were twice as many English women as English men. 'No

[49] *Early Years*, pp. 122-23.
[50] *Early Years*, pp. 127-29.
[51] *Early Years*, pp. 135-38.
[52] *Sketches of the Life*, p. 111; *Early Years*, p. 142.
[53] *Early Years*, pp. 141-44.
[54] *Early Years*, p. 147.
[55] H.R. Reynolds, 'Faithfulness Unto Death', p. 370.
[56] *Early Years*, p. 150.

more than half can become wives. What are the rest doing? I ask the question chiefly of the middle classes'.[57]

Her answer was insistent. Even when due allowance was made for those with family responsibilities or established philanthropic work, and the many 'industrious and capable girls . . . bravely supporting themselves as type-writers, telegraph clerks, photographers, school mistresses, journalists . . .', there remained others, professing Christians some of them, who 'live in lodgings . . . forming no ties, too often unloved and unloving, self-centred, sinking into apathy or fretfulness, and gradually developing all the dreaded features of old maidenhood'.[58] It was to them that Jemima Luke appealed: 'do you feel no compassion for your despairing sisterhood in the East?'

> The Hindoo girls are not like negroes or Malays. Many of them are graceful, beautiful and affectionate, and as capable of intellectual development as English children...I appeal to you to go out now at your own cost and help to lighten their burdens.[59]

And should India prove too expensive, then China might serve since one could work for the China Inland Mission on £50-£70 a year. India, however, remained her focus. It was sixty years since she had been accepted by the London Missionary Society: 'I should have been the first to go from any long-established society, and some time elapsed before any similar offer was sanctioned'.[60]

Jemima Luke remained a woman ahead of her time and of her time. In old age she was excited by the women type-writers, photographers, and journalists. She was up to the mark with current theories of race, perhaps of genetics. She was also weighed down by the white woman's imperial burden, and she was always open to opportunity. In this regard two British missionaries in India had captured her imagination. Mrs R.J. Ward had served with the Church of Scotland Mission in Madras. There she had developed what struck Jemima as 'a feasible and encouraging scheme for the benefit of Indian women'; it was 'a missionary training-home where Anglo-Indian Eurasian Christian women can be prepared for missionary work'.[61] Such women were numerous, on-the-spot, 'intellectually capable' and relatively inexpensive. Perhaps that had been how Mrs Ward had met her husband, a widower who had arrived in Madras in January 1893 to minister to the Congregational Church in Davidson Street and to work among English-speaking Hindus, whose determined assimilation he increasingly deprecated. R.J. Ward, born in the year of *Child's Desire*, was an extrovert. For twenty-eight years he had ministered at Ormskirk Street, St Hel-

---

[57] *Early Years*, p. 151.
[58] *Early Years*, pp. 151-52.
[59] *Early Years*, pp. 152, 153, 154.
[60] *Early Years*, pp. 154, 155.
[61] *Early Years*, p. 163.

en's, prominent in that town's politics, education, temperance, and social work, and on skilful terms with the glass-making Pilkingtons who were steadily stamping that church in their image. He had been doubly influenced, first by Moody and Sankey, whose methods he adapted to the needs of local Congregationalists, and latterly by the Keswick Movement, which had precipitated his passage to India. In November 1892 he left Liverpool for Madras, sailing on the *S.S. Peshawar*. His mission now was to 'save the British Empire'.[62]

Ward combined the qualities – executive, pastoral, evangelistic – of a type of successful Congregational minister. Jemima Luke seized on the evangelism, as expressed in an 'anecdote of thrilling interest' which Ward had clearly picked up on his furlough in England in 1898-99. His telling of it encapsulated her own vicarious experience.[63]

She had been the worst sailor imaginable; it had taken erysipelas to preserve her in 1840 from the perils of ocean crossing. Twenty years later it took Robert Dawson half a year to reach Shanghai. Now, sixty years on, missionaries sailed in 'fine ocean steamers', taking less than half that time.[64] But perils remained, some of them closer to home. On 30 March 1899 the *Stella*, sailing from Southampton to the Channel Islands, hit the Gasquets. On board were a young Christian girl and her father. The girl was put in a lifeboat but there was no room for her father who remained on board, saying: 'Good-bye. We shall meet again. . . . The blood of Jesus Christ, God's Son, cleanseth us from all sin.' So *Stella* went down and the man's soul 'went up to glory'. Asked later if she had been frightened, the girl replied: 'No, I was not afraid to die, because I was trusting in Christ as my Saviour; but I was ashamed to die and to appear before my Lord, because I saw how poor and useless my life had been.'[65]

Such sentiments had changed little in their expression in sixty or even a hundred and sixty years. They made for thrilling communication and they spoke to Jemima Luke's condition. It remains to consider her father, a hero in her own story and, in his way, heroic for his churches.

VI

To judge from the frontispiece portrait to Jemima Luke's *Sketches of the Life and Character* of her father, Thomas Thompson was chubby, rubicund, and benign. He is shown clean-shaven, with fluffy white hair, seated by his study table on a sound mid-Victorian chair in what seems otherwise to be a classically proportioned library. The portrait bears out the man sketched by his daughter

---

[62] For Robert John Ward (1841-1930) see Walter Lazenby, *Thrice Happy Place. The Story of Ormskirk Street Congregational Church and of Congregationalism in St Helens* (St Helens n.d. [1975]); Sibree, *Register*, p. 128; Clyde Binfield, *So Down to Prayers. Studies in English Nonconformity 1780-1920* (London: J.M. Dent & Sons Ltd., 1977), pp. 220, 222.

[63] *Early Years*, p. 156.

[64] *Early Years*, p. 155.

[65] *Early Years*, pp. 156-57.

and its backdrop bears out his informed if old-fashioned taste and his predilection for classical houses in romantic settings. Here is a man who can be placed but not pigeon-holed. Here is an indefatigable joiner of committees, the sort who can always be relied to put his hand in his pocket for a guinea, or five, sometimes for considerably more, although the impact of his giving lay in its consistent strategy rather than its munificence. He was the sort of man who, with irrefutable logic, manifest goodness, and blinding simplicity could propose a course of action which all sensible committee men would immediately recognise as wholly impractical – and yet right. He was also the sort whose good manners, bonhomie, and general common sense helped to reconcile some very awkward personalities and to unravel some difficult situations. Those qualities were charmingly shown in his courtship of his first wife and the manner in which he provided a new gown for the wife of the minister who officiated at his second marriage.[66] They were no less effectively shown in his dealings with John Campbell, the bombastic yet undoubtedly able minister of Moorfields Tabernacle, and with G.C. ('Bo'sun') Smith, the pioneer of the Bethel Seaman's Union, a man with whom few could work for long.[67] They showed him to be a prime, indeed a chronic, facilitator of mission. His missionary impact was consistent, cumulative, unswervingly evangelical, consequently both conservative and catholic. It began with Sunday Schools, which remained – as each successive missionary enthusiasm also remained – a lifelong interest. He became a Sunday School teacher in his late teens, was a founder – still in his late teens – of what became the national Sunday School Union, and at the end of his life he took every opportunity to mention his pride in being the last survivor of that Union's first committee.[68] His practical experience in planting clusters of Sunday Schools wherever he happened to be living was replicated in his support for the Bethel Seaman's Union and the Home Missionary Society, an idea which was exported through his mediation to the United States and which he promoted in Anglican circles with what became the Church Pastoral Aid Society.[69] By the 1820s every weeknight evening was spoken for; and by this time his concern for overseas mission had found its due place on the platform of his public life.[70]

---

[66] *Sketches of the Life*, pp. 12-15, 84-85.

[67] *Sketches of the Life.*, pp. 54-56, 205-208; Robert Ferguson and A. Morton Brown, *Life and Labours of John Campbell DD* (London: Richard Bentley, 1867), pp. 465-67, 513. For Campbell (1795-1867) and George Charles Smith (1782-1863) see *ODNB*.

[68] Charles Chapman, 'Prefatory Note', *Christian Living and Christian Dying: A Sermon on the Occasion of the Death of Thomas Thompson Esq. of Prior Park, Bath, preached at Percy Chapel, Bath, Sunday, December 17, 1865* (London: Jackson, Walford & Hodder, 1866), pp. 6-7; *Sketches of the Life*, p. 9.

[69] *Sketches of the Life*, pp. 37, 41, 76-78.

[70] *Sketches of the Life*, p. 42.

In fact Thompson's interest in foreign mission had from the first been inseparable from his interest in home mission. His daughter dated it to 1803, when he encountered three converted Hottentots brought from the Cape by a Dutch missionary.[71] His Sunday School Union and Bethel Seaman's Union work brought him into regular contact with Baptists and support for the Baptist Missionary Society was a natural corollary; but so was his interest in Wesleyan, Moravian, and Anglican overseas missions.[72] It was, however, the London Missionary Society which was *primus inter pares*: its missionaries had countless practical needs, its directors were invariably in financial straits. Thompson and a few others like him were a band of one-man pump-primers, their response justifying what H.R. Reynolds had in mind in 1859 when he urged Robert Dawson to keep the home front fully informed.

Perhaps Thompson spread his enthusiasms too generously. The expression of his piety could be more diffuse than diffused but his daughter was properly impressed by the consequent 'variety of thought which passed through his mind', charged by his active life, and she was best placed to take note of it since she had so often to discipline its expression.[73] India, Africa, the Caribbean, and China gripped him. China was a particular enthusiasm. In the 1830s he collaborated – usually by paying the costs and ensuring the distribution – in a succession of missionary pamphlets: *Open China! By Two Friends* (1834); *No Opium; or, Commerce and Christianity working together for good in China: A Letter . . . by a Minister and a Layman* (1835); *Baptism for the Dead in China: A voice from the Tombs of Morrison and Milne*.[74] So it was through the 1840s, 1850s and into the 1860s, appeals to raise funds for the London Missionary Society in its latest financial crisis, cunningly well-tried plans like a collecting box in each household, or the provision of 'an extensive and efficient native agency', appeals to old friends.[75] Thus he urged Dr Leifchild to become 'the missionary Whitefield of this era' and he urged Leifchild's congregation, ever an 'animating spectacle', to 'set a noble example to others in the form of a "New Year's gift for the World".'[76] Perhaps most strategic of all, there was his determination in print and publicity to harness Sunday Schools to the missionary cause: 'He believed that the Sunday-school scheme, if properly worked out, might be made, far more than any other, effectual for the moral regeneration of England, and through England of the world'. He envisaged each pastor training his Sunday School teachers, to ensure through them 'a reserved corps from which ministers for home, and missionaries for the heathen, might in a few years be supplied'.[77]

---

71 *Sketches of the Life*, p. 51.
72 *Sketches of the Life*, pp. 51, 73.
73 *Sketches of the Life*, p. 65.
74 *Sketches of the Life*, pp. 69-70.
75 *Sketches of the Life*, pp. 90, 92, 93.
76 *Sketches of the Life*, p. 94.
77 *Sketches of the Life*, pp. 99, 100.

It was in this work that Thomas Thompson and his eldest child were at one. It is impossible not to be impressed by his strategic and catholic grasp of the situation. The enrolment of all classes in an imperial nation's truest needs is not so far away from a galaxy of future worlds: the vision of John R. Mott and the World Student Christian Movement for example; the world of the Boys' and Girls' Brigades, of Scouts and Guides; the world about to dawn nationally and internationally of the YMCA and YWCA. Closer to the London Missionary Society's own territory, this is the mentality that would foreshadow and delight in the formation of the Council for World Mission (1977).[78] Set amidst contemporary realities it must have seemed frustratingly impractical, the well-meaning enthusiasm of an older, simpler age of evangelical mission. Yet was it, in fact, simply so? The experience of Thomas Thompson, Jemima Luke, Henry Robert Reynolds, Robert Dawson, and countless more individuals congregating intelligently in mission suggests otherwise. It is not a wholly simplistic sort of Whig History that sees in such people a constant and sometimes surprising transition, a cumulative evolution.

---

[78] The London Missionary Society ('mission understood as the work of a few dedicated individuals') in 1966 became the Congregational Council for World Mission ('mission understood as the activity of the whole church') and in 1977 this joined the Council for World Mission, the mission council of all the churches that had come into being through the work of the London, Commonwealth (originally Colonial), and Presbyterian Church of England Missionary Societies: D. Preman Niles, 'Preface' in Bernard Thorogood (ed.), *Gales of Change* (Geneva: WCC Publications, 1994), p. vii.

CHAPTER 9

Empire into Commonwealth: the Council for World Mission

Geoffrey Roper

To people in the pews of mid-twentieth century Britain the transition from missionary societies and boards to Council for World Mission (CWM) was seen to resemble and parallel that from empire to Commonwealth, which in some respects it did. Decolonization was not, however, the sole context for CWM's emergence: new thinking about mission and ecumenism through the series of international conferences (sequels to Edinburgh 1910) had impacted on British Free Church leadership along with another factor – perhaps partly a consequence of ecumenical exposure – the fresh ecclesiological understanding among leading British Congregationalists in the mid-twentieth century.

It is often said the London Missionary Society (LMS) turned into Council for World Mission. But that was not all that happened. Several different transformations were taking place, some beginning earlier in the 215 years since the Missionary Society had been formed in London, include moving:

- from a male activity to partnership of women and men which had been fostered with some success;
- from London fund-raising that sent missionary agents to the heathen into international trusteeship of assets to support 31 churches develop their mission; therefore,
- from a Society whose membership was acquired by becoming a subscriber and whose governance was performed by directors capable of getting themselves to meetings in London into a council of churches whose occasional trustee body meetings may be held anywhere in the world; but also, therefore,
- from a lay or rather voluntary movement into a professional church council.
- A hundred and fifty years ago the norm was lifelong service by ordained men missionaries (though there were always exceptions like David Livingstone who left the Society's service to do other things); nowadays the norm is short-service appointment in a church other than one's own under the aegis of that church and for as long as that church requires.

- The old system demanded regular and full reporting to the London mission-house – relayed in quantity to the home constituency so they knew what was happening in 'the mission fields' – nowadays many church members in the traditional sending churches feel out of touch with overseas mission and there has been considerable loss of mission memory.
- The missionary society's contribution to health and education service in the 'mission field' countries probably peaked one hundred years ago: nowadays the mission hospital and schools that exist play a much smaller part (proportionately) in their countries' overall provision.

The complications?

- The London Missionary Society was only one of five predecessor bodies[1] which feed into CWM.
- Seven national Congregational Unions[2] which had not existed in 1795 when the Society was founded developed during its lifetime and saw themselves as its sponsors, though two eventually withdrew.
- Edinburgh 1910 and its aftermath exerted considerable influence on developments, particularly the pressure to integrate missionary society and church more closely. Amsterdam 1948 and its aftermath intensified this pressure but the smaller Congregational Unions stood in the way of attaching the missionary society to a single Church.
- Church unions abroad and in Britain altered the 'geometry' of the church partnerships involved.
- Lack of money and dearth of vocations in the traditional sending countries led to a switch of emphasis from sending missionaries to mounting programmes, especially training and experience immersion – until Council for World Mission discovered its pot of gold.
- All of this took place within and sometimes as part of the decolonisation process, but significant sizeable LMS mission fields had never belonged to the British Empire.

If we nonetheless make the central thread of our narrative the transformation of an organisation, the London Missionary Society, controlled from London by a Board of Directors, into an essentially round-table trusteeship in which each of the partner churches world-wide has an equal voice, it does parallel, in broadest outline, the move from colonies controlled out of Whitehall to the modern Commonwealth of free and equal independent states served by a secretariat

[1] London Missionary Society, Commonwealth (previously 'Colonial') Missionary Society, Presbyterian Church of England, Churches of Christ, Reformed Churches of the Netherlands.

[2] England and Wales (CUEW), Undeb yr Annibynwyr Cymraeg (Welsh Independents), Scotland, Ireland, South Africa, Australia, New Zealand.

which would still be based for convenience in Westminster.[3] Like the Commonwealth, the English language is paramount and social bonds may on occasion be strengthened by discussion of the weather and of cricket while drinking tea.

There are, however, two major currents which run through the story: the move to integrate missionary society and church and the move from western dominance to mutuality.

The change from missionary empire to missionary commonwealth was as lengthy as the political one but not so traumatic; yet they do match in surprising ways. The process by which the Indian Empire and the other colonies won their freedom from British rule was fraught with conflict and controversy throughout. Violent freedom struggles, insurgency, and political tension accompanied the transformation of dependent territories into free independent states. Political solutions of federation, partition and power-sharing were devised and applied, some with disastrous consequences. Struggles over issues of colonial freedom left their mark on domestic British politics for decades. Ultimately, most British people gave up worrying about the countries of their former empire: their government decided to concentrate on relationships in the mainland of Europe although a continuing conscience about third world poverty underlay the agreed commitment to pay over the tiniest tithe in development aid and to ring-fence that commitment even in a period of retrenchment. The Commonwealth, however, reminds us of its presence and our national past by sending students and other citizens to live alongside us in Britain.

To some extent inter-church relationships mirror these changes too. Anglican, Reformed, Methodist and Baptist relationships within Europe bulked a good deal larger by the end of the twentieth century than they did at its beginning. We have among us, both in our churches and in separate black or Asian-led congregations far more Christians originating from the countries of the former mission-fields than were in Britain in 1900, but we know less about Christian activities on those continents – except for our conscience-driven concern for relief and development.

The LMS had an ambivalent relationship with the British empire.

Because the transformation of the London Missionary Society began in the period of imperial twilight and serial decolonization, attitudes and antecedents as well as imperial power relationships played their part. But in many LMS mission fields the Bible had not followed the flag. Their first chosen destination, Tahiti and its neighbouring islands, were never a British colony and are now part of French Polynesia. The great missions in central Africa, starting admittedly from the British-controlled Cape, were pioneered by Moffat and Livingstone well ahead of the British flag. Robert Morrison entered China over 200 years ago and, while missions prospered in the vicinity of European con-

[3] The global office of Council for World Mission remained in Westminster until its transfer to Singapore in 2012.

cessions and in Hong Kong, their influence preceded and extended well beyond any places where British power held sway. Baptist missionaries entered Danish territory in India precisely because the (British) East India Company refused to admit missionaries to theirs. The LMS had to wait to get into Calcutta.

The original object of the missionary society formed in London in 1795 was 'to spread the knowledge of Christ among heathen and other unenlightened nations'. It was deliberately not directed towards evangelistic or pastoral efforts among expatriate Europeans in any territories abroad.

While it can thus be argued that this British Nonconformist protestant mission arrived in its major fields independently of British colonisation, was treated initially as an eccentric nuisance by the East India Company and colonial administrations and was sometimes seen by settlers as 'siding with the natives', the LMS's directors and missionaries did not scruple to look to government ministers in London and to colonial authorities for active intervention on occasions when the going got rough. Though they did not automatically identify with the colonist populations and were not mandated to serve settlers' pastoral needs, there was, inevitably, overlap and interchange between mission stations and colonial churches. Missionaries vary: some assumed settler attitudes; others strenuously withstood them and championed the advance of indigenous peoples, providing educational opportunities, medical treatment and ultimately career advancement for Asians, Africans and the peoples of the South Seas.

So the uneven progress towards what was called 'native agency' and we might call local leadership or indigenous ministry moved at a different rate from the overall advance of native peoples and decolonization. In no country were LMS missionaries shown the door because that country had won political independence: though in the 1950s and 1960s there was anxiety about India possibly closing its frontiers to missionaries and, of course, for the whole second half of the twentieth century missionaries were excluded from the People's Republic of China.

British Nonconformists warmed to the concept of 'commonwealth', an expression first applied to the relationship of nations under the British crown by Lord Rosebery but whose constitutional formulation awaited the Statute of Westminster, 1931. 'Commonwealth' tended to appeal to people who saw the seventeenth century's Puritans as their spiritual forebears. It seemed to combine *koinonia* and egalitarianism. Before 1919 the Welsh minister Hywel Elvet Lewis could contribute a hymn concluding:

> Whom oceans part, O Lord unite
> One commonwealth for God and right
> A ransomed people, strong and free,
> To bring the whole wide world to thee.

which was published by the Colonial Missionary Society (having, unlike the LMS, a major concern for British people overseas).

The historians of this transformation have largely been those who advocated and carried through the changes: Norman Goodall, Robert Latham, Bernard Thorogood. With Ronald Orchard, Maxwell Janes and perhaps (out of sight) Leslie Cooke, they scripted the events, argued for them, modified plans when problems arose and recruited personnel to staff the transformed institutions. A student of these matters in the twenty-first century may question their histories but will find few answers in them except that it was visionary, courageous and all very good.

Twentieth century LMS supporters may have seen the devolution of power to national leaderships and national churches as a development comparable, parallel and related to progress from empire to Commonwealth, but it was not that movement only which motivated the reconstitution of the LMS.

We shall find the central narrative, the transformation of a Society into an international ecclesiastical round-table, wound around a sequence of international conferences.

The World Missionary Conference at Edinburgh in 1910 put the missionary societies centre-stage. Its official continuation committee became the International Missionary Council, but the two movements and conference-series it spawned ('Life & Work' and 'Faith & Order') eventually came together and took over the ecumenical agenda. There were indeed conferences between mission boards and missionary societies at Jerusalem in 1928 and Tambaram (Madras) in December 1938 – though at that latter moment Europeans inevitably had their minds focussed on their own continent. Nonetheless missionary leaders must have thought Tambaram[4] the place where the action was. Ten years later the centre of action had moved. Amsterdam 1948 inaugurated the World Council of Churches, combining Life & Work with Faith & Order, soon creating a post-war reconstruction department, rapidly renamed 'Reconstruction and inter-church Aid'.

In December 1948 Norman Goodall, who had been foreign secretary of the LMS for India and the South Pacific but who by then served the International Missionary Council, addressed the LMS board of directors on 'Amsterdam and the Missionary Societies' saying:

> Amsterdam signifies – amongst much else – that the initiative in the ecumenical movement, hitherto largely exercised by missions, has now been claimed by the churches.

A missionary leader said:

> In its significance as a world gathering Amsterdam had taken the place previously occupied in men's thinking by Tambaram. Whereupon one of the company mur-

4 International Missionary Council, *The World Mission of the Church : Findings and recommendations of the meeting of the International Missionary Council, Tambaram, Madras, India Dec12-29, 1938* (London & New York, 1939).

> mured "They've pinched it!" . . . – I wondered if the historic missionary societies were in danger of "pinching" in return the institutional conservatism against which most of them originally rebelled.[5]

Whoever was going to be institutionally conservative it was not Norman Goodall. He set about welding the LMS to the Congregational Union of England and Wales (CUEW). Periodic reviews and incremental changes had eventually resulted in most directors of the LMS being appointed by the CUEW or its constituent county unions, but Goodall wanted integration. He told the board:

> I don't want a barren repetition of the hoary pros and cons of an old debate. I do want to see a fresh examination of the nature of our churchmanship as a missionary Church . . . this may mean studying, in a new setting, the possibility of making the L.M.S. Board the Missionary Council of the Congregational Union, with the secretary holding the recognized status of a secretary of the Union. It ought not to be beyond our Christian wit and wisdom to achieve this while safeguarding that freedom and catholicity which are the proper pride and responsible legacy of the LMS.

Norman Goodall's wit and wisdom were both considerable but it was beyond him to achieve the kind of merger indicated in that phrase. Nonetheless, the concept of turning the LMS from a separate society into a council of the Church was communicated to many participants in the discussions that followed; it was what many thought would be achieved in the creation of the Congregational Council for World Mission (CCWM) in 1966. They were surprised to find CCWM become more distant from their church denomination than the LMS had been.

'Churchmanship' and 'catholicity' were High Congregational talk in those days, which appealed to New Genevans. 'Freedom' resounded better with the Independent and non-denominational tendencies in Congregationalism. Goodall and R.K. Orchard, in a discussion pamphlet issued by the LMS in 1949, tackled head-on the other major element in the legacy of the LMS, usually known as its Fundamental Principle. The Society's foundation had been heralded as 'the funeral of bigotry'.[6] Its prospectus began by saying:

> [the] design is not to send Presbyterianism, Independency, Episcopacy, or any other form of Church Order and Government (about which there may be differ-

[5] Norman Goodall, 'Amsterdam and the Missionary Societies', *The Congregational Quarterly* Vol XXVII, No 2, April 1949, pp. 110-115 [substantially reproduced in N. Goodall and R.K. Orchard, *Church and Mission: A discussion of the relation of the London Missionary Society to the Congregational Unions* (LMS 1949)].

[6] David Bogue at the inaugural service 1795, quoted in Richard Lovell, *History of the LMS*, (Oxford: OUP, 1899), vol. 1, p. 36.

> ence of opinion among serious persons) but the glorious gospel of the blessed God to the heathen.[7]

So how could it be allied to a specific denomination and labelled definitively 'Congregational'? The truth was that nearly all the Society's support for a hundred years had been given by Congregationalists and a high proportion of the funding came by this time from Congregational sources.[8] The great majority of the British missionaries appointed came from Congregational churches[9] as did the great majority of the directors, but one place was always kept for the Wesleyan Reform Union and occasional Presbyterian, Quaker and Methodist participation has been noted. Although the form of church government was left, in principle, to the converts to decide, what they came up with was always a form of Congregationalism, though often the nineteenth century new urban variant with the missionary or the chief taking the role of mill-owner chapel builder and in Madagascar and some of the Pacific islands such as Samoa, an established-church model reflected social hierarchy in church life.

Goodall and Orchard argued that the second part of the Fundamental Principle had been neglected. After abjuring the export of denominationalism – defined in a characteristically Congregational way by church-government type – the formula went on:

> it shall be left (as it ought to be left) to the minds of the persons whom God may call into the fellowship of his Son from among them to assume for themselves such form of Church Order and Government as to them shall appear most agreeable to the Word of God.

You may hear there a voice nearer to Oliver Cromwell's than to the *laissez-faire* indifference of a 'pack-em-in' Evangelical Revival movement. Goodall and Orchard rejoiced that 'the liberty it gives to the younger churches under the Word of God is too precious a gift to them, and to the cause of Christian unity, to be sacrificed for the sake of a more frequent appearance of the title "Congregationalist" on the ecclesiastical map of the world.' They reinforced the point with this piece of mid-twentieth century Congregational rhetoric:

> our further arguments are all based on the assumption that there is one type of Church in Christendom which in fidelity to its own theological and ecclesiastical presuppositions, can and must discharge its missionary obligation on terms no less

---

7 LONDON MISSIONARY SOCIETY, *Plan and Constitution*, 1796.

8 Norman Goodall, *A History of the London Missionary Society 1895-1945* (Oxford: OUP, 1954), concedes on p. 538, 'No figures are available regarding the total financial contributions to the Society from non-Congregational sources.'

9 But nonetheless 20 Baptists, 16 Anglicans, 10 Methodists and 40 Presbyterians (mostly UFC of Scotland before Scottish church reunion in 1929) were included within the total of approximately 800 appointed by the LMS between 1895 and 1945 (Goodall, *A History*, p. 538).

> catholic than those contained in the fundamental principle of the LMS. That Church is a Congregational Church.

They argued:

> What we are all seeking is a further step by which Congregational churches can become more overtly and responsibly related to their own missionary instrument.

Instead of the LMS Board becoming the missionary council of the CUEW, the scheme was modified to allow for other participants: the CUEW would have a 'Missionary Council of the Congregational Union' which would constitute the greater part of the LMS Board. The other unions (of Scotland, Welsh-speaking Wales, Ireland, Australia and New Zealand) would appoint their missionary councils. For the greater part of each of its agendas the LMS Board would function as the Missionary Council of CUEW and for the remainder as a combined meeting of the missionary councils of all the Unions. There would continue to be places on the Board to represent supporters who were not members of Congregational churches. It is beginning to look like a horse designed by a committee. But the main thrust was still addressed to integrating LMS and CUEW. At this early stage they proposed[10] joint youth work, presses, book-rooms, journals – all of which ultimately came to pass to a greater or lesser extent.

Another personality may have been decisive in this situation. The Revd Leslie Cooke, who became general secretary of the Congregational Union in 1948, had attended the Amsterdam assembly the same year. Goodall told the LMS Board in December:

> Now for most of us in the LMS this [the 'new thing' that had happened at Amsterdam] means that the Congregational Unions of England and Wales (and this is true of its sister Unions) must be able more and more not only to speak as a Church with a world outlook but to act as an instrument of the world mission of the Church. Its representatives in the Assembly of the World Council, those who represent Congregationalism in the departmental activities of the Council and most of all those who sit on the Central Committee and Executive, must be able to act instinctively as leaders in an ecumenical movement which exists to further the Church's world mission. This requires something more than the "missionary spirit" in the individuals who serve in this way. . . . It calls for a close awareness of the whole range of facts, processes and problems which arise *as missionary work is done*[11], whether by independent agencies or in daily, administrative partnership with younger churches. That is to say, it requires inside knowledge and responsibility for the daily business of the LMS. If all this slips into the background of the contribution which the representatives of the Congregational Unions make to the

[10] Goodall and Orchard, *Church and Mission*, p. 16.
[11] Goodall's italics.

> life of the World Council of Churches, something vital will go out of the ecumenical movement.[12]

Is it unjust to read into these words some impatience expressed by Leslie Cooke on his return from Amsterdam? Robert Latham was later to write:

> [T]he Rev. Leslie Cooke was general secretary of the CUEW and he was elected to the central committee of the World Council of Churches. He was a keen supporter of the LMS and an active director, In Geneva he met the leaders of the younger churches as his equals on various committees and was much impressed by their calibre, for example Dr D T Niles of Ceylon and Bishop Samuel of South India. He came to feel that the time was at hand when the churches from which these leaders came should be in direct contact with the churches of Europe and America rather than with the various missionary societies. He was just as frustrated by the constitution of the CUEW. As general secretary he had no authority to speak for British Congregationalism. The general assembly, the 'May meetings' as they were known (reflecting the May meetings of the LMS, since1795), carried no churchly authority. They were consultative and advisory, and the member churches could ignore the resolutions passed, if they so decided. These feelings of frustration he expressed in his own powerful fashion, and they reverberated through the following years. Leslie Cooke moved on to the staff of the World Council of Churches as secretary of the division of inter-church aid, refugee and world service.[13]

There may even have been some anxiety that the new World Council's division of inter-church aid would make a bid for the long-established missionary work in health and education. Norman Goodall hinted at the possibility that the WCC would share in that dimension of missionary agencies' work 'undergirding the life of the younger churches with men and money'.[14]

It was suggested repeatedly over subsequent years that the rapid growth in humanitarian relief and development aid through ecumenical agencies drew strength away from the missionary cause.

The next major missionary conference at Willingen in Waldeck, West Germany in 1952 followed the expulsion of missionaries from China and was titled 'The Missionary Obligation of the Church'. A key statement by a delegate was 'it is no longer sufficient to speak of "Mission and Unity"; the call now is to be

12 Goodall, 'Amsterdam', repeated in Goodall and Orchard, *Church and Mission*, p. 8, with slight modifications.

13 Robert Latham, 'Patterns of the Spirit: Towards a Council', in B. Thorogood (ed.), *Gales of Change: Responding to a Changing Missionary Context. The Story of the LMS 1945-1977* (Geneva: WCC, 1994), pp. 225-26.

14 Goodall, 'Amsterdam', p. 110, repeated in Goodall and Orchard, *Church and Mission*, p. 8, with slight modifications.

"Mission in Unity"'.[15] There was an appraisal of the well-established three-self principle (self-supporting, self-governing and self-propagating);[16] Willingen's critique was that it needed to be reconsidered: 'if self-sufficiency and autonomy are isolated as ends in themselves they lead to a dangerous narrowness of view'. There was evident support for integrating missionary agencies with churches, with the caution that it 'does not in itself produce a missionary-minded church, and there remains a need for the education of the total church membership in the missionary obligation.'

Overall Willingen said: 'Integration in the church rightly gives to mission a constitutive place in the life of the church, but it is necessary to preserve some of the flexibility, spontaneity, and initiative which characterize some of the independent missionary societies.'[17]

A group of 'Younger Church' delegates to Willingen said they were convinced missionary work should be done through the Church. 'We should cease to speak of "missions and churches" and avoid this dichotomy not only in our thinking but also in our actions. We should now speak about the mission of the Church.'

In 1950 the LMS appointed a new general secretary, Maxwell Janes. Robert Latham commented that his

> appointment came as a surprise to many. He was moderator of the southern province of the Congregational Union of England and Wales (CUEW), and, although a member of the Board, he had never taken a leading role. He was regarded as a 'union' man. Several of the senior directors were convinced that the time was coming when the LMS and the Congregational Union should be brought into closer working contact. They used their powers of persuasion on Mr Janes and the board to secure his appointment as general secretary.

In 1952 the London Missionary Society echoed the deliberations of Willingen in a policy document to which Maxwell Janes wrote a popular guide entitled *Servant of the Church*.[18] The main theme was the progress of 'younger churches' to maturity. They were

> growing in numerical strength, in capacity to take responsibility, in providing leaders, and possibly in the ability to find more financial resources for their own work. Their spiritual welfare demands that they be encouraged to stand on their

15 International Mission Council, *The Missionary Obligation of the Church: Willingen 1952* (London: Edinburgh House Press, 1952), Introduction, p. iv.

16 Said to have been adumbrated by Henry Venn (1796-1873) of the Church Missionary Society, for whom see *Oxford Dictionary of National Biography*, and formally drafted at a Shanghai Missionary Conference in 1882.

17 *Missionary Obligation*, p. 14.

18 Maxwell O. Janes, *Servant of the Church* (London: Livingstone Press, 1952).

> own feet, rule their own lives, and take the Gospel to the people of their own neighbourhood and beyond.[19]

Janes also pressed a favourite theme: 'The missionary obligation of the church is laid upon it by its Lord. It is not the fad of the few. It is not something that a Christian accepts if he feels like doing so. It is part of his discipleship.'[20] And again 'It is the whole church that is concerned; not just the missionary enthusiasts' Janes argued further:

> One of the unsatisfactory things about the present organization of Congregationalism in these islands is that the organizations which care for the work of the churches at home, and those which do the same for the churches abroad, have inadequate means of collaboration. The county unions and the LMS auxiliaries are, in most cases, separate from one another though they sometimes co-operate in the county union missionary committee. The Congregational Union of England and Wales and the LMS run along parallel lines with no official machinery for consultation.[21]

In 1955 Canon Max Warren focussed the relationship between older and younger churches in his Merrick Lectures *Partnership: the study of an idea*[22] for the Anglican Church Missionary Society and these were published in book form the following year. In 1956, also, Howard Stanley became general secretary of the Congregational Union of England and Wales and in November 1958 eight Commissions were instituted by CUEW to advise on important issues. Norman Goodall chaired Commission V whose first report echoed the title of the Willingen Conference, being headed 'The Church's Missionary Obligation'. He had addressed a public meeting at the May Assembly that year under the title 'The One Task', sharing a platform (or rather the massive Westminster Chapel pulpit) with the Revd Leslie E. Cooke, now Associate General Secretary of the World Council of Churches. One-ness was all. Even the report of Commission V interlinked with that of the ecclesiologically primary Commission I and was to be read in conjunction with it. The CUEW would be converted into a Church by covenant between all its congregations to fulfil their responsibility to God for work at home and overseas. Formally, the conclusion of Commission V was: 'the time has now come when a serious attempt should be made to create a single organisation responsible under God to the churches for work at home and overseas.'[23] This could then be presented to the LMS and the

[19] *Servant of the Church*, p. 26.

[20] *Servant of the Church*, p. 62.

[21] *Servant of the Church*, pp. 75-76.

[22] Max Warren, *Partnership: the study of an idea* (London: SCM Press, 1956) – the substance of Merrick Lectures, Ohio Wesleyan University, 1955.

[23] Congregational Union of England and Wales, *First Report of Commission V. The Church's Missionary Obligation*, November 1960, p. 6.

other Congregational Unions of Welsh-speaking Wales, Scotland, Ireland, South Africa, Australia and New Zealand.

Robert Latham summarises what followed:

> The negotiations proceeded smoothly, but there was a real tension at the heart of them. The CUEW wanted to have responsibility for its world mission, and be seen to have it, but the existence and participation of the other unions made this appear to be impossible. The LMS, on the other hand, found it beyond acceptance to relinquish its role as the missionary agency for the other six unions, and as a 'mother figure' of many overseas churches which had come into being under its witness.' Norman Goodall and Ronald Orchard were the mediators. The Revd Stuart Craig, foreign secretary for India and the South Pacific, staunchly upheld the unique position of the LMS and had the support of many of the directors, and the representatives of the other unions.[24]

So a council for world mission continuing the work of the London Missionary Society was prefixed by the word 'Congregational' and came into being a few weeks after most of CUEW's congregations had by mutual covenant formed themselves into a Church. CUEW had already abandoned its stated object of establishing *Congregational* churches in other lands but took on responsibility for funding the lion's share of CCWM's budget and recruiting missionary candidates 'whether or not from within Congregationalism'.[25]

In May1966 Maxwell Janes gave the last Chairman's Address of the CUEW with the title 'As Fire . . . by burning' from Emil Brunner's 1931 declaration 'The Church exists by mission, just as a fire exists by burning. Where there is no mission, there is no Church; and where there is neither Church nor mission, there is no faith.'[26] The next day the Congregational Church in England and Wales came into being. Norman Goodall made an official visit to that Assembly as the Free Churches' Moderator[27] and said, with a twinkle, it was a pleasure to greet one of the younger churches.

For most of its short life the headquarters of the Congregational Church in England and Wales shared the offices of the Congregational Council for World Mission at Livingstone House, Carteret Street, London.[28] Staff from the two bodies could meet at meal breaks in the Coffee House, a catering arrangement which claimed continuity with the late eighteenth century coffee-house origins of the LMS. What had been the work of the LMS Home Secretary was transferred to the new Church, of which Robert Latham became an Associate Secre-

---

[24] Latham, 'Patterns of the Spirit', p. 228.

[25] Constitution of the Congregational Church in England and Wales [CCEW], 1966.

[26] Emil Brunner, *The Word and the World* (London: SCM Press, 1931), p. 108.

[27] Revd Dr Norman Goodall was Moderator of the Free Church Federal Council for 1966-67.

[28] CCEW moved from Memorial Hall, Farringdon Street because it was to be demolished and rebuilt and took offices at Livingstone House from June 1968 to October 1972.

tary. Fund-raising, advocacy, publications and missionary deputations moved to the Church and the other Congregational Unions. The missionary magazine *Chronicle* was revamped as *World Mission* and went through fresh incarnations as *Enterprise*, *NewsShare* and *InsideOut* but lost its grip on the imaginations of many supporters. The LMS Prayer Fellowship continued in existence only through publication of a Congregational Prayer Fellowship handbook. CCEW and the six Congregational Unions were presented with a three-year budget for which they were to raise the allotted proportions annually.

The function of CCWM was therefore clearer: it was responsible for sustaining missionaries and supporting the programmes of the receiving churches. It also inherited from the LMS a commitment to support lay ministry overseas, by commissioning and supporting Associates who went abroad from the traditional sending countries, mainly to the historic mission-field countries.

CCWM's first General Secretary, Revd Stuart Craig, had, as Robert Latham said, 'staunchly upheld' the LMS tradition and thus provided reassurance to serving missionaries whose home base might otherwise have seemed insecure. The institution, having lost its responsibility for home-country relationships, no longer needed to promote fund-raising – and as a result perhaps began to lose its rootedness in the hearts and prayers and enthusiasms of the home country constituencies. What was added to the LMS tradition was the work of the Commonwealth Missionary Society, a two-fold activity. This CMS, which only lost its 'Colonial' title ten years before integration into CCWM, supplied ministers to some Congregational churches in the southern hemisphere and fulfilled the normal missionary society function in the Caribbean region, having taken over some of the early LMS work in the islands and (British) Guiana.

CCEW appointed seventy four members of the Congregational Council for World Mission at its foundation in 1966. They could easily have outvoted all the Congregational Unions of the other countries. But the body did not function in the way Norman Goodall first envisaged. CCEW did not have its own Missionary Council. From 1970 the number of CCEW council members shrank to forty two.

In 1972 CCEW united with the Presbyterian Church of England as the United Reformed Church, so CWM was reconstituted as the Council for World Mission (Congregational and Reformed). The new united church increased its delegation to forty six members who sat alongside nine or ten apiece from Welsh-speaking Wales and Australia and smaller numbers from the others. Three members were co-opted from the Presbyterian Church of New Zealand, extending a 'special extra-constitutional relationship' from 1969 since many of the Congregational churches had joined them. Missionary links with Taiwan, Bangladesh, Malaysia, Singapore, Burma and Korea brought new connections with East and South-East Asia. Continuity was provided by Boris Anderson who had carried responsibility for Presbyterian Church of England's Overseas Missions Committee and remained the URC's secretary for World Church and Mission. He still operated certain dedicated Presbyterian funds from Church

House. Integration of the English Presbyterian missions was somewhat gradual. CWM (Congregational and Reformed) was joined after a short interval by the Congregational Federation consisted of some Congregationalists who declined to enter the United Reformed Church.

CWM had committed itself to holding periodic reviews every few years. Bernard Thorogood, who had been general secretary since 1971, worked hard to prepare the most radical review ever undertaken in Singapore in January 1975 with Robert Latham in the chair. Despite their lack of rights to membership in the Council, an equal number of the traditional mission-field representatives attended alongside those from the sending churches. We may note that the International Missionary Council had been brought into the World Council of Churches in 1961 with Norman Goodall steering the committee that negotiated their integration. The resulting Commission on World Mission and Evangelism held influential conferences in Mexico in 1963 on 'Mission in Six Continents' and in Bangkok, on 'Salvation Today', just two years before the CWM review in Singapore. A major theme there was the end of western dominance.[29] The outcome of CWM's Singapore consultation was meant to see the end of western dominance. But the representatives of the 'younger churches' were not calling for moratorium on missionaries, rather mutuality in mission.[30] Codified as 'Sharing in one World Mission'[31] it shaped a new partnership in mission, still to be called Council for World Mission, but with no denominational qualifier, and for the time being (at least) to retain offices in London. It would work on a different basis.[32] All the Churches in the former CCWM and Presbyterian Church of England mission fields were invited to take full membership. There would be an Assembly and a Council where each participant would have equal representation: well, almost equal: the United Reformed Church was allowed four representatives while almost all the other churches were to have only two. Suddenly, churches created through British missionary effort would be in the majority. The model closely resembled what had already become of the Paris Mission: it had transmuted into CEVAA (Communauté d'Eglises en Mission).[33] The Churches in Madagascar and Zambia already belonged to CEVAA and could commend this model of partnership.

---

[29] See Thorogood, *Gales of Change*, p. 15.

[30] See B.G. Thorogood, 'Towards Mutuality in Mission: The Council for World Mission', in *International Review of Mission*, 1976, pp. 163-68. 'When, in January 1975, CWM gathered folk from around the world to discuss the future, the word which seemed to catch the breeze of the Spirit was not "Moratorium" but "Mutuality": If you in the west can be givers, so can we. If you can be missionaries, so can we. If you can hear the calling of the Lord, so can we. Therefore each body in the missionary circle of concern has to be seen as an active participant' (p. 164).

[31] R. Latham and B.G. Thorogood (eds), *Sharing in One World Mission: Proposals for World Mission*, (London: CWM, 1975).

[32] See Thorogood, *Gales of Change.*

[33] Originally Communauté évangélique d'action apostolique.

However, some sceptics who look back now say that the Bangkok Conference of 1972/3 had rejected partnership or said it was not genuine:

> Partnership in mission remains an empty slogan. Even where autonomy and equal partnership have been achieved in a formal sense, the actual dynamics are such as to perpetuate relationships of domination and dependence.[34]

Council for World Mission in its new format was inaugurated in July 1977. One of the important emphases was expressed in a hymn by Caryl Micklem:

> Thanks be to God who now would reach
> his listeners in more global ways;
> now each will send the news, and each
> receive and answer it in praise.

Increasingly missionaries came from anywhere and went everywhere. By September 2010 CWM's website showed that the United Reformed Church had only one missionary serving abroad while the Presbyterian Church of India had twenty one serving through CWM (twelve of them in the south Pacific) and claimed to have a thousand more serving in northern India and twenty others in neighbouring countries which have no CWM member church.

A few further changes took place around 1977. The Congregational Union of Australia joined in the Uniting Church in Australia a few weeks earlier and left CWM. The Congregational Union of Ireland had faded from the scene of collaboration. The CWM lay Associate scheme was terminated. The Presbyterian Church of Wales (the Calvinistic Methodist Church) joined CWM and brought in the vigorous Presbyterian Church in North East India, that is, East of Bangladesh. In 1981 the Re-formed Association of Churches of Christ joined the United Reformed Church and thus brought their partner, Churches of Christ in Malawi, to the table.[35] The Presbyterian Church of Aotearoa New Zealand became a full member. Reformed Churches in the Netherlands[36] joined – the only member which had not been in the historic mission partnerships of the denominations which constituted the United Reformed Church.

---

[34] A Report, *Bangkok Assembly 1973, Minutes and Report of the Assembly of CWME of the WCC*, December 31, 1972 and January 9-12, 1973 (Geneva: WCC, undated), p. 104. Cited in Andrew Prasad, 'Mutual Sharing in Mission: An Analysis of the Structures, Programmes and the Theological Statements of the Council for World Mission 1977-2000' (Ph.D. thesis, University of Birmingham, 2006).

[35] Churches of Christ in Britain had worked in three mission fields: Thailand, India and Malawi (formerly Nyasaland). The Thai churches were served latterly by the American United Christian Missionary Society (UCMS) joined in the united Church of Christ in Thailand. The Indian churches joined the Church of North India (1971) – personal communication from Dr David M. Thompson.

[36] In Dutch, Gereformeerde Kerken in Nederland, since 2004 within the Protestant Church in the Netherlands.

The word 'partnership' has been subjected to close examination[37] in regard to the relationships which constitute CWM. The international missionary conference at Whitby (Canada) in 1947 had emphasised 'partnership in obedience' as the relationship between churches: each was responsible for mission on its own territory. Scepticism around 'partnership' at Bangkok (1975) has been mentioned above. A later conference at El Escorial, Spain in 1987 expanded the understanding of partnership and produced 'Guidelines for the Ecumenical Sharing of Resources'. This approach informed CWM's self-understanding and development as a partnership in mission. Ten years later, at a CWM council meeting in Gaborone, Botswana, frustration was expressed at the slow progress in breaking with the colonial past:

> after twenty years of the organization's founding there were deep dissatisfactions around unfulfilled expectations.[38]

It was felt that western domination still prevailed. This was despite the appointment of successive general secretaries originating from India and Sri Lanka.

A new governance structure was negotiated for CWM in which each member church nominates one trustee. The thirty one trustees determine policy; CWM is also grouped regionally and these world regions are represented in an Executive which operates between trustee body meetings.

The sale of the Nethersole Hospital in Hong Kong for £135 million in 1994 increased CWM's assets by about £100 million, which both enlarged the scope and scale of CWM and its member churches' ability to engage in mission.[39] Referred to as the 'gift of grace', proceeds have been made available to member churches over succeeding years in ways that are reckoned to enhance their mission capacities.

The three main methods employed by CWM are Personnel Sharing (usually that means sending missionaries), Finance Sharing (i.e. grants) and Education in Mission (long-term and short-term training opportunities).

Andrew Prasad in his doctoral thesis[40] of 2006 prefers to speak of mutuality than of partnership. He points out that the three main principles of 'Sharing in One World Mission' are still pursued. They are:

> many-sided understanding of mission; multidimensional sharing of power and resources; and the primacy of local churches in mission.

---

37 Desmond Van Der Water, 'Council for World Mission: A Case Study and Critical Appraisal of the Journey of Partnership in Mission', *International Review of Mission* (2008), pp. 305-22.

38 Van der Water, *Council for World Mission*, p. 315.

39 See the fourth web-page of a brief history of CWM (1977-2007) by Steve de Gruchy http://www.cwmission.org/history/history-of-the-council-for-world-mission/stewards-of-grace accessed on 4 September 2010.

40 Prasad, 'Mutual Sharing in Mission'.

He finds that 'mono-cultural perspectives underlying the Council's structures restricted the participation of non-European Council members.' and also 'Inability to adapt and incorporate other cultural backgrounds and approaches to organisation greatly inhibited CWM's international image'.[41] Keeping the headquarters in London, the finances still subject to British charity law and (for a long while) half the executive staff from Europe, discouraged the emergence of other approaches. Dr Preman Niles was followed by general secretaries from South Africa and Jamaica, respectively.

Prasad observed that 'The Council developed its own identity and became largely independent from the churches, both financially and theologically'. In contrast to the initial approach, in which local churches were paramount, the churches were asked to be accountable to the central Council, particularly after the arrival of the Hong Kong money. The central Council, staff and officers, felt that the constituent churches were unable to articulate a significant mission theology and were therefore dependent on the support of CWM to engage in mission. In fact, he found, they could engage in mission but did not necessarily articulate it in what he calls the 'ecumenical-justice' terms preferred by the in-group. They found creative ways to pursue their mission in their context and according to their own theological bent, but this pursuit had little connection to the central thinking or planning done by CWM.

'Mutual sharing,' he concluded nonetheless, 'remains a major way to live out the ideals of partnership in mission by engaging churches in new and dynamic mode of interaction and relationships, without domination or dependency but approaching with humility.'

As to the conundrum raise by the title of this paper, Prasad left the question open:

> Reference to the issue of former colonial influence is largely absent from the documents relating to the formation of CWM. Further research is required to assess the colonial influence through the work of the predecessors of CWM and to examine CWM's reform in relation to its colonial heritage.[42]

In recent years CWM has engaged theologically with the effect of Empire.

Among the many theological, political and social cross-currents of the twentieth century, CWM's emergence from former mission boards and societies can be seen to have passed through three main stages: a movement of amalgamation, especially a principled move to integrate church and mission; a movement into mutuality intended to give emergent former mission-field churches full weight; and a certain distancing, by which the missionary movement lost impetus in the old home-countries and their church-people largely lost awareness of their world partnership.

---

[41] Prasad, 'Mutual Sharing in Mission', p. 237.

[42] Prasad, 'Mutual Sharing in Mission', p. 243.

BIBLIOGRAPHY

Allison, Neil E., *The Clash of Empires,* volume 1 of the Official History of the United Board (Didcot: United Navy, Army and Air Force Board, 2008).

Barrett, Alfred, *Holy Living: Exemplified in the life of Mrs Mary Cryer, wife of the Rev. Thomas Cryer, Wesleyan Missionary in the south of India. With extracts from her papers and correspondence* (London: John Mason, 1849).

Bartlett, C.J., 'The Question of Religious Toleration in Spain in the Nineteenth Century', *Journal of Ecclesiastical History* 8 (1957), pp. 205-16.

Birtwhistle, N. Allen, 'Methodist Missions', in Rupert Davies, A. Raymond George and Gordon Rupp (eds), *A History of the Methodist Church in Great Britain* (London: Epworth, 1983), vol. 3, pp. 1-116.

Bitton, N., *The Story of Griffith John the Apostle of Central China* (London: Sunday School Union, c.1915).

Blake, Joseph, *The Day of Small Things; or, incitement to Juvenile Activity and Usefulness, founded on practical effort in connection with Christian missions* (London: J. Mason, 1849).

Briggs, J.H.Y., *The English Baptists of the Nineteenth Century* (A History of the English Baptists, vol. 3) (Didcot: Baptist Historical Society, 1994).

Brown, C., *The Story of Baptist Home Missions* (London: Veale, Chifferiel and Co., 1897).

Burder, H.F., *The United Claims of Home and Foreign Missions* (London: R. Baynes, 1824).

Carson, Penelope, *The East India Company and Religion, 1698-1858* (Woodbridge: Boydell, 2012).

Carwardine, R., 'The Evangelist System: Charles Roe, Thomas Pulsford and the Baptist Home Missionary Society,' *Baptist Quarterly* 28 (1980), pp. 209-25.

Cashdollar, Charles D., *A Spiritual Home. Life in British and American Reformed Congregations, 1830-1915* (University Park, PA: Penn State UP, 2000).

Chapman, Charles, *Christian Living and Christian Dying: A Sermon on the Occasion of the Death of Thomas Thompson Esq. of Prior Park, Bath, preached at Percy Chapel, Bath, Sunday, December 17, 1865* (London: Jackson, Walford & Hodder, 1866).

Chilcote, Paul, *Her Own Story: Autobiographical Portraits of Early Methodist Women* (Nashville, TN: Abingdon, 2001).

—. *John Wesley and the Women Preachers of Early Methodism* (Metuchen, NJ: Scarecrow, 1991).

—. *She offered them Christ: The Legacy of Women Preachers in Early Methodism* (Nashville, TN: Abingdon, 1993).

Clough, Benjamin, *Extracts from the Journal and Correspondence of the late Mrs M.M. Clough, wife of the Rev. Benjamin Clough, Missionary in Ceylon* (London: John Mason, 1829).

Cracknell, Kenneth, *In Good and Generous Faith* (London: Epworth Press, 2005).

Crook, William, (ed.), *Report of the Speeches at the Formation of the Hibernian Branch of the Methodist Missionary Society ... 1814* (London: Hamilton, Adams and Co., 1863).

Cust, R.N., *Notes on Missionary Subjects* (London: Elliot Stock, 1889).

Darch, John H., 'Love and Death in the Mission Compound', *Anvil*, 17 (2000), pp. 29-39.

—. *Missionary Imperialists?: Missionaries, Government and the growth of Empire in the Tropics, 1860-1885* (Milton Keynes: Paternoster, 2009).

Davey, Cyril, and Hugh Thomas, *Together Travel On: A History of Women's Work* (London: Cargate Press, 1984).

Davidoff, Leonore, and Catherine Hall, *Family Fortunes: Men and Women of the English Middle Class, 1780-1850* (London: Routledge, 1987).

Evans, Eifion, *Bread of Heaven: The Life and Work of William Williams, Pantycelyn* (Bridgend: Bryntirion Press, 2010).

—. *Daniel Rowland and the Great Evangelical Awakening in Wales* (Edinburgh: Banner of Truth, 1985).

Findlay, G.G., and M.G. Findlay, *Wesley's World Parish* (London: Hodder & Stoughton, 1912).

García, C. Araujo, and Kenneth Grubb, *Religion in the Republic of Spain* (London: World Dominion Press, 1933).

Gibbard, N., *Griffith John: Apostle to Central China* (Bridgend: Gwasg Bryntirion, 1998).

Goodall, Norman, *A History of the London Missionary Society 1895-1945* (Oxford: OUP, 1954).

—. 'Amsterdam and the Missionary Societies', *The Congregational Quarterly* Vol XXVII, No 2, April 1949, pp. 110-15.

Goodall, N., and R.K. Orchard, *Church and Mission: A discussion of the relation of the London Missionary Society to the Congregational Unions* (LMS 1949).

Grass, Tim, *Gathering to His Name* (Bletchley: Paternoster, 2006).

Hannah, John, *The Story of the wreck of the 'Maria' Mailboat, with a Memoir of Mrs Hincksman, the only survivor* (London: C.H. Kelly, n.d.).

Harris, Howell, *Brief Account of the Life of Howell Harris, Esq.* (Trevecka, 1791).

Hayden, Roger, *English Baptist History and Heritage* (Didcot: Baptist Union of Great Britain, 2005[2]).

Hinton, J.H., *Individual Effort and the Active Christian* (London: W. Ball, Arnold and Co., 1859).

—. *The Means of a Religious Revival: A Sermon* (London: 1829).

Horne, C. Silvester, *A Popular History of the Free Churches* (London: James Clarke, 1903).

Howson, P., 'Deaths among Army Chaplains, 1914-1920', *Journal of the Society for Army Historical Research* 83/333 (2008), pp. 63-77.

Hughes, Glyn Tegai, *Williams Pantycelyn* (Cardiff: University of Wales Press, 1983).

Jenkins, D.E., *The Life of the Rev. Thomas Charles of Bala* (Denbigh: Llewelyn Jenkins, 1908).

Jenkins, Nigel, *Gwalia in Khasia* (Llandysul: Alun Books, 1995).

Jones, D. Andrew, 'From Darkness to Light: The Home and Foreign Missions' in J. Gwynfor Jones and M. Beech Hughes (eds.), *The History of Welsh Calvinistic Methodism*, 3 *Growth and Consolidation (c. 1814–1914)* (Presbyterian Church of Wales) (forthcoming).

Kelly, C.H., *Memories*, (London: Robert Culley, 1910).

Lannon, Frances, *Privilege, Persecution, and Prophecy: The Catholic Church in Spain 1875-1975* (Oxford: Clarendon, 1987).

Latham, R., and B.G. Thorogood (eds), *Sharing in One World Mission: Proposals for World Mission*, (London: CWM, 1975).

Lloyd, Gareth, 'Repression and resistance: Wesleyan female public ministry in the generation after 1791', in *Angels and Impudent Women: Women in Methodism* (Wesley Historical Society, 2007), pp. 114-31.

Lloyd, Jennifer M., *Women and the Shaping of British Methodism: Persistent Preachers 1807-1907* (Manchester: Manchester University Press, 2009).

Lloyd, J. Meirion, *History of the Church in Mizoram: Harvest in the Hills* (Aisawl: Synod Publication Board, 1991).

—. (ed.), *Nine Missionary Pioneers: The Story of Nine Pioneering Missionaries in North-East India* (Caernarfon: Mission Board, 1989).

Lovegrove, Deryck W., *Established Church, Sectarian People: Itinerancy and the Transformation of English Dissent, 1780-1830* (Cambridge: Cambridge University Press, 1988).

—. 'Particular Baptist Itinerant Preachers during the late Eighteenth and early Nineteenth centuries,' *Baptist Quarterly* 28 (1979), pp. 127-41.

Lowry, E.P., (ed. H.K.), *Chaplains in Khaki, Methodist Soldiers in Camp, on the Field and on the March* (London: Marshall and Son, 1900).

[Luke, Jemima], *Early Years of My Life. By the Author of 'I Think When I Read that Sweet Story of Old'* (London: Hodder and Stoughton, 1900).

—. *Sketches of The Life and Character of Thomas Thompson* (London: James Nisbet & Co., 1868).

Mack, Phyllis, *Heart Religion in the British Enlightenment. Gender and Emotion in Early Methodism* (Cambridge: CUP, 2008).

Male, A.H., *Scenes through the Battle Smoke*, (London: Dean and Son, 1901).

—. *Through Two Campaigns, Afghanistan and the Soudan* (London: Robert Culley, 1903).
Martin, R.H., *Evangelicals United: Ecumenical Stirrings in Pre-Victorian Britain, 1795-1830* (Lanham, MD: Scarecrow Press, 1983).
May, Andrew J., *Welsh Missionaries and British Imperialism: The Empire of Clouds in North-East India* (Manchester: Manchester University Press, 2012).
Morden, Peter J., *Offering Christ to the World: Andrew Fuller (1754–1815) and the Revival of Eighteenth Century Particular Baptist Life* (Studies in Baptist History and Thought), (Carlisle: Paternoster Press, 2003).
Morgan, Edward, *Ministerial Record; or Brief Account of the Great Progress of Religion under the Ministry of W. Williams, of Pantycelyn* (Llandovery: William Rees, 1847).
Morrell, W.P., *Britain in the Pacific Islands* (Oxford: OUP, 1960).
Morris, J. Hughes, *The History of the Calvinistic Methodists' Foreign Mission to the end of the year 1904* (Liverpool: Calvinistic Methodist Book Room, 1910).
Neill, Stephen, *Colonialism and Christian Missions* (London: Lutterworth Press, 1966).
Nichols, James, *A Report of the Principal Speeches delivered at the Formation of the Methodist Missionary Society for the Leeds District ...1813* (London: Simpkin and Marshall,1840).
Owen, W.T., *Edward Williams DD, 1750-1813. His Life, Thought and Influence* (Cardiff: University of Wales, 1963).
Paton, John G., *John G. Paton, Missionary to the New Hebrides. An Autobiography* [1889] (Edinburgh: Banner of Truth, 1965).
Porter, Andrew, *Religion versus Empire? British Protestant Missionaries and Overseas Expansion, 1700-1914* (Manchester: Manchester UP, 2004).
Rees, D. Ben, (ed.), *Vehicles of Grace & Hope: Welsh Missionaries in India 1870–1970* (Pasadena, CA: William Carey Library, 2002).
Reynolds, Henry Robert, *Notes on The Christian Life. A Selection of Sermons* (London and Cambridge: Macmillan and Co., 1865).
Rinaldi, Frank W., *The Tribe of Dan: The New Connexion of General Baptists 1770-1891* (Studies in Baptist History and Thought) (Milton Keynes: Paternoster, 2008).
Roberts, Gwen Rees, *Memories of Mizoram: Recollections and Reflections* (Cardiff: Presbyterian Church of Wales Mission Board, 2001).
Robson, W., *Griffith John, Founder of the Hankow Mission Central China* (London: F.H. Revell, 1888).
Rule, W.H., *Recollections of my Life* (London: T. Woolmer, 1886).
—. *Wesleyan Methodism in the British Army* (London: T. Woolmer, 1883).
Samson, Jane, *Imperial Benevolence: making British authority in the Pacific Islands* (Honolulu: University of Hawai'i Press, 1998).

Sellars, Ian, 'John Howard Hinton, Theologian', *Baptist Quarterly* 33 (1989), pp. 119-32.

Sharpe, Eric J., *Comparative Religion: A History* (London: Duckworth, 1986 [2nd ed.]),

Stanley, Brian, *The Bible and the Flag. Protestant Missions and British Imperialism in the Nineteenth and Twentieth Centuries* (Leicester: Apollos, 1990).

—. *The History of the Baptist Missionary Society, 1791–1992* (Edinburgh: T and T Clark, 1992).

—. *The World Missionary Conference, Edinburgh 1910* (Cambridge: Eerdmans, 2009).

Thompson, J.H., 'Army Chaplains and the English Presbyterians', *The Journal of the United Reformed Church History Society*, vol. 5, No.7, October 1995, pp. 383-92.

Thorogood, Bernard, (ed.), *Gales of Change* (Geneva: WCC Publications, 1994).

Tudur, Geraint, *Howell Harris: From Conversion to Separation 1735–1750* (Cardiff: University of Wales Press, 2000).

Vickers, John, *Thomas Coke, Apostle of Methodism* (London: Epworth Press, 1969).

Watkins, O.S., *Chaplains at the Front* (London, 1901).

—. *Soldiers and Preachers Too* (London: C.H. Kelly, 1906).

—. *With French in France and Flanders* (London: C.H. Kelly, 1915).

—. *With Kitchener's Army*, (London: S.W. Partridge and Co., 1899).

Webb, Pauline, *Women of our Company* (London: Cargate Press, 1958).

West, Francis, *Memoirs of Mrs Jane Gibson, of Newcastle-upon-Tyne, including selections from her correspondence* (London: Hamilton, Adams, 1837).

Wilson, J., *Memoir of the Life and Character of Thomas Wilson* (London: John Snow, 1849).

Wilson, Linda, *Constrained by Zeal: Female Spirituality Amongst Nonconformists, 1825-1875* (Carlisle: Paternoster, 2000).